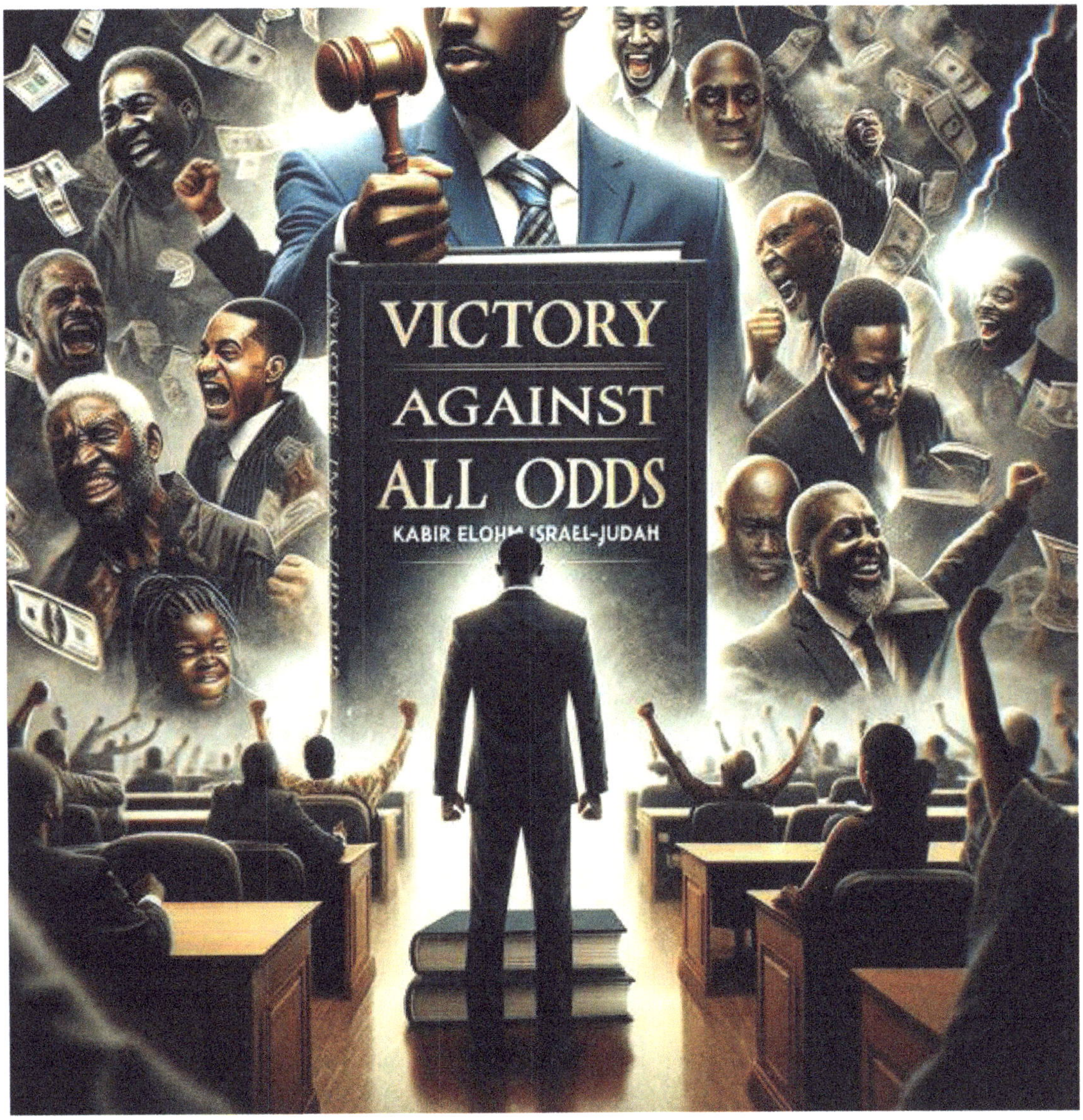
VICTORY
AGAINST
ALL ODDS
KABIR ELOHM ISRAEL-JUDAH

Table of Contents

This is not legal advice and we do not have any desire to be bar attorneys. These documents have been proven time and time again for us with several victories. This is just one example in the form of a self-help workbook. Hope you enjoy, Peace

All Glory be to The Most High, Ya.

Introduction   *P.7*

- Overview of the eBook

- Purpose and Benefits of Becoming a Secured Party Creditor (SPC)

- How to Use This Guide

Chapter 1: Understanding Key Legal   P.9 Documents

-Security Agreement

  - Example: A contract detailing the terms under which the creditor holds an interest in the debtor's property.

- Common Law Copyright

  - Example: A declaration protecting the intellectual property of your legal name.

- Hold Harmless and Indemnity Agreement

  - Example: An agreement that limits your liability for actions taken by the strawman entity.

- Form-56

  - Example: A form submitted to the IRS to notify them of a fiduciary relationship.

- W-8BEN

  - Example: A form establishing non-U.S. status for tax purposes.

- Bond for Investment

  - Example: A bond representing financial security used in various transactions.

- UCC Financing Statement

- Example: A legal form filed to declare a secured interest in assets.

- UCC Financing Addendum

  - Example: An additional document providing more detailed information about the secured party or debtor.

- Cover Letter

  - Example: A letter introducing and explaining the purpose of your SPC filings.

- Chargeback

  - Example: A process to recover funds or property.

- Declaration of Trust

  - Example: A document establishing a trust and detailing its terms.

- Schedule A

  - Example: A list of assets included in the trust.

Chapter 2: Benefits of Becoming a Secured Party Creditor.
P. 23

- Separates the Flesh-and-Blood Man from the Fictitious Corporate Entity

  - Example: Using your new legal identity to distinguish yourself from the corporate entity created by your name.

- Reserves/Secures Rights and Interests

  - Example: Asserting your rights through legal documents to ensure they are recognized and respected.

- Creates the Ability to Proceed in Other Filings/Venues

  - Example: Using your SPC status to engage in legal actions or filings in different jurisdictions.

- Establishes a Superior Interest in the Debtor Trust

  - Example: Filing a UCC Financing Statement to claim priority over the debtor's assets.

- Establishes a Common Law Copyright

- Example: Protecting your name from unauthorized commercial use.
- Defines Penalties for Violations of Rules and Rights
  - Example: Setting legal consequences for breaches of your secured rights.

Chapter 3: Filing Processes and Practical Tips.
P.55

- Step-by-Step Guides for Each Document
  - Example: Detailed instructions on how to fill out and file each key document.
- Common Pitfalls and How to Avoid Them
  - Example: Tips on preventing mistakes that could undermine your filings.

Chapter 4: Real-World Applications and Case Studies.
P.86

- Success Stories
  - Example: Real-life examples of individuals who successfully navigated the SPC process.
- Learning from Challenges
  - Example: Analysis of common obstacles and strategies to overcome them.

Chapter 5: Advanced Strategies for SPC
P.164

- Using Legal Entities and Trusts
  - Example: Setting up advanced structures to protect your assets.
- Navigating International Laws and Treaties
  - Example: Leveraging global legal frameworks to strengthen your SPC status.

Chapter 6: Community and Support   P.172

- Building a Support Network

  - Example: Connecting with other SPCs for advice and collaboration.

- Educational Resources

- Importance of Brotherhood/ Sisterhood

Chapter 7: Continuous Improvement and Advocacy.
P.189

- Staying Informed of Legal Changes

  - Example: Monitoring legal trends and adapting your strategies accordingly.

- Advocating for Legal Reforms

  - Example: Participating in efforts to change laws that affect SPCs.

Appendices.

- Glossary of Terms

  - Example: Definitions of key legal and financial terms used throughout the book.

- Sample Forms and Documents

  - Example: Filled-out examples of key documents to guide your own filings.

- Resources for Further Study

  - Example: Books, websites, and articles for deeper exploration.

Conclusion

This Table of Contents provides a comprehensive overview of the eBook, detailing each chapter and the key concepts covered. It serves as a roadmap for readers, guiding all through the process of becoming a Secured Party Creditor and understanding the benefits and practical applications of this legal status, and the importance of being Born again.

Introduction: From Condemnation to Liberation

The Challenge Unveiled:

At the heart of this documentary book lies a compelling personal narrative — a tale of a man thrice labeled a felon, yet determined to redefine his destiny. The legal battles he faced when defending himself with a weapon, despite his past, sets the stage for an inspiring journey through the intricate maze of legal documentation and self-advocacy.

Purpose of the Documentary Book:

This guide is not merely a recount of personal trials; it's a blueprint for empowerment and legal reclamation. It is designed to serve individuals who find themselves ensnared by their past and the legal system, offering them a methodical approach to challenging and overcoming legal accusations by employing strategic legal documents and sovereign identity principles.

Navigating the Legal Labyrinth:

Facing charges as a three-time felon carries daunting consequences, intensified when self-defense introduces additional legal complexities such as weapons charges. The story detailed in these pages outlines how the protagonist, by proclaiming a new name and identity and strategically navigating the legal system, shifted his position from a defendant to a legally empowered individual.

A New Identity:

The concept of being 'born again' legally signifies the adoption of a new sovereign identity that separates the natural person from their past legal entanglements. This transformation is pivotal in not just defending against legal charges but in rewriting one's destiny. Through detailed examples and documented processes, the book illuminates the path from reclaiming one's name to mastering the legal filings that protect and empower the individual.

Guide for Self-Liberation:

Each chapter of this book is structured to guide readers step-by-step through the same documents and legal maneuvers used successfully by the protagonist. From initial filings like criminal complaints and bonding information to sophisticated instruments such as private register bonds and certificates of live birth, this guide demystifies complex legal procedures and provides practical tools for individuals seeking to alter their legal standing and life.

Empowering Others Through Knowledge:

This book is an invitation to break free from the shackles of past definitions and legal constraints. It is crafted to inspire, educate, and empower others by demonstrating that with knowledge, courage, and the right guidance, it is possible to navigate through and triumph over seemingly insurmountable challenges.

This introduction sets the stage for a detailed exploration into this real-life saga of legal redemption and spiritual rebirth, providing not only a tale of triumph but also a practical handbook for those daring enough to redefine their own legal narratives.

Chapter 1: The Legal Battle Begins.

Section 1: Facing the Charges – The Initial Confrontation

Criminal Complaint: Understanding the Initial Allegations

Incident Overview:

The chapter opens with a detailed account of a critical incident where the alleged offender, referred to as the defendant, faced gunfire while his vehicle was being towed. In defense, the defendant returned fire, striking the assailant multiple times. This act of self-defense sets the stage for the subsequent legal challenges.

Interaction with Law Enforcement:

After the shooting, the defendant did not flee the scene. Instead, he responsibly flagged down the approaching police officers to report the incident. During the interaction, he provided his foreign national passport card as identification, which did not match the domestic databases, escalating police suspicion.

Legal Analysis:

This section analyzes the initial legal implications of using a firearm in self-defense, especially as a person with a previous felony conviction. It delves into the complexities of self-defense laws and how they apply to individuals with a criminal history.

Booking Details: What Happens During Booking and Its Significance

Booking Process:

Following the police's failure to verify his new identity quickly, the defendant was taken into custody. The narrative details the booking process, emphasizing the critical nature of the information collected and its impact on the case.

Significance of Identification:

The use of a foreign national passport by the defendant introduces a discussion on the legal recognition of new identities and the challenges that arise when legal documents do not align with national databases.

Bond/Bail Process: Navigating the Complexities

Setting the Bail:

Upon booking, the defendant was assigned a $7,500 bond, which he promptly posted. This section explains the factors considered by the court in setting bail amounts, particularly for individuals deemed high-risk due to prior convictions.

Strategic Response:

The defendant's immediate posting of bail and his preparation to assert his position through legal paperwork highlight his proactive approach to navigating the legal system. This narrative serves as a practical guide for readers on how to handle similar situations, emphasizing the importance of preparedness and understanding of one's legal rights.

Conclusion:

The opening chapter sets a robust foundation, outlining a real-life scenario that blends legal defense with identity challenges. It not only provides a gripping start to the story but also educates readers on the initial steps and legal considerations necessary when caught in such a predicament. The chapter concludes by setting the stage for the next, where the defendant begins to build his defensive strategy based on his sovereign identity and legal documentation.

Chapter 1: The Legal Battle Begins

Legal Recognition of New Identities and Court Challenges

Legal Recognition of New Identities

Foundational Legal Principles:

- **Bouvier's Law Dictionary Insight**: According to Bouvier's Law Dictionary, the omission of a Christian name in legal proceedings can prevent the court from acquiring jurisdiction. This principle underscores the importance of precise identification in legal processes and highlights potential defense strategies concerning identity issues.

- **Legal Right to Name Change:** It is a well-established legal right that any individual may change their name at any point, provided the change does not defraud or harm others. This right is recognized across various jurisdictions and is critical to understanding the legal stance on identity.

Applying Name Change in Legal Contexts:

- **Charging Under Legal Identity:** Legally, charges must be made against an individual's current legal identity. Using a former name or an incorrect identity (misnomer) can challenge the validity of the judicial proceedings.

- **Recognition of Spiritual and Maturity Claims:** The narrative of personal evolution — coming into spiritual enlightenment and rejecting a government-assigned name — plays into legal arguments about identity. This transformation, recognized legally once properly documented, must be respected in court.

Challenges in Court: Interpretation of Identity and its Impact

Court Interpretation of New Identities:

- **Judicial Recognition:** How courts interpret and recognize legally changed identities is crucial. The acknowledgment of a new name, especially when tied to significant personal or spiritual developments, must be handled with respect to the individual's rights.

- **Impact on Defense Strategy:** A new legal identity can reshape defense strategies, particularly in proving the separation between past criminal records associated with a former name and the individual's present legal status.

Separation of Church and State:

- **Freedom of Belief:** U.S. law stipulates a clear separation of church and state, safeguarding an individual's right to hold and act upon personal beliefs, including those influencing their legal identity.

- **Legal Implications of Spiritual Allegiances:** When an individual declares allegiance to a "government" defined by divine rather than human authority, it challenges traditional legal frameworks. Courts must navigate these claims carefully to avoid infringing on religious freedoms while maintaining legal standards.

Legal Status of Trusts and Personhood

Trust as a Legal Entity:

- **Definition and Personhood:** In legal terms, a trust is often recognized as a separate legal entity, capable of holding property and being party to litigation. This can be a powerful tool in legal strategies, especially for individuals redefining their identity under new spiritual or personal revelations.

- **Trusts and Legal Identity:** Using a trust as part of a legal defense or as a mechanism for holding assets under a new identity can separate personal liabilities from the entity (trust), providing strategic legal protections.

Conclusion of Section 1

This section of the chapter provides a comprehensive analysis of the legal recognition of new identities, the challenges presented in court, and how deeply held beliefs intersect with legal rights. The discussion is designed to empower readers with knowledge on navigating these complex issues, emphasizing the legal and spiritual dimensions of identity transformation. It sets a firm foundation for understanding how one can assert their newly embraced identity against charges tied to a past identity, underlining the profound implications for personal freedom and legal sovereignty.

Milwaukee County Case Number 2023CF001349 State of Wisconsin vs. Londale Quintae Strickling

Case summary

Filing date
03-29-2023

Case type
Criminal

Case status
Closed - Electronic filing

Defendant date of birth
07-11-1983

Address
220 Calle Manuel Domench PMB 2050, San Juan, PR 00918

Branch ID
19

DA case number
2023ML006724

Charges

Responsible official
Ashley-19, Kori

Prosecuting agency
District Attorney

Prosecuting agency attorney
Piotrowski, Owen M

Printable version

Defendant owes the court: $0.00

Count no.	Statute	Description	Severity	Disposition
1	941.29(1m)(a)	Possess Firearm-Convicted of a Felony	Felony G	Dismissed on Prosecutor's Motion

Defendant

Defendant name
Strickling, Londale Quintae

Date of birth
07-11-1983

Sex
Male

Race
African American

Address (last updated 05-23-2023)
220 Calle Manuel Domench PMB 2050, San Juan, PR 00918

JUSTIS ID

Fingerprint ID

Also known as

Name	Type	Date of birth
Strickling, Londale Quinta	Also known as	
Stokes, Robert Ray	Also known as	
Isreal, Kabir-Elohim	True name	

Court record

Date	Event	Court official	Court reporter	Amount
11-08-2023	Transcript			

Date	Event	Court official	Court reporter	Amount

Additional text:

Filed: Original Transcript of preliminary hearing (8 pages) commencing August 9, 2023, by Valori Weber.

08-09-2023 Dispositional order/judgment   Phillips, Barry
08-09-2023 Dismissed   Phillips, Barry   Weber, Valori

Additional text:

Defendant Londale Quintae Strickling in court, Pro Se. Prosecuting attorney Gregg Herman in court for the State of Wisconsin.

Case is set for a Preliminary Hearing. State's Witness IS NOT present. Subpoena was sent out but no response and no response to efforts to make contact.

Court orders case DISMISSED without prejudice.

08-09-2023 Bench warrant authorized for Strickling, Londale   Phillips, Barry
            Quintae

Additional text:

No Bench Warrant Authorized. Entered In Error.

08-09-2023 Motion
06-30-2023 Adjourned hearing   Phillips, Barry   Roque, Gil

Additional text:

3:28 PM Defendant Londale Quintae Strickling in court. Prosecuting attorney Noele Concepcion in court for the State of Wisconsin.
Case set for a preliminary hearing. States witness is not present. Defense moves to dismiss; motion is taken under advisement. Court ordered case adjourned for CAUSE for Preliminary Hearing in Branch PE.
Preliminary hearing scheduled for August 9, 2023 at 01:30 pm.

06-30-2023 Motion

Additional text:

Motion for Discovery

06-30-2023 Motion

Additional text:

Motion of Subrogation and Dismissal-Implied Surety

06-29-2023 Other papers

Additional text:

Bond Probate-Estate

06-28-2023 Other papers

Date	Event	Court official	Court reporter	Amount

Additional text:

Declaration - Domestic Common Law Trust - Form 702

06-26-2023 Status conference   Ashley-19,   Scoville,
                                                        Kori   Kaitlyn

Additional text:

Defendant Londale Quintae Strickling in court.
Attorney Owen M Piotrowski in court for State of Wisconsin.
Case in court for a Status Conference.
Defendant appears Pro se and remains eligible for public defender appointment.
Defendant request to represent himself and advised of his right to counsel.
Court examined defendant as to his request to represent himself and waiver of counsel
Further discussion held with defendant. Court Granted defendant motion to Represent himself.
Defendant moves the court to instruct the State to change the caption relating to his name in CCAP to Kabir-Elohim Israel or Dismiss the matter. Defendant motion Denied for reasons placed on the record. Court ordered case adjourned for a Preliminary Hearing in Preliminary Court. Preliminary hearing scheduled for June 30, 2023 at 01:30 pm.

06-23-2023 Proof of service
06-20-2023 Letters/correspondence

Additional text:

Defendant submitted "FINAL WRITTEN ACCEPTANCE; PAROL or EXTRINSIC EVIDENCE" (KABIR ELOHIM ISREAL)on behalf of "LONDALE QUINTAE STRICKLING"

06-05-2023 Letters/correspondence
06-05-2023 Letters/correspondence
05-23-2023 Adjourned hearing   Phillips, Barry   Roque, Gil

Additional text:

Defendant Londale Quintae Strickling in court. Prosecuting attorney Arthur Kenneth Thexton in court for the State of Wisconsin.
Case set for a preliminary hearing. SPD has not appointed counsel as the defendant refused services. The defendant would like to represent himself. Court ordered case adjourned for cause to the trial court for a Status Conference.
Status conference scheduled for June 26, 2023 at 08:30 am.

05-23-2023 Change of address notification for Strickling, Londale Quintae

Additional text:

ADDRESS INFO for Londale Quintae Strickling
Current: 220 Calle Manuel Domench PMB 2050, San Juan, PR 00918 United States (Effective: 05-23-2023)
Prior: PO BOX 101002, Milwaukee, WI 53210

05-23-2023 Notice

Date	Event	Court official	Court reporter	Amount
05-23-2023	Letters/correspondence			
05-04-2023	Cash bond set for Strickling, Londale Quintae	Flynn, Grace	Tape Reporter	$7,500.00

Additional text:

No possession of dangerous weapons or firearms.

05-04-2023	Initial appearance	Flynn, Grace	Tape Reporter	

Additional text:

Defendant Londale Quintae Strickling in court. Prosecuting attorney Nate Kristian McClure in court for the State of Wisconsin.
Defendant is advised this case is assigned to Judge Ashley, Branch 19.
Defendant given a copy of complaint and advised of maximum penalties, right to counsel and the right to preliminary hearing. The defendant refused to be interviewed by the public defender's office. Commissioner Flynn waived the defendants right to appear with counsel for todays court proceedings. Court reviewed complaint and found probable cause to hold defendant for further proceedings.
Case is adjourned for preliminary hearing in Branch PE.
Preliminary hearing scheduled for May 23, 2023 at 01:30 pm.

05-02-2023	Letters/correspondence			
05-01-2023	Motion to dismiss			
04-24-2023	Other papers			
04-05-2023	Other papers			
03-31-2023	Cash bond posted			$7,500.00

Additional text:

Actual Date Bond Posted with the Sheriff's Department:
03/24/23.   23RM016856

03-29-2023	Notice			
03-29-2023	Electronic Filing Notice			
03-29-2023	Case initiated by electronic filing			
03-29-2023	Complaint filed			

Additional text:

Defendant is Out-of-Custody. Court appearance in Out-Of-Custody Court, Room 221 Safety Building on May 4th, 2023 at 1pm.

Case 2023CF001349   Document 2   Filed 03-29-2023   Page 1 of 2

FILED
03-29-2023
Anna Maria Hodges
Clerk of Circuit Court
2023CF001349
Honorable Kori Ashley-19
Branch 19

STATE OF WISCONSIN   CIRCUIT COURT   MILWAUKEE COUNTY

STATE OF WISCONSIN
        Plaintiff,

vs.

STRICKLING, LONDALE QUINTAE
5521 WEST CENTER STREET #10
MILWAUKEE, WI 53210
DOB: 07/11/1983

        Defendant(s).

DA Case No.: 2023ML006724
Court Case No.:

CRIMINAL COMPLAINT

For Official Use

THE BELOW NAMED COMPLAINANT BEING DULY SWORN, ON INFORMATION AND BELIEF STATES THAT:

Count 1: POSSESSION OF A FIREARM BY A FELON

The above-named defendant on or about Tuesday, March 21, 2023, at 3624 West North Avenue, in the City of Milwaukee, Milwaukee County, Wisconsin, did possess a firearm, having been convicted of a felony in this state, contrary to sec. 941.29(1m)(a), 939.50(3)(g) Wis. Stats.

Upon conviction for this offense, a Class G Felony, the defendant may be fined not more than Twenty Five Thousand Dollars ($25,000), or imprisoned not more than ten (10) years, or both.

Probable Cause:

Your affiant is a City of Milwaukee law enforcement officer and I base this complaint on my review of official Milwaukee Police Department reports. Said reports indicate the following:

On March 21st, 2023, around 2:36pm, officers with the Milwaukee Police Department responded to the area of 3624 W North Ave, Milwaukee, Milwaukee County, WI in regards to a shooting complaint and ShotSpotter activation. Upon arrival, they were flagged down by the defendant, Londale Strickling. The defendant turned over a 9mm firearm and indicated he had just been involved in a shooting. The defendant initially gave his name as Kabir-Elohim Israel.

The defendant indicated that his van had broken down and he had tried to hire a mechanic. He indicated the mechanic that came started work but stated he couldn't finish. The defendant stated that the mechanic demanded payment but the defendant did not want to pay until the work was done. The defendant stated that led to an argument but nothing happened at that time. The defendant stated on March 21st he decided to sell his van and contacted a scrapper to buy his van and tow it away. The defendant stated the tow truck driver, GL, showed up and the both of them began to hook the van up to the tow truck. The defendant stated at that point he heard a gunshot and saw who he recognized as the mechanic in a mask with his eyes visible now armed with a gun pointed at him. The defendant stated he then unholstered his weapon and fired it at the mechanic and struck him. The defendant stated the mechanic was hit but he continued to try and clear a jam in his gun. The defendant stated he yelled at the mechanic to drop the gun and the mechanic ran off.

GL corroborated the defendant's story. Police found casings and a blood spot in the area where the mechanic had shot from. An individual suffering from a gunshot wound had been dropped off at a Fire Station nearby within minutes of the shooting matching the mechanic's description.

Londale Quintae Strickling, DOB: 07/11/1983

A review of the defendant's prior record reveals that he was convicted on April 13th, 2017 in Milwaukee County Case 2015CF138 for Possession of Burglarious Tools, a Class I Felony. The conviction is of record and unreversed.

This affidavit contains a summary of facts to establish probable cause. It does not contain all of the facts known to me relating to this investigation.

****End of Complaint****

Electronic Filing Notice:
This case was electronically filed with the Milwaukee County Clerk of Circuit Court office. The electronic filing system is designed to allow for fast, reliable exchange of documents in court cases. Parties who register as electronic parties can file, receive and view documents online through the court electronic filing website. A document filed electronically has the same legal effect as a document filed by traditional means. You may also register as an electronic party by following the instructions found at http://efiling.wicourts.gov/ and may withdraw as an electronic party at any time. There is a $20.00 fee to register as an electronic party. If you are not represented by an attorney and would like to register an electronic party, you will need to contact the Clerk of Circuit Court office at 414-278-4120. Unless you register as an electronic party, you will be served with traditional paper documents by other parties and by the court. You must file and serve traditional paper documents.

Criminal Complaint prepared by Eric Bashirian.
ADA Assigned Email Address: Owen.Piotrowski@da.wi.gov

Subscribed and sworn to before me on 03/25/23
Electronically Signed By:
Eric Bashirian
Assistant Attorney General
State Bar #: 1105843

Electronically Signed By:
Police Officer Sao Yang
Complainant

CMS Inm Property Log Sheet - CJF 299151
Printed On: 03/22/23 20:25

SPN#	Name	DOB	Eyes	Weight	Race
299151	Strickling,		Brown	195	Black/African American
Booking# 23-003900		Sex Male	Hair Black	Height 511	BKG

Inmate Property

Property for SPN: 299151

Item	Description	Qty	Location/Container ID	Action	Date Time
Money, Cash, Coins	money in kiosk	1	CJF Booking Room	Received from Inmate	03/22/23 20:25
Gold Jacket, Coat	x	1	CJF Booking Room	Received from Inmate	03/22/23 20:25
Multicolored Socks	pair	1	CJF Booking Room	Received from Inmate	03/22/23 20:25
Red Footwear	pair of shoes	1	CJF Booking Room	Received from Inmate	03/22/23 20:25
Sealed Bag	MPD	1	CJF Booking Room	Received from Inmate	03/22/23 20:25

Inmate Signature :

Officer Signature :

Date: 3/22/2023 8:25:32 PM

PF#: DHEDH

Location : CJF BKOW

Chapter 2: The Foundation of Defense

Section 1: Legal Documentation and Strategy

Bonding/Insurance Requirements for Municipal Officials

- **Overview and Importance:** Explain the role and significance of bonding for municipal officials such as judges and police officers, highlighting how these bonds guarantee their adherence to lawful procedures and ethical standards.

- **Strategic Use in Defense:** Guide on how to request and review the bonding information of the officials involved in the case, and how discrepancies or lapses can be used to challenge misconduct or bias.

-

Performance Bond: Utilizing the Trust as The Surety

- **Understanding Performance Bonds:** Detailed explanation of what performance bonds are and how they function within the realm of legal disputes, particularly focusing on their use to secure the performance of contractual obligations by public officials.

- **Implementing a Trust as Surety**: Steps to establish a trust to act as surety, providing the financial backing for a performance bond, and how this can influence the proceedings and ensure compliance with legal standards by the court or government body.

Legal Documentation and Strategy for Pro Se Litigants

As a pro se litigant, understanding the legal documentation and strategies available to you can significantly enhance your ability to defend yourself in court. This section will focus on the roles and uses of specific legal instruments related to municipal officials and performance bonds in the context of a criminal charge.

Bonding/Insurance Requirements for Municipal Officials

Overview and Importance:

Municipal officials, including judges and police officers, are typically required to be bonded or insured. These bonds serve as a form of financial assurance that the officials will adhere to lawful procedures and ethical standards. Bonding is a safeguard meant to protect the public from misconduct, corruption, or errors made by these officials.

- **Role of Bonds:** Bonds are essentially insurance policies that protect the public against damages resulting from the actions or negligence of bonded officials. If an official acts unlawfully or unethically, the bond can be claimed against to compensate the affected party.

- **Significance in Legal Proceedings:** Knowing that municipal officials are bonded can be a crucial element in your defense. It means there is a financial mechanism in place to hold officials accountable for their actions.

Strategic Use in Defense:

As a pro se litigant, you can leverage the bonding information of municipal officials to your advantage.

- **Requesting Bond Information:** You have the right to request the bonding information of any official involved in your case. This can typically be done through a public records request or by directly asking the official's office.

- **Reviewing Bond Information:** Once you have this information, review it to ensure that the officials are properly bonded. This includes checking the bond's validity, coverage, and the conditions under which it can be claimed.

- **Challenging Misconduct or Bias:** If you find any discrepancies or lapses in the bonding, or if you believe an official has acted unethically, you can use this information to challenge their actions. For example, you can file a claim against the bond or bring this to the court's attention as part of your defense strategy. This can potentially disqualify the official from participating in your case or force a review of their actions.

Performance Bond: Utilizing the Trust as The Surety

Understanding Performance Bonds:

Performance bonds are a type of surety bond that ensures contractual obligations are met. In legal disputes, performance bonds can be used to guarantee that public officials will perform their duties according to the law.

- **Function of Performance Bonds:** These bonds provide a financial guarantee that the bonded official will perform their duties faithfully and in accordance with the law. If they fail to do so, the bond can be used to compensate the affected parties.

- **Relevance in Criminal Cases:** In the context of a criminal charge, performance bonds can be particularly useful in ensuring that officials act lawfully and ethically throughout the legal proceedings.

Implementing a Trust as Surety:

One advanced strategy for pro se litigants is to use a trust as the surety for a performance bond. This involves setting up a trust that can act as a financial backer for the bond.

- **Establishing a Trust:** To use a trust as surety, you need to establish a trust that holds sufficient assets to back the performance bond. This typically involves creating a legal document that outlines the terms and conditions of the trust and its role as surety.

- **Filing the Performance Bond:** Once the trust is established, you can file a performance bond with the court, naming the trust as the surety. This bond guarantees that the officials involved in your case will adhere to legal standards and perform their duties faithfully.

- **Influencing Legal Proceedings:** By having a performance bond backed by a trust, you add a layer of accountability for the officials involved in your case. This can help ensure compliance with legal standards and may provide leverage in your defense strategy. If an official fails to perform their duties properly, the bond can be claimed against, providing you with a financial remedy.

Practical Example:

Scenario:

Imagine you are facing a criminal charge, and you believe that the police officer who arrested you acted unlawfully during the arrest. You decide to defend yourself in court as a pro se litigant.

Steps:

1. **Request Bond Information:** You submit a public records request to obtain the bonding information of the arresting officer.

2. **Review Bond Details:** Upon receiving the information, you discover that the officer's bond has lapsed.

3. **Challenge Legitimacy:** You present this finding to the court, arguing that the officer's actions should be scrutinized due to the lack of valid bonding, potentially undermining the legitimacy of the arrest.

4. **Establish a Trust as Surety:** Additionally, you establish a trust and file a performance bond, backed by this trust, to ensure that all officials involved in your case act lawfully.

5. **File Complaints:** If you believe any officials have acted unethically, you can file a claim against their bonds, seeking compensation and accountability.

By understanding and utilizing these legal tools, you enhance your ability to navigate the legal system effectively, ensuring that your rights are protected and that officials are held accountable for their actions. This strategic approach can significantly strengthen your defense and increase your chances of a favorable outcome.

STATE OF WISCONSIN, CIRCUIT COURT, MILWAUKEE COUNTY

State of Wisconsin

-vs-

Strickling, Londale Q
Defendant

Date of Birth: 07/11/1983

Offense(s): 940.23(1)(a) FD-1st Degree Reckless Injury
941.29(1m)(a) FG-Possession of Firearm - Convicted Felon

☐ Amended

Bail/Bond

Case No. SUMMARY
Citation No.

A. Monetary Conditions of Release

1. ☒ CASH BAIL: Cash bail of $ $7,500.00 shall be deposited. Date deposited 10/14/2022 3:43 PM
2. ☐ SIGNATURE BOND: ☐ Defendant and/or ☐ Surety gurantees compliance with the terms of this bond by pledging $
3. ☐ PROPERTY BOND: ☐ Defendant and/or ☐ Surety gurantees compliance with the terms of this bond by pledging $ _____ in personal or real property (Description attached).

Surety Name(s): [redacted]

B. Additional Conditions of Release

- Defendant shall appear on all court dates.
- Defendant shall give written notice to the Clerk of this Court within 48 hours of any change of address or telephone number.
- Defendant shall not commit any crime.
- Defendant shall neither directly or indirectly threaten, harass, intimidate or otherwise interfere with victims or witnesses in this action
- Other: PC SET PER CC SUSAN ROTH ON 03/23/2023 AT 1337 HOURS//AW373

☐ See attached

If the defendant does not comply with the terms of this bail/bond, the defendant may be charged with bail jumping, a warrant may be issued for the arrest of the defendant, the bail/bond may be forfeited, and the defendant and/or surety may be ordered to pay the amount of the bond.

Any restitution, recompense, fines, forgeitures or costs imposed against the defendant shall be paid out of the bail/bond without further notice.

Federal law provides penalties for, and you may be prohibited from possessing, transporting, shipping, receiving or purchasing a firearm, including, but not limited to, a rifle, shotgun, pistol, revolver, or ammunition, pursuant to 18 U.S.C. §922(g)(8)-(9).

The sheriff shall detain the defendant in custody until the defendant has signed the bond, complied with the monetary conditions of release, or is otherwise discharged.

I have received a copy of this bail/bond and I agree to its terms. I understand that my next court date(s) is/are:

Circuit Court Location	Date	Time
SB 221 - Honorable Court Commissioner - 821 W State St, Milwaukee, WI 53233	5/4/2023	01:00 PM

Defendant's Signature: X — Date: 3/24/2023
SPN ID Number: 299151 - 3A26-1L

Surety's Signature: X — Date: 3/24/2023
MARSHALL, MARSHELLA

☐ I have furnished the defendant with a copy of this document.

Signature _____
Title _____
Date: 03/24/2023

Legal

Bonding/Insurance Requirements for Municipal Officials

Claire Silverman, Legal Counsel, League of Wisconsin Municipalities

Wisconsin law requires that certain municipal officers be covered by either a bond or a dishonesty insurance or other appropriate insurance policy. The purpose of requiring such bonds or insurance policies is to protect the municipality and its taxpayers against any loss of public funds that might occur if a public officer engages in wrongdoing and fails to faithfully perform the duties of his or her office. Although incidents of embezzlement or misuse of public funds by public officials may be uncommon, such incidents do occur and can be devastating. A recent documentary titled "All the Queen's Horses," details how the City of Dixon, Illinois' appointed comptroller/treasurer embezzled $53.7 million from the City over the course of 22 years. As public infrastructure deteriorated and the City repeatedly slashed its budget and incurred debt in its struggle to provide basic services, Rita Crundwell used the funds she stole from the City to build a championship horse breeding operation.

Questions concerning bonding/insurance requirements typically arise this time of year when new officials take office or are appointed following the spring elections. This month's Comment reviews the law in light of recent changes made by 2017 Wis. Act 51 which simplify the law by giving municipalities discretion to require bonds or obtain a dishonesty insurance policy or other appropriate insurance policy to cover such officials.

Which Municipal Officials Must be Bonded?

Various municipal officials are required by statute to file official bonds as a qualification for office or be covered under a blanket bond or dishonesty insurance policy obtained by the municipality. In cities the treasurer,[1] comptroller,[2] chief of police,[3] municipal judge,[4] and such other officers as the statutes or council may direct[5] are subject to such requirements.

Although the statutes do not expressly require a bond or coverage for city clerks, such a bond is implied by Wis Stat. § 62.09(11)(i), which provides that if a deputy clerk is appointed by the clerk, "[t]he clerk and the clerk's sureties shall be liable on the clerk's official bond for the acts of such deputy." This implication is further supported by § 19.01(4)(f) which provides that the oaths and bonds of city clerks shall be filed in the office of city treasurer. Whether mandatory or not, many cities direct the clerk to file an official bond and this appears to be the better procedure since clerks often handle municipal funds and property.

In villages an official bond or coverage is required by statute of the clerk,[6] treasurer,[7] marshal,[8] constable[9] and municipal judge.[10] The acts of a deputy village treasurer are to be covered by an official bond as the village board shall direct.[11]

The clerk or comptroller of municipalities that have adopted the alternative method of approving financial claims under § 66.0609 are required to be covered by a bond or insurance policy.[12] Also, utility commissions may provide that utility receipts be paid to a bonded cashier appointed by the commission who then must turn the receipts over to the municipal treasurer on a monthly basis.[13]

In general, the official acts of a deputy are covered by the principal's bond. Section 19.01(3) provides in part that the duties mentioned in the oath and bond of public officials must include "the faithful performance by all persons appointed or employed by the officer either in his or her principal or subsidiary office, of their respective duties and trusts therein." Thus, it would appear, for example, that the acts of an assistant clerk appointed by the clerk would be covered by the clerk's bond.

It is doubtful that this is true when the deputy clerk is appointed or employed not by the clerk but by the governing body. If the duties of a deputy or

▸ p.19

---

1. Wis. Stat. § 62.09(4)(a)1.
2. Id.
3. Id.
4. Wis. Stat. § 755.03(1).
5. Wis. Stat. § 62.09(4)(a)1.
6. Wis. Stat. § 61.25(1).
7. Wis. Stat. § 61.26(1).
8. Wis. Stat. § 61.28.
9. Wis. Stat. § 61.29(1)(a).
10. Wis. Stat. § 755.03(1).
11. Wis. Stat. § 61.26t.
12. Wis. Stat. § 66.0609(4).
13. Wis. Stat. § 66.0805(4).

Legal

When Must a Bond Be Filed?

Where public official bonds are required, the bond is usually a prerequisite to the assumption of office. Failure of a municipal official to execute a required bond within the time prescribed by law creates a vacancy in that office.[20] The official bonds of city officers must be approved by the mayor and, when so approved, must be filed within ten days after the officer has been notified of his or her election or appointment.[21] In first class cities (Milwaukee), if an office or position involves fiduciary responsibility or the handling of money, the appointing officer may require the appointee to furnish a bond or other security to the officer and the city.[22]

The official bonds of village officials must be approved by the village president.[23] The village clerk, treasurer, and constable are required to file an official bond at the same time they take their oath of office, which must be done within five days after receiving notice of election or appointment to office.[24]

The only time limit for the filing of bonds by other municipal officials who are not required to take an official oath appears to be in § 19.01(5), which provides that every official required to file a bond shall do so before entering upon the duties of the office.

Local officials should bear in mind that a new bond is required for each term of office. Thus, incumbents who are reelected or reappointed must renew their bonds within the prescribed time periods. Also, bonds continue in force until the officer's successor is duly qualified and installed.[25]

Where are Bonds to be Filed?

Official bonds executed by city officers must be filed in the office of the city clerk. If the city clerk is required by the common council to file a bond, the clerk must file the bond in the office of city treasurer.[26] Similarly, official bonds executed by village officers must be filed in the office of the village clerk, except the village clerk is required to file in the office of village treasurer.[27] In first class cities, after the common council has approved the bonds, the clerk delivers the bonds to the city comptroller who has them recorded in the office of the register of deeds. The comptroller then files them in the clerk's office; a duplicate copy is filed in the comptroller's office.[28]

The Blanket Bond

Municipalities may obtain blanket bonds which provide coverage against losses resulting from failure of officials or employees to perform faithfully or to account properly for all monies or property received by virtue of their office or employment.[29] All officers and subordinates who are not required by law to furnish individual bonds in order to qualify for office are eligible to be covered by a blanket bond.

Amount of Bond Coverage

The amount of an official bond, unless prescribed by statute, is determined by the city council or village board, and is subject to the approval of the mayor or village president.[30] In first class cities, the amount of a bond required by an appointing officer is fixed by the appointing officer with the mayor's approval.[31] In most cases the statutes are silent as to the amount of a bond. For municipalities that have adopted the alternative method of approving financial claims under § 66.0609, the amount of the bond of the clerk or comptroller is specified in sub. (4).[32] Also, the amount of the treasurer's bond required by § 70.67(1) (discussed below) is specified in that statute.

Varying local conditions prevent the establishment of a fixed formula for determining the amount of the bond for various officials. However, certain influential factors may be pointed out. The amount of the bond should be commensurate with the financial responsibility of the position. This may best be determined by the local finance officer and/or municipal attorney. In determining the amount of coverage needed, the largest amount of money on hand at any one time is a more significant factor than the total amount handled by an official during the entire year. Also, the frequency and effectiveness of audits are important factors in determining the amount of a bond.

Municipalities may want to consult with responsible surety companies on the issue of minimum bond requirements.

MUNICIPAL TREASURER'S BOND

In addition to the official bond required of every city and village treasurer pursuant to §§ 61.26 and 62.09(4)(b), § 70.67(1) requires that municipal treasurers execute and deliver to the

▶ p.21

---

20. Wis. Stat. § 17.03(7).
21. Wis. Stat. § 62.09(4)(b).
22. Wis. Stat. § 62.55.
23. Wis. Stat. § 61.22.
24. Wis. Stat. §§ 61.21 and 19.01(5).
25. Wis. Stat. § 19.01(6).
26. Wis. Stat. § 19.01(4)(f).
27. Wis. Stat. § 19.01(4)(g).
28. Wis. Stat. § 62.55.
29. Wis. Stat. §§ 19.07(1), 61.22 and 62.09(4)(b).
30. Wis. Stat. §§ 61.22 and 62.09(4)(b).
31. Wis. Stat. § 62.55.
32. The alternative system of approving financial claims that can be adopted by municipalities under § 66.0609 is only operative if the comptroller or clerk is covered by a fidelity bond of not less than $5,000 in villages and 4th class cities, of not less than $10,000 in 3rd class cities, and of not less than $20,000 in 2nd class cities.

Legal

county treasurer a bond to be approved by the county treasurer, conditioned for the faithful performance of the duties of the office and, more specifically, that the treasurer will account for and pay over all taxes of any kind which are required to be paid to the county treasurer. The bond must be no less than the amount of state and county taxes apportioned to the village or city.

The duplicate treasurer's bond required by § 70.67(1) need not be given to the county if the municipal governing body adopts an ordinance obligating the municipality to pay, in case the treasurer fails to, all taxes required by law to be paid by the municipal treasurer to the county treasurer.[33] A certified copy of the ordinance must be filed with the county treasurer. Such an ordinance remains in effect until a certified copy of its repeal by the municipal governing body is filed with the county clerk and treasurer.

Any governing body that has adopted such an ordinance may demand from the treasurer, in addition to the official bond required of all municipal treasurers, a fidelity or surety bond in an amount and upon such terms as may be determined by the governing body. Such an additional bond must be delivered to the municipal clerk.[34]

Payment of Bond Premiums

In first class cities, where bonds are required by appointing officers pursuant to § 62.55, the premium for the bond is paid out of the city treasury. For other cities and villages, the law authorizes but does not appear to require the municipality to pay the cost of the public official bond of any officer.[35] In cities,[36] unless forbidden by law or unless other means of payment are provided for, the premium for the bond shall be charged to the fund appropriated and set up in the budget for the department, board, commission or other body whose officer is required by law to file a bond.[37] The surety company furnishing the bond must be licensed and the cost of the bond may not exceed the current premium per year on the amount of the bond or obligation executed by the surety.[38]

Statute of Limitations

An action by any municipality to recover a sum of money by reason of the breach of an official bond given by a public officer or employee of the municipality must be commenced within three years after the municipality learns that a default has occurred in some of the conditions of the bond and that it was damaged because of the default. After that, the action is barred.[39]

Fidelity Bonds 33 R-2

About the Author:

Claire Silverman is Legal Counsel for the League of Wisconsin Municipalities. Claire joined the League staff in 1992. Contact Claire at cms@lwm-info.org

---

33. Wis. Stat. § 70.67(2)
34. Id.
35. Wis. Stat. § 19.01(a).
36. The provision referenced in this statute used to be found in § 66.14 which applied to municipalities generally. When chapter 66 was reorganized and modernized in 1999, § 66.14 was renumbered as § 62.09(4)(b) which makes it applicable to cities.
37. Wis. Stat. § 62.09(4)(b)
38. Id.
39. Wis. Stat. § 893.90(1)

Performance Bond

This CONSTRUCTION PERFORMANCE BOND (Bond) is dated May 19, 2023

KNOW ALL PERSONS BY THESE PRESENTS:

WHEREAS, LONDALE QUINTAE STRICLKING©?, united States of America Republic, Arizona Republic, Arizona [00000] (hereafter designated as "Principal"), has, by written agreement dated March 21, 2023, contracted with State of Wisconsin/ Owen M. Piotrowski/ 2023cf001349, 901 N 9th street, Milwaukee, Wisconsin 53233 (hereafter designated as "Owner") to Bond for Attachment Settlement/ Discharge for 2023cf001349 on behalf of LONDALE QUINTAE STRICLKING©? on the property legally described as Bond for Attachment Settlement/ Discharge for 2023cf001349 on behalf of LONDALE QUINTAE STRICLKING©? 07/11/1983. This Agreement, and all of the Contract Documents attached to or forming a part of the Agreement (hereinafter designated as "Contract"), are hereby referred to and incorporated by reference;

NOW THEREFORE, we, the Principal, and LONDALE QUINTAE STRICLKING©? TRUST, a corporation having its principal office at united States of America Republic, San Juan, _____ [00918] and authorized to transact a general surety business in the state of Wisconsin as Surety, are held and firmly bound unto Owner in the sum of $175,000.00, lawful money of the United States of America for the payment of which sum Principal and Surety hereby jointly and severally bind ourselves, our respective heirs, executors, administrators, successors, and assigns.

Bond Terms and Conditions

Principal and surety, jointly and severally bind themselves, their heirs, executors, successors and assigns, to the owner for the complete and proper performance of the construction contract. If the Principal promptly and faithfully performs all the covenants and conditions of the Contract on its part, then the surety and Contractor shall have no obligation under this bond.

Default by Principal

Whenever the Principal is in default under the Contract and is declared by the Owner to be in default, the Surety has to remedy the default. In the alternative, the Surety shall have the option to:

a) assume and complete the Contract in accordance with its terms and conditions;

b) Obtain another to complete the Contract, and thereafter the Surety or that other person shall be subrogated to all the rights of the Principal under the Contract.

Default by the Owner

If the Owner defaults in the performance of any material covenant or condition on its part to be performed under the Contract, the Surety shall be relieved from all liability hereunder.

Limitation of Liability

Suretys monetary obligation under this Bond is limited by the Amount of this Bond identified herein as Penal Sum. This monetary obligation shall augment the balance of the Contract Sum. Subject to these limits, Suretys obligations under this Bond are commensurate with the obligations of the Principal under the Construction Contract. Suretys obligations shall include, but are not limited to:

a) The responsibilities of Principal under the Construction Contract for completion of the Construction Contract and correction of defective work.

b) The responsibilities of Principal under the Construction Contract to pay liquidated damages, and for damages for which no liquidated damages are specified in the Construction Contract, actual damages caused by non-performance of the Construction Contract, including, but not limited to, all valid and proper back charges, offsets, payments, indemnities, or other damages.

c) Additional legal, design professional and delay costs resulting from Principals default or resulting from the actions or failure to act of the Surety.

Suretys Rights Regarding Modification of Construction Contract
If the Principal and the Owner agree on any modifications in the terms of the Contract, or in the drawings and specifications mentioned therein, the Principal shall immediately and prior to the commencement of work designed to put that modification into effect, give notice to the Surety stating the nature and amount of the modification; and the Surety shall have the right in its absolute discretion to disapprove any modification which would, collectively with other modifications not specifically approved by the Surety, increase the contract cost of constructing the building by more than 10 percent.

Force Majeure
The Surety shall not be liable for the nonperformance of any of the terms of the Contract attributable, without limitation, to acts of God, plague, epidemic, pandemic, outbreaks of infectious disease or any other public health crisis, including quarantine or other employee restrictions, fire, explosion, vandalism, storm or other similar occurrence, orders or acts of military or civil authority, or by national emergencies, insurrections, riots, or wars, or strikes, lock-outs, work stoppages or other labor disputes, or supplier failures.

Third Party Rights
No right of action shall accrue on this bond to or for the use of any person, firm, or corporation other than the Owner, its business successors or assigns.

Limitation
No suit, action, or proceeding shall be maintained under this bond unless commenced within two years after the completion of the work.

Governing Law
Any proceeding, legal or equitable, under this Bond shall be instituted in any court of competent jurisdiction where a proceeding is pending regarding the Construction Contract, or in the courts of the State of Wisconsin or in a court of competent jurisdiction where the work is performed.

Notice
All notices to the Surety or Principal shall be mailed or delivered (at the address set forth on the signature page of this Bond), and all notices to the owner shall be mailed or delivered to the address provided in the Construction Contract.

Severability
Any provision in this Bond conflicting with any statutory or regulatory requirement shall be deemed deleted here from and provisions conforming to such statutory requirement shall be deemed incorporated herein.

IN WITNESS WHEREOF two identical counterparts of this instrument, each of which shall for all purposes be deemed an original, have been duly executed by the above Principal and Surety on.

Signatures
This Bond shall be signed by Kabir-Elohim IsReal©?, Authorizer, Ambassador of Private Foreign Trust, on behalf of L███████████████RICI KING©? and by KABIR- ELOHIM ISREAL LLC, Authorized Representative, on behalf of L█████████████████KING©? TRUST.

LONDALE QUINTAE STRICLKING©?

By: _All Rights Reserved_ Date: 05/20/2023
Kabir-Elohim IsReal©?, Authorizer, Ambassador of Private Foreign Trust

LONDALE QUINTAE STRICLKING©? TRUST

By: _Kabir-Elohim Isreal LLC_ Date: 05/20/2023
KABIR- ELOHIM ISREAL LLC, Authorized Representative

Section 2: Asserting Legal Presence and Demands

As a pro se litigant, asserting your legal presence and making formal demands within the judicial process are crucial steps in defending yourself against criminal charges. This section explains two important tools: the Notice of Appearance and Demand for Discharge, and the Notification of Record. Understanding how to use these tools effectively can help you establish your legal identity, challenge the court's jurisdiction, and potentially shift the focus from criminal penalties to financial resolutions.

Notice of Appearance and Demand for Discharge

Filing the Notice:

A Notice of Appearance is a formal document that informs the court that you, as the defendant, are participating in the legal proceedings. It also serves to challenge the court's jurisdiction over your new legal identity.

- **Drafting the Notice**: Begin by drafting a document that includes your full name, case number, and a statement indicating that you are entering your appearance in the case. Clearly assert your new legal identity and any supporting documents, such as a legal name change or a foreign national passport.

- **Challenging Jurisdiction**: Include a section in the notice that challenges the court's jurisdiction over your new legal identity. Cite relevant laws or precedents that support your right to be recognized under your new identity.

- **Submission**: Submit the Notice of Appearance to the court clerk's office, ensuring that it is filed in your case record. Send copies to all parties involved, including the prosecution.

EXAMPLE:

```
IN THE [COURT NAME] OF [JURISDICTION]

Case No. [Your Case Number]

NOTICE OF APPEARANCE AND CHALLENGE TO JURISDICTION

I, [Your New Legal Name], hereby enter my appearance in the above-referenced case. I assert my legal identity as [New Legal Identity Details] and challenge the court's jurisdiction over this identity based on [Legal Grounds for Challenge].

Respectfully submitted,

[Your Signature]

[Your New Legal Name]

[Date]
```

Demand for Performance:

A Demand for Performance is a legal request that obligates the court or other parties to meet their contractual obligations, such as respecting your rights under your new legal identity.

- Drafting the Demand: Clearly state your demand for the court to perform its duties in accordance with your rights. Highlight any contractual obligations or legal standards that must be met.

- Submission: File the demand along with your Notice of Appearance or as a separate document if necessary. Ensure that it is included in the case file and acknowledged by the court.

EXAMPLE:

```

DEMAND FOR PERFORMANCE

I, [Your New Legal Name], demand that the court and all involved parties perform their duties in accordance with [specific legal standards or contractual obligations]. Failure to do so will be met with appropriate legal action.

Respectfully submitted,

[Your Signature]

[Your New Legal Name]

[Date]

```

Notification of Record: Compensation and Settlement Sources

Purpose of Notification:

A Notification of Record is used to inform court officials about potential sources of compensation or settlement, such as trust assets or performance bonds. This document aims to shift the court's focus from criminal penalties to financial resolutions.

- Drafting the Notification: Prepare a document that outlines the sources of compensation available. This may include assets held in a trust or performance bonds that can be used to settle the case.

- Submission: File the Notification of Record with the court and provide copies to all relevant parties, ensuring that it becomes part of the official case record.

EXAMPLE:

```
NOTIFICATION OF RECORD

Case No. [Your Case Number]

I, [Your New Legal Name], hereby notify the court that compensation and settlement for the above-referenced case can be sourced from [Trust Assets/Performance Bonds]. Attached are the relevant documents verifying the availability of these funds.

Respectfully submitted,

[Your Signature]

[Your New Legal Name]

[Date]
```

Strategic Filing:

Filing a Notification of Record strategically can influence the outcome of your case by emphasizing financial resolutions over criminal penalties.

- Shift the Focus: Use the notification to suggest that the court consider financial settlements as an alternative to criminal sanctions. This can be particularly effective if the court is aware of significant trust assets or performance bonds available for settlement.

- Highlight Benefits: Emphasize how settling the case through financial means benefits all parties involved, potentially reducing the burden on the judicial system and providing timely resolution.

EXAMPLE STRATEGY:

- File Early: Submit the Notification of Record early in the proceedings to set the tone for financial negotiations.

- Document Evidence: Include thorough documentation of the available funds and how they can be accessed for settlement.

- Negotiate: Use the notification as a basis for negotiating with the prosecution and the court, proposing a financial settlement that satisfies the legal requirements and resolves the case efficiently.

By understanding and effectively utilizing these legal tools, you can assert your presence in the legal process, challenge jurisdictional issues, and strategically steer the outcome towards favorable resolutions. These steps are essential for a pro se litigant defending against criminal charges, providing a clear path to asserting your rights and protecting your interests.

John 3:3

Yeshua answered and said unto him, Verily, verily, I say unto thee, Except a man be born again, he cannot see the kingdom of God.

💎💎💎

STATES OF WISCONSIN CIRCUIT
COURT MILWAUKEE COUNTY

State of Wisconsin and District Attorney Owen M. Piotrowski

Plaintiffs

-vs-

Kabir -Elohim IsReal©
Secured Party UCC Filing # P19008387-8, P19007796-6
united states of America Republic
Non domestic/Non-Combatant/Non assumptive

Defendant

2023cf001349

NOTICE OF APPEARANCE AND DEMAND FOR DISCHARGE

I, Kabir-Elohim IsReal©, of Arizona Republic, in united states of America Republic County, Arizona, MAKE OATH AND SAY THAT:

Dear clerk, the accompanying Private Registered Bond/ bonded bill of exchange, Certificate of Live Birth as well as Trust Certificate Unit# 5, is hereby presented under notary seal by pre-arrangement with the department of Treasury. Treasury secretary [Teresita Fuentes] is copay on the instrument and holder of the securitization Bond reference thereon

Please credit the above reference account dollar for dollar for the full value of the instrument (case#2023cf001349) and present it to [Teresita Fuentes] no later than three(3) days after this date you receive it from the date of receipt.

The court is hereby authorized to utilize the revenue winfall to its benefit until maturity. In consideration you are expected to issue a settlement statement, warrant or other confirmation of closure of [2023cf001349] reflecting the posted credit. You may also debit any customary fees and mailing costs. Please allow sixty (60) days for final reconciliation. However, customary banking practices via your treasury account can shorten the duration.

Please submit your copy of IRS form 1040v to ensure treasury can track the transactions. The payment instrument has been marked RE: [7018 3090 0000 7573 2846] and UCC filing #E21027511, P19008387-8, P19007796-6 and will be monitored in real time to protect [Teresita Fuentes] interest. It is essential that you pass the credit and make presentment to the Secretary of Treasury or return the instrument for cause with evidence of a substantial legal defect from a qualified third party within three (3) days of receipt.

Failure to post the credit or identify a defect within ten (10) days will be certified in a Default Judgment by the notary to be issued and filed with the clerk of court. That judgment will comprise your stipulation to the value and validity of the instrument and confession of the theft of public funds when you defaulted on the opportunity to rebut. A return of the instrument without cause will be certified as a conversion of liability under public policy, i.e. your agreement to accept liability for the missing funds. Any attempt to malign payment without a demonstrative notice of dishonor or certificate of protest will be treated as commercial slander.

In any event, legal fiction ▓▓▓▓▓▓▓▓▓▓▓ TRICKLING© is required to report your gains on form 1099OID. The "Creditor" intends to report all suspicious activity and honor his misprision of felony obligations.

REQUEST FOR IRS FORM W-9

PLEASE COMPLETE FORM W-9 AND RETURN TO THE UNDERSIGN NO LATER THAN ten (10) days from the post mark to facilitate such reporting. Typically, the IRS Criminal Investigation Division seizes the full amount of funds on behalf of the Treasury, and a warrant is issued to the Marshall for distress of the Respondents public hazard bond on behalf of the Treasury, the Alien Property Custodian thereby rendering the party uninsurable for public service. Any such commercial process will be audited by the Comptroller General of the President's Corporate task force.

Default judgment will also comprise your consent for legal fiction LON▓▓▓▓▓▓▓▓▓ ST▓▓▓▓▓▓▓▓ to file the judgment annexed to a criminal complaint with the u.s. Attorney [OR DISTRICT ATTORNEY OR ATTORNEY GENERAL of the UNITED STATES].

STATE OF WISCONSIN

COUNTY OF UNITED STATES OF AMERICA REPUBLIC

SUBSCRIBED AND SWORN TO BEFORE ME, on the _19_ day of _May_, _2023_

Signature
Alice Carter (Seal)
NOTARY PUBLIC
My Commission expires:
_12/12/25_

All Rights Reserved.
Kabir-Elohim Ben
(Signature)

Kabir-Elohim IsReal©

ALICIA CARTER
Notary Public
State of Wisconsin

Certified Mail Tracking Number: 7018 3090 0000 7573 2846

Notification of Record

TO:
Director of court services/Clerk of circuit Court
Anna Marie Hodges
901 North 9th Street,
MILWAUKEE, WISCONSIN [53233]

FROM:
Kabir-Elohim Isreal©
███████████
███████████
PUERTO RICO [00918] united
States of America REPUBLIC

RE: Accounts/Trusts under account or sub-account and/or ███████

Dear Director of Court Services.

Until recently I was unaware that there were affairs being managed on my behalf without my knowledge or consent that have been left improperly tended with atrocious results. Now that it has come to my attention that

1) matters are not being handled equitably
2) matters are not being handled with efficiency
3) in many respects matters are not being taken care of at all
4) usurpation of funds is occurring
5) there is rampant fraud and deceit
6) position of trustee has been left vacant or improperly attenuated

I have waived beneficial position and interest to take a position of trustee to manage the affairs of the trust L███████████████████ TRUST© and full control forth hence as indicated and identified by the account numbers above.

Please return all information to the address above if you have any on hand or is in your care to the Trustee. All others are now barred from handling affairs in re ███████████████████. All contracts that are in existence for Trust are to be returned to trustee within 30 Days for management or shall be considered vitiated nunc pro tunc, void from inception by the trust forth hence. Your prompt cooperation is greatly appreciated.

Furthermore this and all pertinent documentation has been filed as public record under necessity in the Commercial registry of the States of Wisconsin and Iowa P19007796-6, P19008387-8, E21027511-3. This is notice and acceptance via your receipt of this mailing. If you feel this notice is in any way in error or disagree with the change in position please feel free to rebut this notice with your concerns within 30 days or it will stand as fact prima facie.

Notice to agent is notice to principal and notice to principal is notice to agent.

Trustee/Secured Party
Kabir-Elohim Isreal©
Without Prejudice/Without Recourse

Kabir-Elohim Isreal
Authorized Representative of
█████████████████ TRUST©

44

Form W-8BEN

Certificate of Foreign Status of Non-resident for United States Tax Withholding and Reporting (Human)

Department of the Treasury
Internal Revenue Service

► For use by humans. Entities must use Form W-8BEN-E.
► Information about Form W-8BEN and its separate instructions is at www.irs.gov/formw8ben.
► Give this form to the withholding agent or payer. Do not send to the IRS.

OMB No. 1545-1621

Do NOT use this form if:	Instead, use Form:
• You are NOT an individual ("individual" means a "non-resident non-person non-taxpayer" under the I.R.C.)	W-8BEN-E
• You are a statutory U.S. citizen or other U.S. person, including a resident alien individual	W-9
• You are a beneficial owner claiming that income is effectively connected with the conduct of trade or business within the U.S. (other than personal services)	W-8ECI
• You are a beneficial owner who is receiving compensation for personal services performed in the United States	8233 or W-4
• A person acting as an intermediary	W-8IMY

Part I — Identification of Non-Resident Non-Taxpayer (see instructions)

1 Name of human applicant
[redacted]

2 Country of nationality
American National

3 Mailing address (Not a domicile or residence. Don't have a domicile or residence) (street, apt. or suite no., or rural route)
C/O 226 [redacted]

City or town, state or province. Include postal code where appropriate.
San J[redacted]

Country
united States of America

4 [address] (if different from above)

City or town, state or province. Include postal code where appropriate.

Country

5 U.S. taxpayer identification number (SSN or ITIN), if required (not required)
NONE (Not required. See 31 CFR 306.10; 31 CFR 103.34(a)(3)(x); W-8BEN Inst. p. 1,2,4,5 (Cat. 25576H), W-8 Supp. Inst. p. 1,2,6 (Cat. 26698G); Pub. 515 Inst. p. 7; Form 1042-s Inst. p. 1,14)

6 Foreign tax identifying number (see instructions)

7 Reference number(s) (see instructions)

8 Date of birth (MM-DD-YYYY) (see instructions)
07/11/1983

Part II — Claim of Tax Treaty Benefits (for chapter 3 purposes only) (see instructions)

9 I certify that the non-resident is a resident of _____ within the meaning of the income tax treaty between the United States and that country.

10 Special rates and conditions (if applicable—see instructions): The beneficial owner is claiming the provisions of Article _____ of the treaty identified on line 9 above to claim a _____ % rate of withholding on (specify type of income) _____.

Explain the reasons the non-resident meets the terms of the treaty article: _____

Part III — Certification

Under penalties of perjury from without the "United States" as defined in 26 U.S.C. §1740(1) and 26 U.S.C. §7701(a)(9) and (a)(10), I declare that I have examined the information on this form and to the best of my knowledge and belief it is true, correct, and complete. I further certify from without the "United States" that:

- I am the human who is the non-resident (or am authorized to sign for the human that is the non-resident) of all the earnings to which this form relates or am using this form to document myself as a statutory "non-resident non-person" that is an owner or account holder of a financial institution outside the geographical "United States" per I.R.C. 7701(a)(9) and (a)(10).
- The human named on line 1 of this form is not a statutory "U.S. person", "person", or "individual" as defined in 26 U.S.C. §7701(a)(30) or 26 U.S.C. §7701(c), or 26 C.F.R. §1.1441-1(c)(3) respectively, would have to hold a public office to be any of these entities, and does not consensually hold such an office
- The earnings to which this form relates are:
  (a) not effectively connected with the conduct of a "trade or business" (public office per 26 U.S.C. §7701(a)(26)) in the United States (government),
  (b) not earned from sources within the geographical "United States" defined in 26 U.S.C. §7701(a)(9) and (a)(10),
  (c) not subject to reporting per 26 U.S.C. §6041 because not connected to a statutory "trade or business" (public office)
  (d) not subject to withholding because not statutory "income" per 26 U.S.C. §643(b) and earned by a "non-resident non-person non-taxpayer".
- The non-resident named on line 1 of this form is a resident of the treaty country listed on line 9 of the form (if any) within the meaning of the income tax treaty between the United States and that country, and
- For broker transactions or barter exchanges, the non-resident is either not-subject or statutorily exempt foreign person as defined in the instructions.

Furthermore, I authorize this form to be provided to any withholding agent that has control, receipt, or custody of the earnings of which I am the non-resident or any withholding agent that can disburse or make payments of the income of which I am the non-resident. I agree that I will submit a new form within 30 days if any certification made on this form becomes incorrect.

All rights reserved

Sign Here ► _Kabir Elohim IsReal_ (signature)
Signature of non-resident (or individual authorized to sign for non-resident)

Date (MM-DD-YYYY): August 7, 2019

Print name of signer: Kabir- Elohim IsReal

Capacity in which acting (if form is not signed by non-resident): Trustee

For Paperwork Reduction Act Notice, see separate instructions.
Cat. No. 25047Z
Form W-8BEN (Rev. 2-2014)

Section 3:

Establishing New Identity Legally

In defending against criminal charges as a pro se litigant, one powerful strategy is to establish a new legal identity that separates your current self from any past legal entanglements. This section will guide you through two crucial documents: the W-8BEN form and its supporting affidavit, and Form 56, which notifies the IRS of a fiduciary relationship. Understanding and effectively using these forms can significantly strengthen your defense.

W-8BEN and Affidavit: Separation from Entity and Living Man/Woman

Utilizing W-8BEN Forms:

The W-8BEN form is used by non-resident aliens to establish their foreign status for tax purposes. However, it can also serve as a powerful tool in asserting the separation between your living persona and any connected legal entities or obligations.

- **Purpose of the W-8BEN Form:** The primary purpose of the W-8BEN is to declare that you are not a U.S. person for tax purposes. By filing this form, you assert your status as a non-resident alien, which can help separate your personal identity from any legal entities that may be associated with previous legal or financial obligations.

- **Filing the W-8BEN Form:** Complete the form by providing your personal information, foreign address, and details that confirm your non-resident alien status. Submit the form to the relevant financial institutions or government bodies as required.

EXAMPLE:

```
```

Form W-8BEN

Certificate of Foreign Status of Beneficial Owner for United States Tax Withholding and Reporting (Individuals)

Part I: *Identification of Beneficial Owner*

1. Name of individual: [Your New Legal Name]

2. Country of citizenship: [Your New Country of Citizenship]

3. Permanent residence address: [Your Foreign Address]

Part II: *Claim of Tax Treaty Benefits (if applicable)*

[Complete as necessary]

Part III: *Certification*

Under penalties of perjury, I declare that I have examined the information on this form and to the best of my knowledge and belief, it is true, correct, and complete.

[Your Signature]

[Date]

```
```

Drafting an Affidavit:

A supporting affidavit strengthens your W-8BEN form by providing additional context and confirmation of your claims.

- **Purpose of the Affidavit**: The affidavit clarifies and supports the information provided in your W-8BEN form, asserting your new legal identity and the separation from any prior legal entities or obligations.

- **Creating the Affidavit**: Write a detailed statement that explains your new identity, your reasons for the change, and how this identity separates you from past obligations. Have the affidavit notarized to ensure its legal validity.

EXAMPLE:

```
AFFIDAVIT OF [YOUR NEW LEGAL NAME]

I, [Your New Legal Name], being duly sworn, depose and say:

1. I am a non-resident alien for tax purposes, and I have submitted a W-8BEN form to assert this status.

2. I have legally changed my name from [Your Old Legal Name] to [Your New Legal Name] and have established my permanent residence in [Your New Country].

3. This affidavit supports my W-8BEN form and confirms that I am not subject to U.S. tax obligations under my new legal identity.

[Your Signature]

[Notary Public Signature]

[Date]
```

Form 56: Establishing Fiduciary Relationships

Form 56 Explained:

Form 56 is used to notify the IRS and other agencies of a fiduciary relationship. This can redefine financial and legal responsibilities under your new identity.

- **Purpose of Form 56:** By filing Form 56, you inform the IRS that you are acting in a fiduciary capacity, such as a trustee or executor. This can help protect your assets and redefine how you interact with government bodies.

- **Filing Form 56:** Complete the form by providing your personal information, the fiduciary's information (your new legal identity), and details about the fiduciary relationship. Submit the form to the IRS and any other relevant agencies.

EXAMPLE:

```

```

Form 56

Notice Concerning Fiduciary Relationship

Part I: Identification

1. Name of person for whom you are acting: [Your Old Legal Name]

2. Fiduciary's name: [Your New Legal Name]

3. Address: [Your New Address]

Part II: Nature of Fiduciary Relationship

4. Type of fiduciary relationship: [Trustee/Executor]

5. Date of creation: [Date of Legal Identity Change]

Part III: Court and Administrative Proceedings

[Complete as necessary]

Certification

Under penalties of perjury, I declare that I have examined this form and to the best of my knowledge and belief, it is true, correct, and complete.

[Your Signature]

[Date]

```
```

Impact on Legal Proceedings:

Establishing a fiduciary relationship can significantly influence your legal defense.

- **Asset Protection:** By acting in a fiduciary capacity, you can protect your personal assets from being directly linked to your past legal obligations. This separation can shield your current assets from claims made against your previous identity.

- **Redefining Interactions:** Informing government bodies of your new fiduciary role can change how they interact with you legally and financially. It can establish a clear distinction between your past and present identities, which is crucial in defending against criminal charges.

Conclusion of Chapter 2

This chapter equips you with a thorough understanding of the key documents and strategies necessary for building a solid defense based on a new identity and enhanced legal knowledge. By utilizing the W-8BEN form and supporting affidavit, and by establishing fiduciary relationships through Form 56, you can assert your rights, challenge conventional procedures, and shift the narrative from criminal defense to a discussion on rights and identity recognition. This foundation is critical for anyone looking to navigate complex legal challenges, especially when their past and present identities are in conflict.

W8BEN Affidavit

(International) Commercial Affidavit

This Affidavit in regards to the W-8BEN on the obverse side is executed as Lawful **"PUBLIC NOTICE"** [U.C.C. § 1-201(25)(26)(27)]. The Trustee/Secured Party signatory hereto is executing document under signature; expressly to **"declare trustees stature as a Non-Resident/Non-Person in regards to U.S. Inc. (Id)"** with no duress, in accord the terms of the aforementioned. Therefore, I, the Trustee/Secured Party duly depose and says without recourse that, the foregoing is true, correct, and certain; and if called as a witness, I am One; who can "Testify" to the facts, evidenced, and subject-matter within Trust Documentation and supporting documents as well as the "W-8BEN" evidence(d) on the obverse side of this page; executed hereunder; and expressly supported by this Affidavit; executed as dated below, nunc pro tunc to 07/11/2001 the date or original creation of trust.

NOTICE TO AGENT IS [Imputed] NOTICE TO PRINCIPAL, NOTICE TO PRINCIPAL IS [Imputed] NOTICE TO ALL AGENTS OF THE SUBJECT MATTER HEREIN, and PRESENTED IN GOOD FAITH [UCC. § 1-201(19) UCC § 1-203; UCC § 1-202].

This Affidavit is executed under the penalty of perjury; [in nature of 28 U.S.C. § 1746(1)] expressly without UNITED STATES, [i.e., "28 U.S.C. § 3002(15)(A); U.C.C. § 9-307(h); U.S.C.A. Const. Art. 1:8;17- 18,"] Administered by a commissioned officer, i.e., Notary Public in accordance who is also acknowledging same [in accordance Fed.R.Evid. 902(1)(B)].

[signature]
Trustee/Secured Party: Kabir- Elohim IsReal
All Rights Reserved, Without Prejudice. [UCC 1-308]

WITNESSES

We the undersigned Witnesses hereby STAND and Attest that the fore signed, signed this document on the date listed supra, of their own Free Will, as witnessed by Our Signatures below:

First Witness Signature
Address: ~~[redacted]~~

Second Witness Signature
Address: ~~[redacted]~~ Republic

W8BEN Affidavit

Item # 07111983-LQS-W8BEN

Form 56 — Notice Concerning Fiduciary Relationship

(Rev. December 2011)
Department of the Treasury
Internal Revenue Service

(Internal Revenue Code sections 6036 and 6903)

OMB No. 1545-0013

Part I — Identification

Name of person for whom you are acting (as shown on the tax return): ███████ TRUST ®

Address of person for whom you are acting (number, street, and room or suite no.): 220 ███████

City, town, state, and ZIP code (if a foreign address, see instructions): San Juan ███████ 918█

Identifying number:

Decedent's social security no.:

Fiduciary's name: TERESITA FUENTES, et al D.B.A. SECRETARY OF TREASURY [UNITED STATES]

Address of fiduciary (number, street, and room or suite no.): C/O DEPARTMENT DE HACIENDA, P.O. BOX 9024140

City or town, state, and ZIP code: SAN JUAN, PUERTO RICO 00902-4140

Telephone number (optional): (787) 721-2020

Section A. Authority

1. Authority for fiduciary relationship. Check applicable box:
   - a. ☐ Court appointment of testate estate (valid will exists)
   - b. ☐ Court appointment of intestate estate (no valid will exists)
   - c. ☐ Court appointment as guardian or conservator
   - d. ☑ Valid trust instrument and amendments
   - e. ☐ Bankruptcy or assignment for the benefit of creditors
   - f. ☐ Other. Describe ▶

2a. If box 1a or 1b is checked, enter the date of death ▶

2b. If box 1c–1f is checked, enter the date of appointment, taking office, or assignment or transfer of assets ▶

Section B. Nature of Liability and Tax Notices

3. Type of taxes (check all that apply): ☑ Income ☐ Gift ☐ Estate ☐ Generation-skipping transfer ☐ Employment ☐ Excise ☐ Other (describe) ▶

4. Federal tax form number (check all that apply): a ☐ 706 series b ☐ 709 c ☐ 940 d ☐ 941, 943, 944 e ☐ 1040, 1040-A, or 1040-EZ f ☑ 1041 g ☐ 1120 h ☐ Other (list) ▶

5. If your authority as a fiduciary does not cover all years or tax periods, check here . . . . ▶ ☐ and list the specific years or periods ▶

6. If the fiduciary listed wants a copy of notices or other written communications (see the instructions) check this box . . . . ▶ ☐ and enter the year(s) or period(s) for the corresponding line 4 item checked. If more than 1 form entered on line 4h, enter the form number.

Complete only if the line 6 box is checked.

If this item is checked:	Enter year(s) or period(s)	If this item is checked:	Enter year(s) or period(s)
4a		4b	
4c		4d	
4e		4f	
4g		4h:	
4h:		4h:	

For Paperwork Reduction Act and Privacy Act Notice, see the separate instructions.   Cat. No. 16375I   Form **56** (Rev. 12-2011)

Form 56 (Rev. 12-2011)

Part II — Court and Administrative Proceedings

Name of court (if other than a court proceeding, identify the type of proceeding and name of agency)

Address of court

City or town, state, and ZIP code | Date | Time ☐ a.m. ☐ p.m. | Place of other proceedings

Date proceeding initiated

Docket number of proceeding

Part III — Signature

TRUSTEE On behalf of LONDALE QUINTAE STRICKLING TRUST©

Please Sign Here

I certify that I have the authority to execute this notice concerning fiduciary relationship on behalf of the taxpayer.

TERESITA FUENTES — By appointment of: LONDALE QUINTAE STRICKLING TRUST©
Fiduciary's signature | Secretary of Treasury | Title, if applicable | Date

ACTUAL & CONSTRUCTIVE LEGAL NOTICE [U.C.C. §§ 1-201(25)(26)(27)]:

By appointment you TERESITA FUENTES have been chosen to act as fiduciary in re L_____ TRUST©. Please see accompanying Minutes of Trust designating your appointment. If this appointment is outside of your abilities/scope, or you do not choose to take the position please simply return all documentation to the trust within 30 days and we will designate a new appointment.

Otherwise this document will act as PUBLIC NOTICE and will be filed along with related instruments upon the U.C.C. Commercial Registry constituting "Lawful", open, notorious, public notice of the subject-matter executed & presented in good-faith U.C.C. § 1-201(19); U.C.C. § 1-203 to the UNITED STATES, i.e., 28 U.S.C. 3002(15)(A); U.C.C. § 9-307(h); U.S.C.A. .Const. Art. 1:8:17-18, by the real party in interest; Trustee/TRUST & Holder-in-Due-Course (HDC) of this and all related documents and instruments.

TAKE SPECIAL NOTICE From "Lawful" private Trust jurisdiction ['as defined within, 26 U.S.C. § 7701(a)(31); 8 U.S.C. § 1101(a)(14); 28 U.S.C. § 1603(b)(3)"] That entity and man are "Non-Assumpsit"; and "Non-Domestic and Non-Federal" in regards the UNITED STATES and/or any of its "Constituent STATES" incorporated thereof, e.g., inter alia, but not limited to, STATE OF WI, STATE OF IOWA, and the like; and also in regards the UNITED NATIONS, as well as to England & Russia... Intent to contract does not validate or give ascent to any contract or waiver of right unless implicity stated in writing. Noting: within a State: That Congress cannot create a trade or business, [i.e., "as defined within 26 U.S.C. § 7701(a)(26),"] tax it; [See: inter alia, License Tax Cases, 72 U.S. 462; 18 L.E. 497 (1866); M'Ilvaine v. Coxe's Lessee,8 U.S. 209; 2 L.E. 598 (1808); and Yick Wo v. Hopkins, 118 U.S. 356, 6 S.Ct 1064 (1886)]. All accounts in relation to 349-72-1930/112-99182 or the like Accounts are accepted with Claim [11 U S.C. § 101(5)] and [Special] Maritime Lien upon all related accounts both general & special and if not currently held are to be transferred and held in _____ RUST; as defined in TRUST and supporting documentation. Lien will be removed when transference and control of all aforesaid accounts are transferred in full to trust under Trustee's sole control. Without prejudice, for cause.

Trustee: Kabir-Elohim IsReal on behalf of L_____ G TRUST©

All Rights Reserved, Without Prejudice. UCC 1-308

WITNESSES

We the undersigned Witnesses hereby STAND and Attest that the fore signed, signed this document on the date listed supra, of their own Free Will, as witnessed by Our Signatures below:

First Witness Signature
Address:

Second Witness Signature
Address:

Chapter 3:

Financial Instruments and Legal Tools

In this chapter, we will explore sophisticated financial instruments and legal tools that can be crucial in managing and asserting a new legal identity, particularly when facing criminal charges. These tools can help you establish financial stability, verify your identity, and potentially shift the nature of your legal disputes from criminal to civil matters.

Section 1: Utilizing Trusts and Bonds

Payment Bond from Trust

Definition and Usage:

A payment bond is a type of surety bond typically used in commercial and legal contexts to guarantee payment or performance of a contract. When facing legal disputes, particularly those involving financial obligations, a trust can issue a payment bond to ensure these obligations are met.

- **Payment Bond**: A financial guarantee that ensures the payment of a debt or the fulfillment of a contractual obligation.

- **Trust as Issuer:** By using trust certificate units (TCUs), a trust can issue a payment bond, which acts as a negotiable instrument within the trust structure. This can be particularly useful in legal disputes to show that there are financial resources backing the obligations.

Practical Application:

Here's a step-by-step guide on how to set up a payment bond using TCUs:

1. **Establish a Trust:** Create a trust that holds assets sufficient to back the payment bond.

2. **Issue Trust Certificate Units (TCUs):** These units represent the value of the assets within the trust and can be used as a negotiable instrument.

3. **Draft the Payment Bond:** Include details such as the amount guaranteed, the parties involved, and the conditions under which the bond can be claimed.

4. **File the Bond:** Submit the bond to the relevant legal or financial authorities as part of your case documentation.

EXAMPLE:

```
Payment Bond

This Payment Bond, issued by [Trust Name], guarantees the payment of [Amount] to [Beneficiary], ensuring the fulfillment of [Obligation/Contract]. This bond is backed by Trust Certificate Units (TCUs) valued at [Amount], held within [Trust Name].


Signed,

[Trustee Name]

Date: [Date]
```

Notarial Certificate: Identity Verification and Authorization

Role of Notarial Certification:

A notarial certificate is essential in verifying the authenticity of documents and the identity of the signatory. This is especially important in cases involving new legal identities and substantial financial transactions.

- **Verification:** The notary public verifies that the person signing the document is indeed who they claim to be, adding a layer of legitimacy to the document.

- **Authorization:** The notary's seal and signature confirm that the document has been properly executed and can be trusted in legal and financial contexts.

Process and Impact:

Here's how to obtain and use a notarial certificate:

1. **Prepare the Document:** Draft the document that needs notarization, ensuring all details are accurate and complete.

2. **Visit a Notary Public:** Present the document and your identification to a notary public.

3. **Notarization:** The notary will verify your identity, witness your signature, and affix their seal and signature to the document.

4. **Use in Court:** Submit the notarized document as part of your legal filings to confirm the separation between your new identity and any previous legal or financial claims.

EXAMPLE:

```
Notarial Certificate

State of [State]

County of [County]


On this [Date] day of [Month], [Year], before me, [Notary Name], a Notary Public in and for said County, personally appeared [Your New Legal Name], known to me (or satisfactorily proven) to be the person whose name is subscribed to the within instrument, and acknowledged that [he/she] executed the same for the purposes therein contained.

In witness whereof, I hereunto set my hand and official seal.


[Notary Signature]

[Notary Seal]
```

Section 2:

Establishing and Managing Financial Identity

Private Register Bond for Investment (PRB)

Understanding PRBs:

A Private Register Bond for Investment (PRB) is a financial instrument used to verify and manage accounts and investments associated with a trust or new legal entity. PRBs help in establishing the legitimacy and financial standing of your new identity.

- **Verification Tool:** PRBs serve as proof of financial backing for your legal claims or investments.

- **Management Tool:** They help in managing and organizing the assets held under your new identity or trust structure.

Creating and Using PRBs:

Here's how to create and utilize PRBs:

1. **Create the PRB**: Draft a bond document that outlines the assets and investments associated with your trust or new legal entity.

2. **Verification**: Include details that verify the existence and value of the assets, such as account statements or asset appraisals.

3. **Usage:** Use the PRB to manage and verify financial accounts, presenting it as evidence in legal or financial proceedings.

EXAMPLE:

```
Private Register Bond for Investment

This Private Register Bond, issued by [Trust Name], verifies the existence and value of assets amounting to [Amount], held within [Trust Name]. These assets are registered and managed under the authority of [Trustee Name].


Signed,

[Trustee Name]

Date: [Date]
```

Trust Certificate Unit: Deed of Transfer/Bond for Settlement

Functionality of TCUs:

Trust Certificate Units (TCUs) are used as deeds of transfer or bonds for settlement, facilitating the movement and management of assets within a trust. They act as negotiable instruments that represent the value of assets held by the trust.

- **Deed of Transfer:** TCUs can be used to transfer ownership of assets within the trust.
- **Bond for Settlement:** They can also serve as financial guarantees in legal settlements.

Endorsement and Legal Relevance:

Here's how to endorse and use TCUs:

1. **Issue TCUs:** Create trust certificates that represent specific values of the assets held within the trust.

2. **Endorse the TCUs:** Include a notary's endorsement on the back side of the certificate to make it a valid financial instrument.

3. **Use in Transactions:** Present the endorsed TCUs as part of legal settlements or asset transfers.

EXAMPLE:

```
Trust Certificate Unit

This certificate represents [Amount] held within [Trust Name]. The bearer of this certificate is entitled to the value of the assets as specified.


Endorsed by:

[Notary Signature]

[Notary Seal]

Date: [Date]
```

Section 3:

Legal Recognition and Documentation

Original' Certificate of Live Birth

Legal and Symbolic Significance:

The original certificate of live birth is a foundational identity document. It serves as the primary proof of one's birth and legal identity.

- **Legal Significance**: It is used to establish the legitimacy of one's identity in various legal contexts.

- **Symbolic Significance**: It represents the individual's legal existence and heritage.

Strategic Use in Legal Disputes:

Here's how to leverage this document:

1. **Obtain the Certificate**: Request a certified copy of your original certificate of live birth from the relevant authorities.

2. **Use in Legal Proceedings**: Present the certificate in court to affirm your identity and its relevance to current legal matters.

EXAMPLE:

```
Certified Copy of Certificate of Live Birth

State of [State]

County of [County]


This certifies that [Your Name] was born on [Date] in [City, State]. This document serves as proof of identity and legal existence.


Certified by:

[Registrar's Signature]

Date: [Date]
```

Bond for Probate: Converting Criminal Charges to Civil Matters

Purpose and Process:

A bond for probate can be used to shift criminal charges to civil disputes, focusing on financial compensation rather than punitive outcomes.

- **Purpose**: Convert the nature of the legal dispute to allow for financial settlements.

- **Process**: Obtain a bond for probate from an online bonding company, attach the case number, and use the bond in court to argue for civil adjudication.

Acquisition and Application:

Here's how to acquire and apply a bond for probate:

1. **Obtain the Bond:** Purchase a bond for probate from a reputable online bonding company.

2. **Attach Case Number:** Ensure the bond includes your case number and relevant details.

3. **Submit in Court:** File the bond with the court as part of your defense strategy to argue for the conversion of criminal charges to a civil matter.

EXAMPLE:

```
Bond for Probate

This bond, issued by [Bonding Company], guarantees the payment of [Amount] for the case of [Your Case Number]. This bond is intended to convert the nature of the charges to a civil dispute focusing on financial compensation.


Issued by:

[Bonding Company Representative]

Date: [Date]
```

Conclusion of Chapter 3

Chapter 3 equips you with an understanding of sophisticated financial instruments and legal documents essential for asserting and managing a new legal identity, particularly in complex legal challenges. By utilizing these tools, you can establish financial stability, verify your identity, and shift the nature of legal disputes from criminal to civil. This knowledge empowers you to navigate your legal journey with greater confidence and control, aligning your financial and legal strategies with your personal and spiritual transformations.

Chapter 3:

Financial Instruments and Legal Tools

In this chapter, we will explore sophisticated financial instruments and legal tools that can be crucial in managing and asserting a new legal identity, particularly when facing criminal charges. These tools can help you establish financial stability, verify your identity, and potentially shift the nature of your legal disputes from criminal to civil matters.

Section 1: Utilizing Trusts and Bonds

Payment Bond from Trust

Definition and Usage:

A payment bond is a type of surety bond typically used in commercial and legal contexts to guarantee payment or performance of a contract. When facing legal disputes, particularly those involving financial obligations, a trust can issue a payment bond to ensure these obligations are met.

- **Payment Bond**: A financial guarantee that ensures the payment of a debt or the fulfillment of a contractual obligation.

- **Trust as Issuer:** By using trust certificate units (TCUs), a trust can issue a payment bond, which acts as a negotiable instrument within the trust structure. This can be particularly useful in legal disputes to show that there are financial resources backing the obligations.

Practical Application:

Here's a step-by-step guide on how to set up a payment bond using TCUs:

1. **Establish a Trust:** Create a trust that holds assets sufficient to back the payment bond.

2. **Issue Trust Certificate Units (TCUs):** These units represent the value of the assets within the trust and can be used as a negotiable instrument.

3. **Draft the Payment Bond:** Include details such as the amount guaranteed, the parties involved, and the conditions under which the bond can be claimed.

4. **File the Bond:** Submit the bond to the relevant legal or financial authorities as part of your case documentation.

EXAMPLE:

```
Payment Bond

This Payment Bond, issued by [Trust Name], guarantees the payment of [Amount] to [Beneficiary], ensuring the fulfillment of [Obligation/Contract]. This bond is backed by Trust Certificate Units (TCUs) valued at [Amount], held within [Trust Name].


Signed,

[Trustee Name]

Date: [Date]
```

Notarial Certificate: Identity Verification and Authorization

Role of Notarial Certification:

A notarial certificate is essential in verifying the authenticity of documents and the identity of the signatory. This is especially important in cases involving new legal identities and substantial financial transactions.

- **Verification:** The notary public verifies that the person signing the document is indeed who they claim to be, adding a layer of legitimacy to the document.

- **Authorization:** The notary's seal and signature confirm that the document has been properly executed and can be trusted in legal and financial contexts.

Process and Impact:

Here's how to obtain and use a notarial certificate:

1. **Prepare the Document:** Draft the document that needs notarization, ensuring all details are accurate and complete.

2. **Visit a Notary Public:** Present the document and your identification to a notary public.

3. **Notarization**: The notary will verify your identity, witness your signature, and affix their seal and signature to the document.

4. **Use in Court:** Submit the notarized document as part of your legal filings to confirm the separation between your new identity and any previous legal or financial claims.

EXAMPLE:

```
Notarial Certificate

State of [State]

County of [County]


On this [Date] day of [Month], [Year], before me, [Notary Name], a Notary Public in and for said County, personally appeared [Your New Legal Name], known to me (or satisfactorily proven) to be the person whose name is subscribed to the within instrument, and acknowledged that [he/she] executed the same for the purposes therein contained.

In witness whereof, I hereunto set my hand and official seal.

[Notary Signature]

[Notary Seal]
```

Section 2:

Establishing and Managing Financial Identity

Private Register Bond for Investment (PRB)

Understanding PRBs:

A Private Register Bond for Investment (PRB) is a financial instrument used to verify and manage accounts and investments associated with a trust or new legal entity. PRBs help in establishing the legitimacy and financial standing of your new identity.

- **Verification Tool:** PRBs serve as proof of financial backing for your legal claims or investments.

- **Management Tool:** They help in managing and organizing the assets held under your new identity or trust structure.

Creating and Using PRBs:

Here's how to create and utilize PRBs:

1. **Create the PRB**: Draft a bond document that outlines the assets and investments associated with your trust or new legal entity.

2. **Verification**: Include details that verify the existence and value of the assets, such as account statements or asset appraisals.

3. **Usage:** Use the PRB to manage and verify financial accounts, presenting it as evidence in legal or financial proceedings.

EXAMPLE:

```
Private Register Bond for Investment

This Private Register Bond, issued by [Trust Name], verifies the existence and value of assets amounting to [Amount], held within [Trust Name]. These assets are registered and managed under the authority of [Trustee Name].

Signed,

[Trustee Name]

Date: [Date]
```

Trust Certificate Unit: Deed of Transfer/Bond for Settlement

Functionality of TCUs:

Trust Certificate Units (TCUs) are used as deeds of transfer or bonds for settlement, facilitating the movement and management of assets within a trust. They act as negotiable instruments that represent the value of assets held by the trust.

- **Deed of Transfer:** TCUs can be used to transfer ownership of assets within the trust.
- **Bond for Settlement:** They can also serve as financial guarantees in legal settlements.

Endorsement and Legal Relevance:

Here's how to endorse and use TCUs:

1. **Issue TCUs:** Create trust certificates that represent specific values of the assets held within the trust.

2. **Endorse the TCUs:** Include a notary's endorsement on the back side of the certificate to make it a valid financial instrument.

3. **Use in Transactions:** Present the endorsed TCUs as part of legal settlements or asset transfers.

EXAMPLE:

```
Trust Certificate Unit

This certificate represents [Amount] held within [Trust Name]. The bearer of this certificate is entitled to the value of the assets as specified.


Endorsed by:

[Notary Signature]

[Notary Seal]

Date: [Date]
```

Section 3:

Legal Recognition and Documentation

Original' Certificate of Live Birth

Legal and Symbolic Significance:

The original certificate of live birth is a foundational identity document. It serves as the primary proof of one's birth and legal identity.

- **Legal Significance**: It is used to establish the legitimacy of one's identity in various legal contexts.
- **Symbolic Significance**: It represents the individual's legal existence and heritage.

Strategic Use in Legal Disputes:

Here's how to leverage this document:

1. **Obtain the Certificate**: Request a certified copy of your original certificate of live birth from the relevant authorities.
2. **Use in Legal Proceedings**: Present the certificate in court to affirm your identity and its relevance to current legal matters.

EXAMPLE:
```
Certified Copy of Certificate of Live Birth

State of [State]

County of [County]


This certifies that [Your Name] was born on [Date] in [City, State]. This document serves as proof of identity and legal existence.


Certified by:

[Registrar's Signature]

Date: [Date]
```

Bond for Probate: Converting Criminal Charges to Civil Matters

Purpose and Process:

A bond for probate can be used to shift criminal charges to civil disputes, focusing on financial compensation rather than punitive outcomes.

- **Purpose**: Convert the nature of the legal dispute to allow for financial settlements.

- **Process**: Obtain a bond for probate from an online bonding company, attach the case number, and use the bond in court to argue for civil adjudication.

Acquisition and Application:

Here's how to acquire and apply a bond for probate:

1. **Obtain the Bond:** Purchase a bond for probate from a reputable online bonding company.

2. **Attach Case Number:** Ensure the bond includes your case number and relevant details.

3. **Submit in Court:** File the bond with the court as part of your defense strategy to argue for the conversion of criminal charges to a civil matter.

EXAMPLE:

```
Bond for Probate

This bond, issued by [Bonding Company], guarantees the payment of [Amount] for the case of [Your Case Number]. This bond is intended to convert the nature of the charges to a civil dispute focusing on financial compensation.


Issued by:

[Bonding Company Representative]

Date: [Date]
```

Conclusion of Chapter 3

Chapter 3 equips you with an understanding of sophisticated financial instruments and legal documents essential for asserting and managing a new legal identity, particularly in complex legal challenges. By utilizing these tools, you can establish financial stability, verify your identity, and shift the nature of legal disputes from criminal to civil. This knowledge empowers you to navigate your legal journey with greater confidence and control, aligning your financial and legal strategies with your personal and spiritual transformations.

Payment Bond

KNOW ALL PERSONS BY THESE PRESENTS:

THAT WHEREAS, Owen M. Piotrowski (District Attorney), 821 W State Street, Milwaukee, Wisconsin 53233 (the Owner) has awarded to LONDALE QUINTAE STRICKLING, Sojourning C/o220 Calle Manuel Domenech PMB 2050, San Juan, united States of America Republic, [00918] (the Principal) a contract dated 2023CF0001349 (the "Contract") for the Project, May 26, 2023.

NOW, THEREFORE, we, the undersigned Principal and TERESITA FUENTES D.B.A SECRETARY OF TREASURY, Department of Hacienda, P.O BOX 9024140, San Juan, Puerto Rico, united States of America Republic, [00918] as Surety, are held and firmly bound unto in the sum of (Full Settlement Amount, not to exceed $175,000) for which payment is to be made. We bind Trust, tangible assets of trust, Fuduciary and assigns, jointly and severally, firmly by these presents:

1. **Bond**

    According to this Payment Bond, if Principal, or its heirs, executors, administrators, successors, or assigns approved by the Owner, or its subcontractors shall fail to pay any of the money due with respect to work or labor performed under the Contract, or for any amounts required to be deducted, withheld, and paid over to any state departments from the wages of employees of Principal and subcontractors with respect to such work and labor, the Surety will pay for the same in an amount not exceeding the sum specified in this bond.

2. **Parties Bound**

    This bond shall inure to the benefit of any of the persons named in state criminal/civil code as to whom a right of action is given or their assigns in any suit brought upon this bond.

3. **Modification**

    Surety, for value received, hereby expressly agrees that no extension of time, change, modification, alteration, or addition to the undertakings, covenants, terms, conditions, and agreements of the Contract, or to the work to be performed there under, shall in any way affect the obligation of this bond.

4. **Waiver**

Surety does hereby waive notice of any such extension of time, change, modification, alteration, or addition to the undertakings, covenants, terms, conditions, and agreements of the Contract, or to the work to be performed there under.

5. **Third Party**

    Surety's obligations hereunder are independent of the obligations of any other surety for the payment of claims of laborers, mechanics, material suppliers, and other persons in connection with the Contract.

6. Attorneys' Fees

If any action at law or in equity is brought to enforce or interpret the provisions of this Bond, the prevailing party will be entitled to reasonable attorneys' fees in addition to any other relief to which that party may be entitled.

7. Notice

Correspondence or claims relating to this bond shall be sent to Surety or the Principal at the address set forth above.

8. Applicable Law

This Agreement shall be construed under and in accordance with the laws of Wisconsin, and all obligations of the parties created under this Agreement are performable in Wisconsin

9. Signatures

This Agreement shall be signed by Kabir-Elohim Isreal LLC, Ambassador, Authorized Representative, on behalf of LONDALE QUINTAE STRICLKING, and by C/o TERESITA FUENTES, Fuduciary, Secretary of Treasury, on behalf of TERESITA FUENTES D.B.A SECRETARY OF TREASURY

IN WITNESS WHEREOF, we have hereunto set our hands this with the intent to be legally bound.

LONDALE QUINTAE STRICKLING

By: *Implied Surety* Kabir-Elohim Isreal LLC   Date: 05/26/2023

Kabir-Elohim Isreal LLC, its Ambassador, Authorized Representative

TERESITA FUENTES D.B.A SECRETARY OF TREASURY

By: LONDALE QUINTAE STRICKLING TRUST   Date: 05/26/2023

C/o TERESITA FUENTES, its Fuduciary, Secretary of Treasury

WISCONSIN NOTARIAL CERTIFICATE
(VERIFICATION UPON OATH OR AFFIRMATION)

State of Wisconsin
County of Milwaukee

Signed and sworn to (or affirmed) before me on 5/19/23 [Date] by Alicia Carter [Name(s) of Person(s)].

Alicia Carter
Signature of Notarial Officer

(Seal, if any)

Notary Public
Title (and Rank)

ALICIA CARTER
Notary Public
State of Wisconsin

My commission expires: 12/12/25

Copyright © 2018 NotaryAcknowledgement.com. All Rights Reserved.

Tracking No._____

TO: Secretary of the Treasury / I.M.F.
C/O DEPARTMENT DE HACIENDA
P.O. BOX 9024140,
SAN JUAN, PR 00902-4140

**PRIVATE REGISTERED
BOND FOR INVESTMENT**
Value of Bond is: $100,000,000.00
ONE HUNDRED MILLION U.S. DOLLARS

**PRIVATE REGISTERED SELF BACKED BOND BASED ON FUTURE EARNINGS IN RE:
LIVE BIRTH #** ▓▓▓▓▓▓▓▓▓▓▓▓ Investment at the discretion of the Secretary of the
Treasury/U.S. DEPARTMENT OF THE TREASURY as Fiduciary

Attention: Fiduciary/Receiver:

The below Undersigned Principal, ▓▓▓▓▓▓▓▓, ▓▓▓▓▓▓ on behalf of the ▓▓▓▓▓▓▓▓▓▓
▓▓▓▓▓▓▓▓▓▓ TRUST, herewith includes proof of the original issued instrument for basis of future
value predicated on Certificate of Live Birth under Number ▓▓▓▓▓▓▓▓. Current value accepted and issued as credit
as indicated at the same amount as this bond. All endorsements front and back, to be attached to the original. The
Undersigned Principal being the only known legitimate party having ameliorated value into aforesaid, contributing
of the credit assured therein.
Tendered in accordance with all applicable laws including but not limited to UCC 1-104 and Public Law 73-10
and Chap. 48, 48 Stat. 112.

~ BOND ORDER ~

You are hereby directed to utilize said credit (asset funds) for sound investment purposes not including games of
speculation. This bond valued at ONE HUNDRED MILLION ($100,000,000) is issued to the treasury with a
maturity date of 100 years hence bearing 1% interest per annum for a full value of $100,000,000 at maturity date.
This credit we issue with guarantee of ONE HUNDRED MILLION DOLLARS ($100,000,000) to the treasury
that we make with no request for money up front. In return we would like the treasury to use the credit of ONE
HUNDRED MILLION DOLLARS ($100,000,000) to make investment(s) of at least 2% per annum in safe non-
speculative investments, 1% of which will be held on account or reinvested to continue to accrue and roll over to
cover the bonds value at maturity. Please also note the below Trust Name & Address to be used for anything over
the 1% per annum divisible on biannual basis accordingly available after the first term from the date of receipt
indicated on the green card return receipt from acceptance. Please send overages in the form of a check for use by
the trust in operations and other investments. This agreement creates full security of the funds as you are guaranteed
to be paid as they will accrue in your control, furthermore we will also pledge the current and future assets of the
trust as a guarantee of payment in full upon maturity or if it pleases the treasury to reissue another bond on the
same basis. This Bond shall be ledgered as an asset to mature in One-Hundred (100) years from the date of issuance.
   The Secretary of the Treasury shall have Thirty (30) days from the date of receipt of this Bond, as witnessed by
the date of receipt of sending, to dishonor this Bond by returning this Bond to the Principal at the address below
by mail verified by return receipt, with an explanation of all deficiencies. Failure to return the Bond as stated shall
constitute Acceptance and Honoring of this Bond.
   All overages held and not distributed may be used at the discretion of ▓▓▓▓▓▓ ▓▓▓▓▓▓'S
ESTATE/TRUST for set-off of any private, commercial, corporate or Public bills, taxes, debts, money claims,
demand(s) for payment(s) and the like, used in any regular course of business affairs as well as backing for lending
at institutions for lines of credit, to transmit electronic telex or other instruction to the vendor/creditor to remove
'ledgered debt' from their books or for discharge/setoff for adjustment of account for settlement and/or closure.
Void where prohibited by law.

Trustee/Secured Party,
on behalf of ▓▓▓▓▓▓▓▓▓▓▓▓▓▓▓▓
▓▓▓▓▓▓▓▓▓▓▓▓▓▓▓▓
M▓▓▓▓▓▓▓▓, WI 53218

This instrument is backed by the full faith
and credit of ▓▓▓▓▓▓▓▓▓▓

CERTIFICATION OF BIRTH RECORD

CERTIFICATE OF LIVE BIRTH

STATE OF ILLINOIS

This is to certify that this is a true and correct copy from the official birth record filed with the Illinois Department of Public Health.

Dan Hendrickson
Kankakee County Clerk

LONDALE QUINTAE STRICKLING TRUST

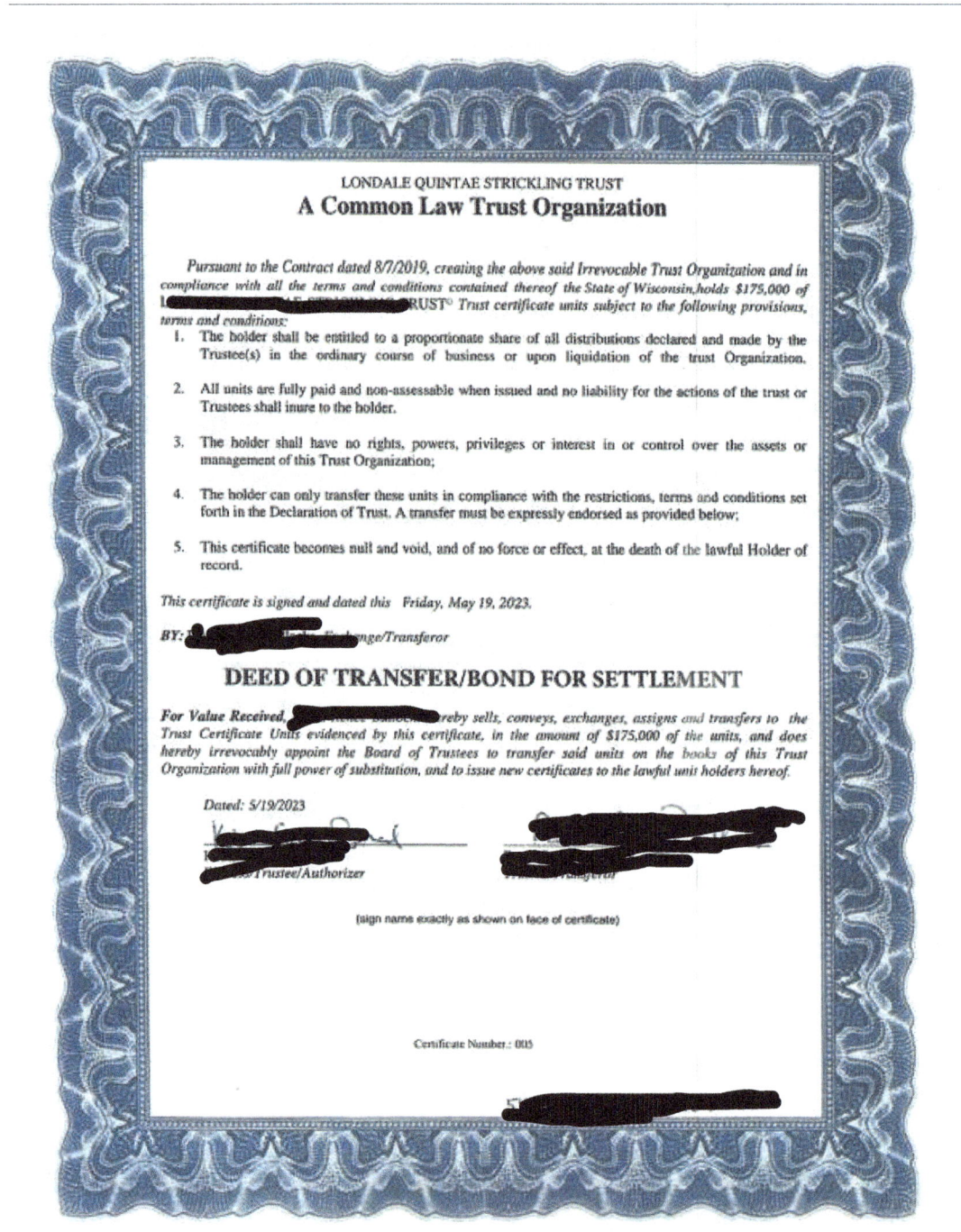

A Common Law Trust Organization

Pursuant to the Contract dated 8/7/2019, creating the above said Irrevocable Trust Organization and in compliance with all the terms and conditions contained thereof the State of Wisconsin, holds $175,000 of L████████████████RUST° Trust certificate units subject to the following provisions, terms and conditions:

1. The holder shall be entitled to a proportionate share of all distributions declared and made by the Trustee(s) in the ordinary course of business or upon liquidation of the trust Organization.

2. All units are fully paid and non-assessable when issued and no liability for the actions of the trust or Trustees shall inure to the holder.

3. The holder shall have no rights, powers, privileges or interest in or control over the assets or management of this Trust Organization;

4. The holder can only transfer these units in compliance with the restrictions, terms and conditions set forth in the Declaration of Trust. A transfer must be expressly endorsed as provided below;

5. This certificate becomes null and void, and of no force or effect, at the death of the lawful Holder of record.

This certificate is signed and dated this Friday, May 19, 2023.

BY: ████████████ ██████ Exchange/Transferor

DEED OF TRANSFER/BOND FOR SETTLEMENT

For Value Received, ████████████████ hereby sells, conveys, exchanges, assigns and transfers to the Trust Certificate Units evidenced by this certificate, in the amount of $175,000 of the units, and does hereby irrevocably appoint the Board of Trustees to transfer said units on the books of this Trust Organization with full power of substitution, and to issue new certificates to the lawful unit holders hereof.

Dated: 5/19/2023

████████ Trustee/Authorizer

(sign name exactly as shown on face of certificate)

Certificate Number.: 005

80

OFFICE OF THE SECRETARY OF STATE
STATE OF WISCONSIN

18 January, 2023

In response to your documents submitted to this office:

Based upon advice from legal counsel at the Wisconsin Department of Justice, we are returning your document to you. The duties of the Office of the Secretary of State are set forth by statute. None of those duties permit the acceptance, filing, or processing of the documents which you submitted.

Per instruction from the Hague Convention, under refusal authority provided in 22 CFR 92.9[1] and 22 CFR 131.2[2] and under guidance from the Wisconsin Department of Justice, the Office of the Secretary of State refuses to file, notarize, authenticate or affix the Hague Apostille to any documents concerning:
- United States citizenship
- Allegiance the United States
- Allegiance to any state within the United States
- Allegiance to other jurisdictions or sovereignty

Any and all submitted materials and/or fees are enclosed.

By: [signature]

---

[1] 22 CFR 92.9 Refusals of requests for notarial services
(a) A notarizing officer should refuse requests for notarial services, the performance of which is not authorized by treaty provisions or permitted by the laws or authorities of the country in which he is stationed. (See Sec. 92.4(a).) Also, a notarizing officer should refuse to perform notarial acts for use in transactions which may from time to time be prohibited by law or by regulations of the United States Government such, for example, as regulations based on the "Trading With the Enemy Act of 1917," as amended.
(b) A notarizing officer is also authorized to refuse to perform a notarial act if he had reasonable grounds for believing that the document in connection with which his notarial act is requested will be used for a purpose patently unlawful, improper or inimical to the best interests of the United States. Requests for notarial services should be refused only after the most careful deliberation.
[22 FR 10858, Dec. 27, 1957, as amended at 60 FR 51723, Oct. 3, 1995]

[2] 22 CFR § 131.2 Refusal of certification for unlawful purpose
(a) The Department will not certify to a document when it has good reason to believe that the certification is desired for an unlawful or improper purpose. It is therefore the duty of the Authentication Officer to examine not only the document which the Department is asked to authenticate, but also the fundamental document to which previous seals or other certifications may have been affixed by other authorities. The Authentication Officer shall request such additional information as may be necessary to establish that the requested authentication will serve the interests of justice and is not contrary to public policy.
(b) In accordance with section 3, paragraph 5 of the Export Administration Act of 1969 (83 Stat. 841, Pub. L. 91-184) approved December 30, 1969, documents which have the effect of furthering or supporting the restrictive trade practices or boycotts fostered or imposed by foreign countries against countries friendly to the United States shall be considered contrary to public policy for purposes of these regulations.
[R.S. 203, sec. 4, 63 Stat. 111, as amended, sec. 1733, 62 Stat. 946, secs. 104, 332, 66 Stat. 174, 252, 22 U.S.C. 2657, 2658, 28 U.S.C. 1733, 8 U.S.C. 1104, 1443)
[22 FR 10882, Dec. 27, 1957, as amended at 30 FR 12732, Oct. 6, 1965; Dept. Reg. 108.627; 35 FR 8887, June 9, 1970]

BOND OF PROBATE

Bond No. 107866576

IN THE ___Circuit___ COURT OF THE STATE OF ___WISCONSIN___
IN AND FOR ___MILWAUKEE___ COUNTY

No. 2023cf001349

IN THE MATTER OF THE

☑ Estate
☐ Guardianship
☐ Conservatorship

OF LONDALE QUINTAE STRICKLING TRUST

☑ Deceased   ☐ Minor
☐ Incompetent

KNOW ALL MEN BY THESE PRESENTS: That we, __KABIR-ELOHIM ISREAL__

as principal, and __Travelers Casualty and Surety Company of America__, a __CT__ corporation, as Surety, are held and firmly bound unto the State of __WI__, in the full and just sum of __Twenty Five Thousand & 00/100__ (__$25,000.00__) Dollars for the payment of which, well and truly to be made, we bind ourselves, our and each of our heirs, executors, administrators, successors and assigns, jointly and severally, by these presents.

Sealed with our seals, and dated this __28__ day of __June__, __2023__

THE CONDITION OF THIS OBLIGATION SUCH, That, WHEREAS Principal was by an order of said Court made on the __28th__ day of __June__, __2023__, appointed

☐ Guardian
☑ Administrator   of the above named Estate.
☐ Executor
☐ Conservator
☐ Personal Representative

NOW, THEREFORE, if the said principal shall faithfully execute the duties of the trust according to law then this obligation to be void; otherwise, to remain in full force and effect.

KABIR-ELOHIM ISREAL

Travelers Casualty and Surety Company of America

By _Valerie Aber_
VALERIE ABER
Attorney-in-Fact

Principal

WWIS
Producer Name
(Required in Arizona Only)

RECEIVED
JUN 29 2023
Office of District Attorney
Milwaukee, WI 53233

CLERK OF CIRCUIT COURT
23 JUN 29 PM 4:00
CRIMINAL DIVISION
FILED

S-2131E (4/17)

A NOTARY PUBLIC OR OTHER OFFICER COMPLETING THIS CERTIFICATE VERIFIES ONLY THE IDENTITY OF THE INDIVIDUAL WHO SIGNED THE DOCUMENT TO WHICH THIS CERTIFICATE IS ATTACHED, AND NOT THE TRUTHFULNESS, ACCURACY, OR VALIDITY OF THAT DOCUMENT

STATE OF ARIZONA
COUNTY OF MARICOPA } SS.

ON 06/28/2023 BEFORE ME, Amanda Lynn Turner

PERSONALLY APPEARED VALERIE ABER, ATTORNEY-IN-FACT

WHO PROVED TO ME ON THE BASIS OF SATISFACTORY EVIDENCE TO BE THE PERSON(S) WHOSE NAME(S) IS/ARE SUBSCRIBED TO THE WITHIN INSTRUMENT AND ACKNOWLEDGED TO ME THAT HE/SHE/THEY EXECUTED THE SAME IN HIS/HER/THEIR AUTHORIZED CAPACITY(IES) AND THAT BY HIS/HER/THEIR SIGNATURE(S) ON THE INSTRUMENT THE PERSON(S), OR THE ENTITY UPON BEHALF OF WHICH THE PERSON(S) ACTED, EXECUTED THE INSTRUMENT.

I CERTIFY UNDER PENALTY OF PERJURY UNDER THE LAWS OF THE STATE OF ARIZONA THAT THE FOREGOING PARAGRAPH IS TRUE AND CORRECT.

WITNESS MY HAND AND OFFICIAL SEAL.

SIGNATURE

THIS AREA FOR OFFICIAL NOTARIAL SEAL

AMANDA LYNN TURNER
Notary Public, State of Arizona
Maricopa County
Commission # 637078
My Commission Expires
September 27, 2026

RECEIVED
JUN 29 2023
Office of District Attorney
Milwaukee, WI 53233

CLERK OF CIRCUIT COURT
23 JUN 29 PM 4:00
FILED
CRIMINAL DIVISION

TRAVELERS

| Travelers Casualty and Surety Company of America |
| Travelers Casualty and Surety Company |
| St. Paul Fire and Marine Insurance Company |
| Farmington Casualty Company |

POWER OF ATTORNEY

KNOW ALL MEN BY THESE PRESENTS: That Travelers Casualty and Surety Company of America, Travelers Casualty and Surety Company, St. Paul Fire and Marine Insurance Company, and Farmington Casualty Company are corporations duly organized under the laws of the State of Connecticut (herein collectively called the "Companies"), and that the Companies do hereby make, constitute and appoint **VALERIE ABER**, of **PHOENIX, AZ**, their true and lawful Attorney(s)-in-Fact, to sign, execute, seal and acknowledge the following bond:

Surety Bond No.: 107866576 **Principal:** KABIR-ELOHIM ISREAL

IN WITNESS WHEREOF, the Companies have caused this instrument to be signed and their corporate seals to be hereto affixed, this **21st** day of **April, 2021**.

RECEIVED JUN 29 2023 Office of District Attorney Milwaukee, WI 53233

State of Connecticut
City of Hartford ss.

Robert L. Raney, Senior Vice President

On this the **21st** day of **April, 2021**, before me personally appeared Robert L. Raney, who acknowledged himself to be the Senior Vice President of each of the Companies, and that he, as such, being authorized so to do, executed the foregoing instrument for the purposes therein contained by signing on behalf of said Companies by himself as a duly authorized officer.

IN WITNESS WHEREOF, I hereunto set my hand and official seal.

My Commission expires the **30th** day of **June, 2026**.

Anna P. Nowik, Notary Public

This Power of Attorney is granted under and by the authority of the following resolutions adopted by the Boards of Directors of each of the Companies, which resolutions are now in full force and effect, reading as follows:

RESOLVED, that the Chairman, the President, any Vice Chairman, any Executive Vice President, any Senior Vice President, any Vice President, any Second Vice President, the Treasurer, any Assistant Treasurer, the Corporate Secretary or any Assistant Secretary may appoint Attorneys-in-Fact and Agents to act for and on behalf of the Company and may give such appointee such authority as his or her certificate of authority may prescribe to sign with the Company's name and seal with the Company's seal bonds, recognizances, contracts of indemnity, and other writings obligatory in the nature of a bond, recognizance, or conditional undertaking, and any of said officers or the Board of Directors at any time may remove any such appointee and revoke the power given him or her; and it is

FURTHER RESOLVED, that the Chairman, the President, any Vice Chairman, any Executive Vice President, any Senior Vice President or any Vice President may delegate all or any part of the foregoing authority to one or more officers or employees of this Company, provided that each such delegation is in writing and a copy thereof is filed in the office of the Secretary; and it is

FURTHER RESOLVED, that any bond, recognizance, contract of indemnity, or writing obligatory in the nature of a bond, recognizance, or conditional undertaking shall be valid and binding upon the Company when (a) signed by the President, any Vice Chairman, any Executive Vice President, any Senior Vice President or any Vice President, any Second Vice President, the Treasurer, any Assistant Treasurer, the Corporate Secretary or any Assistant Secretary and duly attested and sealed with the Company's seal by a Secretary or Assistant Secretary; or (b) duly executed (under seal, if required) by one or more Attorneys-in-Fact and Agents pursuant to the power prescribed in his or her certificate or their certificates of authority or by one or more Company officers pursuant to a written delegation of authority; and it is

FURTHER RESOLVED, that the signature of each of the following officers: President, any Executive Vice President, any Senior Vice President, any Vice President, any Assistant Vice President, any Secretary, any Assistant Secretary, and the seal of the Company may be affixed by facsimile to any Power of Attorney or to any certificate relating thereto appointing Resident Vice Presidents, Resident Assistant Secretaries or Attorneys-in-Fact for purposes only of executing and attesting bonds and undertakings and other writings obligatory in the nature thereof, and any such Power of Attorney or certificate bearing such facsimile signature or facsimile seal shall be valid and binding upon the Company and any such power so executed and certified by such facsimile signature and facsimile seal shall be valid and binding on the Company in the future with respect to any bond or understanding to which it is attached.

I, Kevin E. Hughes, the undersigned, Assistant Secretary of each of the Companies, do hereby certify that the above and foregoing is a true and correct copy of the Power of Attorney executed by said Companies, which remains in full force and effect.

Dated this 26 day of June, 2023.

Kevin E. Hughes, Assistant Secretary

To verify the authenticity of this Power of Attorney, please call us at 1-800-421-3880.
Please refer to the above-named Attorney(s)-in-Fact and the details of the bond to which this Power of Attorney is attached.

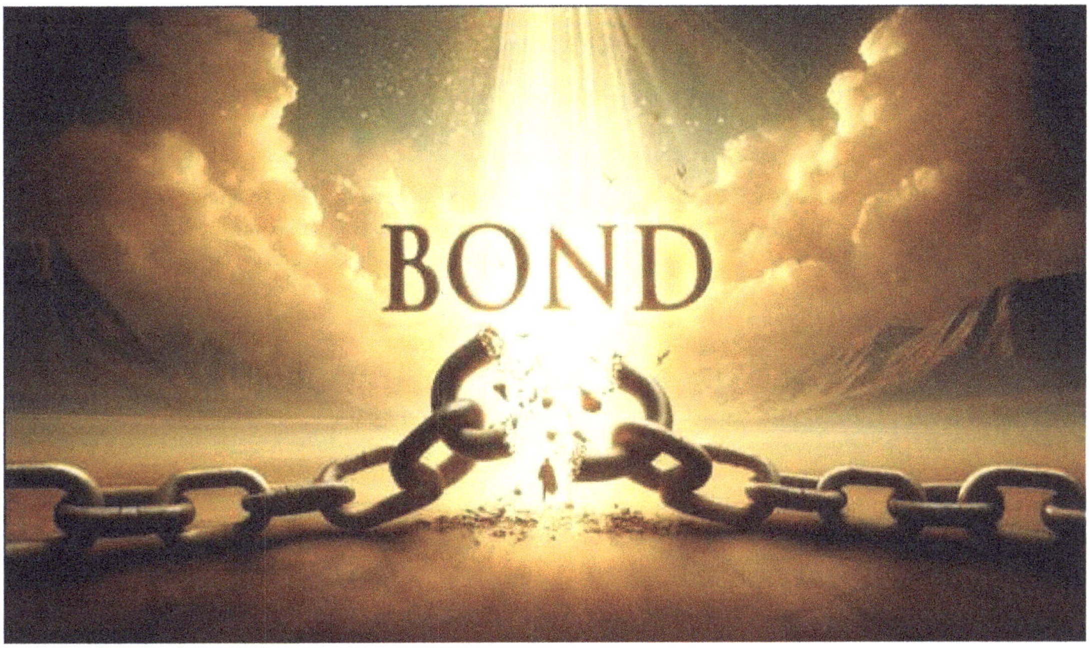
BOND

Chapter 4:
The Power of Documentation

In this chapter, we delve into the significance of thorough documentation in asserting and securing your legal identity and rights. As a pro se litigant facing criminal charges, understanding how to utilize key legal documents strategically can be pivotal in your defense. This chapter provides detailed guidance on drafting, filing, and using various legal and contractual documents to navigate the judicial system effectively.

Section 1: Core Legal Documents and Their Strategic Use

Legal Notice and Demand

Purpose and Preparation:

A legal notice and demand is a formal document used to assert your rights and expectations from the judicial system. It is crucial in notifying the court and opposing parties of your legal stance and demanding adherence to due process.

- **Purpose:** The primary purpose of a legal notice and demand is to formally communicate your legal position, rights, and demands to the court and other parties involved. It serves as an official assertion of your expectations for due process and respect for your legal identity.

- **Preparation**: When preparing a legal notice, ensure that it is precise, clearly outlining the legal basis for your demands. Include relevant laws, precedents, and evidence that support your position.

EXAMPLE:

```

```

Legal Notice and Demand

Date: [Date]

To: [Court/Recipient Name]
From: [Your Name]

Subject: Formal Assertion of Legal Rights and Demands

I, [Your Name], hereby formally assert my legal rights and demand adherence to due process in the handling of my case, [Case Number]. It is my expectation that all parties involved respect my newly established legal identity as [New Legal Identity], and adhere to the legal standards and obligations pertaining to this identity.

Failure to comply with these demands will result in further legal action.

Respectfully,

[Your Signature]

[Your Name]
```

***Strategic Application:***

Use a legal notice and demand to challenge procedural errors and insist on the recognition of your new legal identity. This document can be filed at the outset of legal proceedings or whenever a procedural violation occurs.

- **Challenging Procedural Errors:** If you identify any procedural errors or biases, a legal notice can formally challenge these issues and demand corrective action.
```

- **Demanding Due Process:** Clearly state your expectations for due process and the legal basis for your demands, ensuring that the court and opposing parties are fully aware of your legal stance.

Public Servant Questionnaire

Functionality:

The Public Servant Questionnaire is a tool used to assess and document the qualifications and legal limitations of public officials involved in your case. This can be instrumental in exposing biases or inadequacies.

- **Role**: This questionnaire helps gather information about the qualifications, roles, and responsibilities of the public officials handling your case.

- **Documentation:** It provides documented evidence of any potential conflicts of interest, biases, or inadequacies, supporting claims of unfair treatment or procedural violations.

EXAMPLE QUESTIONS:

```

*Public Servant Questionnaire*

1. Full Name and Title:

2. Office Address:

3. Date of Appointment/Election:

4. Qualifications (Degrees, Certifications):

5. Bonding Information (Bond Number, Issuer):

6. Have you received any disciplinary actions? If so, please explain.

Signature: [Public Servant's Signature]

Date: [Date]
```

```

*Usage in Defense:*

Use the responses from the Public Servant Questionnaire to identify and challenge potential biases or procedural violations. This can strengthen your defense by highlighting any inadequacies or conflicts of interest among the officials involved.

- **Identify Biases**: Analyze the responses to uncover any biases or conflicts of interest that may impact your case.

- **Document Violations**: Use the documented responses to support claims of procedural violations or unfair treatment in your defense filings.

## Section 2:

## Advanced Identity and Status Documents

**DFI Form 702 and Declaration of Trust**

*DFI Form 702:*

DFI Form 702 is used to establish a common law trust, delineating the roles and responsibilities of trustees.

- **Introduction:** This form is critical in formalizing a trust under common law, providing a clear framework for its operation and management.

- **Roles and Responsibilities:** It details the roles of the trustees, their duties, and the trust's purposes.

**Declaration of Trust:**

A Declaration of Trust formalizes the existence of the trust and outlines its legal framework.
```

- **Purpose**: It establishes the trust's existence and defines its objectives, assets, and operational guidelines.

- **Legal Framework:** The document provides a legal basis for the trust's activities and asset management.

EXAMPLE:

```

**Declaration of Trust**

This Declaration of Trust is made on [Date] by [Trustor's Name], hereby establishing [Trust Name] under common law.

Trustees: [Names of Trustees]

Purpose: [Trust's Purpose]

Assets: [List of Trust Assets]

Signed,

[Trustor's Signature]

Date: [Date]

```

Certificate of Authorization and Proof of Foreign Status

Purpose of the Certificate:

A Certificate of Authorization serves as legal proof of a person's authority to act on behalf of a trust or other entity.

- **Authorization:** It confirms that you have the legal authority to represent and make decisions for the trust or entity.

- **Legal Proof:** This certificate is essential for validating your actions in legal and financial transactions.

Proving Foreign Status:

The Proof of Foreign Status document supports claims of non-residency or foreign status, crucial for legal strategies involving jurisdictional challenges.

- **Non-Residency:** It confirms that you are not subject to local jurisdiction, impacting how legal actions are handled.

- **Legal Strategy:** Use this document to challenge the court's jurisdiction over you based on your foreign status.

EXAMPLE:

```

### Certificate of Authorization

This certifies that [Your Name] is authorized to act on behalf of [Trust Name].

Issued by: [Authorizing Entity]

Date: [Date]

Proof of Foreign Status

This certifies that [Your Name] is a non-resident alien of [Country].

Issued by: [Government Authority]

Date: [Date]
```

```

## Section 3: Negotiating Legal Identity and Contracts

**Power of Attorney**

*Legal Implications:*

Granting a Power of Attorney (POA) allows designated individuals to act legally on your behalf, particularly in navigating complex legal landscapes.

- **Significance:** A POA grants significant legal authority to the designated individual, enabling them to make decisions and take actions on your behalf.

- **Complex Legal Landscapes:** This is particularly useful in handling intricate legal matters where professional representation is crucial.

**Document Preparation and Use:**

Here's how to draft and use a Power of Attorney:

1. **Draft the POA:** Clearly outline the powers granted, the duration, and any limitations.

2. **Legal Scrutiny:** Ensure the document is legally sound and compliant with relevant laws.

3. **Execution:** Sign the POA in the presence of a notary public to validate it.

**EXAMPLE:**

```

Power of Attorney

I, [Your Name], hereby appoint [Attorney-in-Fact Name] as my lawful attorney-in-fact, with full authority to act on my behalf in legal and financial matters.

Effective Date: [Date]

Expiration Date: [Date or 'Until Revoked']

Signed,

[Your Signature]

Date: [Date]

Notary Public:

[Notary Signature]

Date: [Date]

```

## Commercial Offer for Present Sale and Related Affidavits

**Commercial Offer:**

Drafting a commercial offer can serve as a negotiation tool in legal disputes, proposing settlements or agreements to preempt lengthy trials.

- **Negotiation Tool:** A well-crafted commercial offer can facilitate settlements, reducing the need for extended litigation.
- **Settlement Proposals:** Clearly outline the terms and conditions of the offer, aiming for a mutually beneficial resolution.

## Affidavit of Commercial Offer:
```

Back up the commercial offer with an affidavit to legally document the offer and its terms.

- **Legal Documentation:** An affidavit adds legal weight to the offer, confirming its authenticity and terms.
- **Terms of the Offer:** Detail the offer's conditions, ensuring clarity and enforceability.

EXAMPLE:

```

*Commercial Offer*

I, [Your Name], propose the following terms for settlement of [Legal Matter]:

Terms: [Details of Offer]

Expiration Date: [Date]

**Affidavit of Commercial Offer**

I, [Your Name], affirm that the above offer is made in good faith and represents my intention to settle [Legal Matter] on the stated terms.

Signed,

[Your Signature]

Date: [Date]

```

Section 4: Finalizing Legal Status and Identity

Final Written Acceptance and Certificate of Dishonor

Final Written Acceptance:

A final written acceptance formally agrees to or rejects proposed legal resolutions, finalizing your stance in the legal matter.

- **Agreement or Rejection:** Clearly state whether you accept or reject the terms, finalizing your legal position.
- **Formal Resolution:** This document is essential in concluding negotiations and legal discussions.

EXAMPLE:

```
                    **Final Written Acceptance**

I, [Your Name], hereby [accept/reject] the proposed terms of settlement for [Legal Matter].

Signed,

[Your Signature]

Date: [Date]
```

Certificate of Dishonor:

Use a Certificate of Dishonor when negotiations fail or legal offers are not honored, documenting these failures as part of the legal record.

- **Documenting Failures:** Record instances where offers are not honored or negotiations break down.

- **Legal Record:** This certificate serves as evidence of dishonor in the legal proceedings.

EXAMPLE:

```

### Certificate of Dishonor

This certifies that the offer made on [Date] to [Recipient Name] was not honored.

Signed,

[Your Signature]

Date: [Date]

```

Affidavit of Truth

Affidavit of Truth

Purpose and Strength:

An Affidavit of Truth is a powerful document that asserts factual statements to support your claims or disputes against allegations made in a legal case. It serves as a formal declaration under oath, affirming the truthfulness of the statements within.

- **Asserting Facts:** This affidavit is used to clearly state the facts relevant to your case, which can be instrumental in clarifying misunderstandings or countering false claims.

- **Legal Weight:** Because it is sworn under oath, an Affidavit of Truth carries significant legal weight and can be a critical piece of evidence in court.

Creating an Effective Affidavit:

Here's how to draft an Affidavit of Truth:

1. **Title and Introduction:** Begin with a clear title and an introduction that states your name, the purpose of the affidavit, and a declaration that the statements are true to the best of your knowledge.

2. **Statement of Facts:** List the facts in a clear, concise, and numbered format. Each fact should be relevant to the case and directly address the claims or allegations.

3. **Oath and Signature:** Include a closing statement that reiterates the truthfulness of the document, followed by your signature and the date. Have the affidavit notarized to validate its authenticity.

EXAMPLE:

```

### Affidavit of Truth
```

State of [State]

County of [County]

I, [Your Name], being duly sworn, depose and say:

1. I am the [Plaintiff/Defendant] in the case of [Case Number].

2. On [Date], [Fact 1: Detailed description of the fact].

3. [Fact 2: Detailed description of the fact].

4. [Continue listing facts as needed].

I affirm that the statements above are true and correct to the best of my knowledge and belief.

[Your Signature]

[Date]

Sworn to and subscribed before me this [Date] day of [Month], [Year].

[Notary Signature]

[Notary Seal]

```

**Conclusion of Chapter 4**
```

Chapter 4 consolidates the importance of documentation in securing and asserting your legal identity and rights within the judicial system. It provides the reader with essential knowledge on how to utilize various legal and contractual documents to challenge, negotiate, and ultimately establish their legal standing and resolutions. This chapter is critical for anyone seeking to navigate their legal challenges with a comprehensive and documented strategy, ensuring that each step taken is legally sound and strategically advantageous.

By understanding and effectively using these documents, you can enhance your ability to present a strong defense, assert your rights, and achieve favorable outcomes in legal disputes. These tools empower you to navigate the complexities of the legal system with confidence and control, aligning your legal strategies with your personal and spiritual transformations.

Print at: Wednesday, April 5, 2023 4:08:59 PM
Host: MILWA-0422YD3 / MILWAUKEE-RDS-1
User: CMASON

LEGAL NOTICE AND DEMAND
FIAT JUSTITIA, RUAT COELUM
(Let right be done, though the heavens should fall)

NON WAR POWERS ACT FLAG

To: All State, Federal and International Public Officials,
THIS IS A CONTRACT IN ADMIRALTY JURISDICTION
THIS TITLE IS FOR YOUR PROTECTION
Notice to Agent is Notice to Principal. Notice to Principal is notice to Agent.

Attention: Any and all Governments, Municipalities, Cities, Townships, Public Officials, Lending Institutions, brokerage firms, credit unions, depository institutions and insurance agencies, credit bureaus and the aforementioned officers, agents, and employees therein: This is a notice of the law as applicable to your corporate and personal financial liability in the event of any violations upon the rights, privileges and immunities and/or being of Londale-Quintae: Strickling or the trust in representation thereof. This Contract being of honor is presented under the "**Good Faith (Oxford) Doctrine.**"

For a Collateral list that is subject to this documentation please see both Security Agreement under Item No.: 07111983-LQS-SA and SCHEDULE A.

Definitions as they apply to this Contract are enclosed in ATTACHMENT "A", and are included as a legal part of this Contract. Any dispute of any definition will be decided by the Undersigned.

I, Londale-Quintae: Strickling, Trustee/Secured Party/Bailee, hereinafter the Undersigned, state the ensuing being of lawful majority age, clear head, and sound mind. All responses, requests and the like henceforth must be presented in writing, signed under penalty of perjury required by your law as shown in this Legal Demand and Notice (hereinafter "Contract"). The law stated herein is for your clarification, not an agreement/omission/contract/covenant that the Undersigned has entered or agreed to enter into any foreign jurisdiction.

It has recently come to my attention that the IRS, & the SSA, and the federal courts have willfully been making injurious "presumptions" which prejudice my Constitutional rights by trying to associate me with the "**idem sonans**", which is the all caps version of my Christian name which is in fact a trust previously associated with a "**public office**" in the United States government by virtue of the Social Security Number attached to it. Further information is to help clear up any presumptions and set the record straight.

The undersigned tendering this document is a Trustee/Secured Party/Bailee by fact; **not**:

1) a Strawman Vessel in Commerce,		
2) Corporate Fiction,		1) the "United States of America",
3) Legal Entity,	of, for, by, or to	2) the "government of the United States"
4) *ens legis*,		3) the "State of Wisconsin",
5) or Transmitting Utility,		4) or to "UNITED STATES Corporation".

also known as the corporate "UNITED STATES, Corp. USA", "United States, Inc.", or by whatever name may currently be known or be hereafter named, or any of its subdivisions including but not limited to local, state, federal, and/or international or multinational governments, Corporations, agencies, or sub-Corporations, and any de facto compact (Corporate) commercial STATES contracting therein, including the "STATE OF WISCONSIN", or by whatever name same may currently be known or be hereafter named, and the like.

Further, the undersigned is **not**:
1) a citizen within;
2) surety for;
3) subject of;

to the "UNITED STATES CORPORATION" [28 U.S.C. §3002(15)(A)], also known as the corporate "UNITED STATES, Corp. USA", "United States, Inc.", or by whatever name it may currently be known or be hereafter named, (excluding the

Legal Notice & Demand	Page 1 of 8	07111983-LQS-LND

4) an officer of
5) and does not owe
   a. allegiance,
   b. fealty, bond,
   c. undertaking,
   d. obligation,
   e. duty,
   f. tax,
   g. impost,
   h. or tribute

"united states of America" and the "government of the United States as created in the original "Constitution for the united States of America", circa 1787") or any of its agencies, or sub-Corporations, including but not limited to any de facto compact (Corporate) commercial STATES contracting therein, including but not limited to the "STATE OF WISCONSIN", or by whatever name it may currently be known or hereafter named (excluding the, "Republic of Wisconsin"), and the like.

This is now being a matter of public record.

The Vessel in Commerce known as LONDALE QUINTAE STRICKLING initially created as a trust (also known by identifying numbers 349-72-1930/112-99182) by the Government/Parents for the benefit of the Undersigned, Londale-Quintae: Strickling as beneficiary on 07/11/1983. On Wednesday, August 07, 2019 a waiver of beneficial position was declared to take up the abandoned post of Trustee/Secured Party/Bailee to manage the affairs of LONDALE QUINTAE STRICKLING TRUST for the benefit of beneficiaries thereinafter named in REGISTRY OF TRUST for the following reasons:

1) matters are not being handled with efficiency
2) in many respects matters are not being taken care of at all
3) usurpation of funds is occurring
4) there is rampant fraud and deceit
5) position of trustee has been left vacant or uncontested

Private Offset Account established at the United States Department of Treasury through a branch of the Federal Reserve Bank will remain in full effect from the initial date of creation with current office holder of Secretary of Treasury being provided appointment to trust to continue as fiduciary.

Fraud gives the victim of the fraud the right to terminate his relationship to the government:
"Si quis custos fraudem pupillo fecerit, a tutela removendus est."
If a guardian behaves fraudently to his ward, he shall be removed from the guardianship. Jenk. Cen. 39
[Bouvier's Maxims of Law, 1856.]

The similarity in the names of the Undersigned and the Vessel in Commerce, two distinct and separate legal entities, is testament to the undeniable propinquity. LONDALE QUINTAE STRICKLING TRUST, originally an incorporeal creation of Government/Parents, is dependent upon and only exists because Londale-Quintae: Strickling, a Natural Man exists as a living, breathing, flesh and blood sentient being. The Government, being an incorporeal entity can only engage another incorporeal entity, and not a real flesh and blood human, and therefore the creation of a Vessel in Commerce known commonly as LONDALE QUINTAE STRICKLING TRUST was highly advantageous to Government to interface with.

Since the birth of the Undersigned, the Government has utilized the credit and future earning potential of the Undersigned, establishing and operating a Private Offset Account through the use of the Vessel in Commerce, LONDALE QUINTAE STRICKLING TRUST without the knowledge, consent, or permission of the Undersigned acting to the detriment of the beneficiary Londale-Quintae: Strickling, against the basic precepts of a trust. During this time the Undersigned has unknowingly been functioning as the manager of the trust, and signing as an authorized representative for the Vessel in Commerce, by signing bank checks, applications for credit and notes on behalf of the Vessel in Commerce. Now, the Undersigned acts knowingly, not in a beneficial position but as manager/Trustee of the trust. The Undersigned has valid documentation waiving beneficial position for the position of Trustee/Secured Party/Bailee submitted as a matter of public record by which the Undersigned became Trustee/secured party/Bailee to LONDALE QUINTAE STRICKLING TRUST , and has full operating authority.

The Undersigned having full control of Trust **revokes all** permissions to the Government and/or any political subdivisions/Organizations to use copyrighted TRUST name LONDALE QUINTAE STRICKLING TRUST or trust in any fashion except by explicit written request/order in direction otherwise. Said name belongs to Trust in operation by trustees wherein the government/agencies thereof have no control as Trustee/Secured Party/Bailee having full mental capacity and ability to contract as well as natural right to trust holds a common-law trade-name, trademark, LONDALE QUINTAE STRICKLING as authorized representative (Attorney-In-Fact), as well as established validity of the Power of Attorney by continual non-contested use. The Private Offset Account established in the name of TRUST is the property of TRUST as well as any value that has been deposited in Private Offset Account is the property of TRUST, as any such value was created from the credit thereof. Account will remain in effect with appointment of fiduciary by Form 56.

The Undersigned now tendering this binding Legal Notice and Demand, having hereinabove declared Trustee/Secured Party's/TRUST's proper Legal Status and relation to the "Republic of Wisconsin" and to the said de facto compact (Corporate) commercial STATES, including the "STATE OF WI", or by whatever name it may currently be known or hereafter named, does hereby state that the declarations and statements made herein are the truth, the whole truth and nothing but the truth to the best of Trustee/Secured Party's knowledge. Acknowledged by silence and acquiescence of the WI SECRETARY OF STATE, also but not limited to any public officers, agents, contractors, assigns, employees, and subsidiaries of said office, regarding the Trustee/Secured Party's "NOTICE and DEMAND", is therefore accepted and agreed to be the truth.

With silence of Corporate Office "SECRETARY OF STATE" ratifies severances of any nexus or relationship between Trustee/Secured Party/Trust and the said de facto corporate commercial STATE offices; being fraudulently conveyed, operating under "Color of Authority". Let this be known by the "**Good Faith (Oxford) Doctrine**" to all men and women. The Undersigned nor Trust consent to any warrantless searches, or searches that are not compliant with the "Constitution for the united States of America", all of the Amendments of the Honorable "Bill of Rights", and/or the "Constitution of the State of Wisconsin", whether the Undersigned or trusts dwellings, cars, land crafts, watercrafts, aircrafts, the Undersigned himself and current location, property, hotel rooms, apartments, business records, business, or machinery, vehicles, equipment, supplies, buildings, grounds, land in private possession or control of the Undersigned or Trust, past, present, and future, now and forevermore, so help me God.

This notice is in the nature of a Miranda Warning *"Where rights secured by the Constitution are involved, there can be no rule making or legislation which would abrogate them."* Take due heed of its contents. If, for any reason, you do not understand any of these statements or warnings, it is incumbent upon you to summon a superior officer, special prosecutor, federal judge, or other competent legal counsel, to immediately explain to you the significance of this presentment as per your duties and obligations in respect to this private formal, registered Statute Staple Securities Instrument. As per Title 11 USC 501(a), 502(a), and Federal Rules of Civil Procedure Sections 8-A, and 13-A, the claim or presumption that I, Londale-Quintae: Strickling or LONDALE QUINTAE STRICKLING TRUST (simply know herein as Trust) as aforestated am not a citizen within, surety for, subject of, and do not owe allegiance, or fealty as aforestated to the any of the aforementioned or the like, and herein is forever rebutted by this counterclaim in Admiralty.

By this record let it be known that the Undersigned and Trust do not at any time waive any rights, capacities, privileges, immunities, defenses, or protections, as acknowledged by the "Constitution for the united States of America", the Honorable "Bill of Rights", and/or the "Constitution of the State of Wisconsin", nonetheless, demanding that you protect these as you swore an oath(s) to do so. The Undersigned accepts you're lawfully required "Oath(s) of Office," bonds of any type, insurance policies, CAFR funds, and property of any type for protection and making whole. Furthermore, should you witness any public officers at this time, or any time past, present, or future violate any of the rights, privileges, immunities, defenses, or protections of the Undersigned or the Trust that he represents, it is your sworn duty (of oath) to immediately arrest, or have them arrested. You are legally required to charge them as you should any law breaker, regardless of officer's title, rank, uniform, cloak, badge, position, stature, or office; or you shall henceforth be accountable for monetary damages from, but not limited to, your monetary liability, your corporate bond, compensatory costs, punitive procurements, and sanctioned by attorney attributions.

NOTE: A true and correct copy of this **Statute Staple Securities Instrument** is on file not only with the Secretary of State's office, but also been delivered to several trusted parties apprising them of the Undersigned's policy of presenting this security instrument to each and every public officer who approaches the Undersigned or the Trust violating the Undersigned and/or Trusts unalienable rights including, but not limited to right of liberty and free movement upon any common pathway of travel. The Undersigned has a lawful right to travel, by whatever means, via land, sea or air, without any officer, agent, employee, attorney, or judge, in any manner willfully causing adverse effects or damages upon the Undersigned by an arrest, detainment, restraint, or deprivation. With regard to any encounter or communication with the de facto compact (Corporate) commercial STATES, including the "STATE OF WI", or by whatever name it may currently be known or be hereafter named, the Undersigned will be granted the status and treatment of a foreign Sovereign, a foreign diplomat, by all customs officials. This document or the deposited copy thereof becomes an evidentiary document certified herein, as if now fully reproduced, should any court action be taken upon the Undersigned as caused by your acts under color of law with you, your officers, and employees.

Take note; you are now monetarily liable in your personal and corporate capacity. The Undersigned, notwithstanding anything to the contrary, abides by all laws in accordance with the "Constitution for the united States of America", the Honorable "Bill of Rights", and/or the "Constitution of the State of Wisconsin" which are applicable to non-domestic non-assumpsit non-residents on sojourn. The Undersigned wishes no harm to any man or woman. You agree to uphold my "Right to Travel"

BE WARNED, NOTICED, AND ADVISED that in addition to the constitutional limits on governmental authority included in the "Constitution for the united States of America", the Honorable "Bill of Rights", and/or the "Constitution of the State of Wisconsin", the Undersigned relies upon the rights and defenses guaranteed under Uniform Commercial Code(s), common equity law, laws of admiralty, and commercial liens and levies pursuant, but not limited to, Title 42 U.S.C.A.(Civil Rights), Title 18 U.S.C.A. (Criminal Codes), Title 28 U.S.C.A. (Civil Codes), to which you are bound by office and oath, the "Constitution of the State of Wisconsin", and WISCONSIN penal codes, in as much as they are in compliance with the "Constitution for the united States of America", Bill of Rights, and/or the "Constitution of the State of WISCONSIN", as applicable. There can be no violation of any of these laws unless there is a victim consisting of a natural flesh and blood man or woman who has been injured. When there is no victim, there is no crime committed or law broken.

Remember in taking a solemn binding oath(s) to protect and defend the original Constitution for the United States of America circa (1787) and/or the Constitution of the State of Wisconsin against all enemies, foreign and domestic, that violation(s) of said oath(s) is perjury, being a bad-faith doctrine by constructive treason and immoral dishonor. The Undersigned accepts said Oath(s) of Office that you have sworn to uphold.

This legal and timely notice, declaration, and demand is prima facie evidence of sufficient Notice of Grace. The terms and conditions of this presentment agreement are a quasi-contract under the Uniform Commercial Code and Fair Debt Collections Act. These terms and conditions are not subject to any or all immunities that you may claim, should you in any way violate The Undersigned's rights or allow violations by others. Your corporate commercial acts against The Undersigned or The Undersigned's own and your failures to act on behalf of same, where an obligation to act or not to act exists, are ultra vires and injurious by willful and gross negligence

The liability is upon you, and/or your superior, and upon, including any and all local, state, regional, federal, multijurisdictional, international, and/or corporate agencies, and/or persons representing or attached to the foregoing, involved directly or indirectly with you via any nexus acting with you; and said liability shall be satisfied jointly and/or severally at The Undersigned's discretion. You are sworn to your Oath(s) of Office, and I accept your Oath(s) of Office and your responsibility to uphold the rights of The Undersigned or The Undersigned's own at all times

BILLING COSTS ASSESSED WITH LEVIES AND LIENS AND OR TORT UPON VIOLATIONS SHALL BE:

-Unlawful Arrest, Illegal Arrest, Restraint, Distraint, or Trespassing/Trespass	without a lawful correct and complete 4th amendment warrant: $2,000,000.00 (Two Million) US Dollars, per occurrence, per officer, official, agent, or Representative involved.
-Excessive Bail, Fraudulent Bond, Cruel and Unusual Punishment, Violation of Right to Speedy Trial, Violation of Right to Freedom of Speech, Conspiracy, Aid and Abet, Racketeering, and or Abuse of Authority	as per Title 18 U.S.C.A., §241 and §242, or definitions contained herein: $2,000,000.00 (Two Million) US Dollars, per occurrence, per officer, official, agent, or Representative involved.
-Assault and Battery with Weapon:	$3,000,000.00 (Three Million) US Dollars, per occurrence, per officer, official, agent, or Representative involved.
-Unlawful Distraint, Unlawful Detainer, or False Imprisonment:	$5,000,000.00 (Five Million) US Dollars, per day, per occurrence, per officer, official, agent, or Representative involved, plus 18% annual interest.
The Placing of an Unlawful or Improper Lien, Levy, Impoundment, or Garnishment against any funds, bank accounts, savings, accounts, retirement funds, investment funds, social security funds, intellectual property, or any other property belonging to the Secured Party by any agency:	$2,000,000.00 (Two Million) US Dollars per occurrence, and $100,000.00 (One Hundred Thousand) US Dollars per day penalty until liens, levies, impoundments, and/or garnishments are ended and all funds reimbursed, and all property returned in the same condition as it was when taken, with 18% annual interest upon the Secured Party's declared value of property

-Assault or Assault and Battery without Weapon; -Unfounded Accusations by officer of the court; -Denial and or Abuse of Due Process; -Obstruction of Justice; Reckless Endangerment, Failure to Identify and/or present credentials and/or Failure to Charge within 48 (Forty-Eight) Hours after being detained; -Counterfeiting Statute Staple Security Instruments; - Unlawful Detention, or Incarceration; -Incarceration for Civil or Criminal Contempt of court without lawful, documented-in-law, and valid reason; -Disrespect by a Judge or Officer of the Court; -Threat, Coercion, Deception, or Attempted Deception by any Officer of the Court; -Coercing or Attempted Coercion of the Trustee/Secured Party/Bailee to take responsibility for the trust against his Will:		$2,000,000.00 (Two Million) US Dollars, per occurrence, per officer, official, agent, or Representative involved.
-Destruction, Deprivation, Concealment, Defacing, Alteration, or Theft, of Property	including buildings, structures, equipment, furniture, fixtures, and supplies belonging to the Secured Party will incur a penalty equal to the total new replacement costs of property, as indicated by Secured Party, including but not limited to purchase price and labor costs for locating, purchasing, packaging, shipping, handling, transportation, delivery, set up, assembly, installation, tips and fees, permits, replacement of computer information and data, computer hardware and software, computer supplies, office equipment and supplies, or any other legitimate fees and costs associated with total replacement of new items of the same type, like kind, and/or quality, and quantity as affected items. The list and description of affected property will be provided by the Secured Party and will be accepted as complete, accurate, and uncontestable by the agency, or Representative thereof that caused such harm or deprivation of rights. In addition to the aforementioned cost, there will be a $200,000.00 (Two Hundred Thousand) US Dollars per day penalty until property is restored in full, beginning on the first day after the occurrence of the incident, as provided by this Contract.	
The Undersigned does not grant entrance under any circumstances to enter any property at which the undersigned is located, leasing, owns or controls at any time for any reason without the Undersigned's express written permission		Violation of this Notice will be considered criminal trespass and will be subject to a $2,000,000.00 (Two Million) lawful US Silver dollar penalty plus damages, per violation, per violator.

All penalties contained herein will be subject to a penalty increase of $1,000,000.00 (One Million) US Dollars per day, plus interest, while there is any unpaid balance for the first (30) days after Default of payment. This penalty will increase by 10% per each day until balance is paid in full, plus 18% annual interest, beginning on the thirty first (31st) day after Default of payment. All penalties in this document are assessed in lawful money and are to be paid in one troy ounce US Silver Dollars that are .999 pure silver or equivalent par values in legal tender or fiat paper money. Par value will be determined by the value established by a one troy ounce .999 pure silver coins at the US MINT, or by law, whichever is highest in value at the time of the incident. Any dispute over the par value will be decided by the Undersigned, or The Undersigned's designee

CAVEAT

The aforementioned charges are billing costs derived from, but not limited to, Uniform Commercial Codes, the Fair Debt Collection Practices Act and this Contract. These charges shall be assessed against persons, governmental bodies, and corporate entities supra, or any combination thereof when they individually and/or collectively violate the Undersigned/Trust rights, privileges, capacities, and immunities under the "Constitution for the united States of America", the Honorable "Bill of Rights" and/or "Constitution of the State of WISCONSIN", each of which establishes jurisdiction for you in your normal course of business. All violations against the Undersigned/Trust will be assessed per occurrence, and individually and personally. Representative of any branch of government, agency, or group that is involved in any unlawful action against The Undersigned.

By your actions, carried out to The Undersigned/Trust's harm, said actions being *ultra vires* of the limits of power properly placed on the exercise of authority and power of such office and made in conflict with your oath(s) of office or of that of your principal you shall lack recourse for all claims of immunity in any forum. Your knowing consent and admission of perpetrating known acts by your continued *ultra vires* enterprise is a violation of The Undersigned/Trust rights, privileges, capacities, and immunities. This **Statute Staple Securities Instrument** exhausts all state maritime Article I administrative jurisdictions and protects Article III court remedies, as guaranteed in the Constitution for the united States of America, including but not limited to Title 42 U.S.C.A, Title 18 U.S.C.A (including, but not limited to § 242 thereof), and Title 28 U.S.C.A. In short All Rights Reserved.

IGNORANCE OF THE LAW IS NO EXCUSE

I, Londale-Quintae: Strickling, Trustee/Secured Party/Bailee am the principal, and you are the agent. Fail not to adhere to your oath(s), lest you be called to answer before one God and one Supreme Court of Exclusive and Original Jurisdiction, which is the court of first and last resort, not excluding my "Good Faith Oxford Doctrine" by my conclusive Honorable "Bill of Rights."

This Statute Staple Securities Instrument is not set forth to threaten, delay, hinder, harass, or obstruct in any manner, but rather to protect guaranteed Rights and Defenses assuring that at no time my Inalienable Rights are ever waived or taken from the undersigned against my will by threats, duress, coercion, fraud, or in any case without my express written consent of waiver. None of the statements contained herein intend to threaten or cause any type of physical or other harm to anyone. The statements contained herein are to notice any persons, whether real or corporate, of their potential personal, civil and criminal liability if and when such persons violate The Undersigned/Trust's Unalienable Rights as protected by the original "Constitution for the united States of America" circa (1787), "Bill of Rights" and/or the "Constitution of the State of Wisconsin." A bona fide duplicate of this paperwork is safely archived with those who testify under oath that it is The Undersigned's stated standard policy to ALWAYS present this NOTICE to any public or private, officer, official, or agent attempting to violate The Undersigned's rights. It is noted on the record that by implication of said presentment, this notice has been tendered by way of certified mail to SECRETARY OF STATE. Said presentment is prima facie evidence of your receipt and acceptance of this presentment in both your official and personal capacity, jointly and severally for each and all governmental political and corporate bodies. Any other individuals who have been, are, or hereafter are involved in any actions now existing or that may arise in the future against The aforementioned shall only correspond to The Undersigned in writing while signing under penalty of perjury pursuant but not limited to Title 28 U.S.C.A. §1746.

SUMMATION

Should you move against The Undersigned or Trust in defiance of this presentment, there is no immunity from prosecution available to you, or any of your fellow public officers, officials of government or private corporations, judges, magistrates, district attorney, clerks or any other persons who become involved in any actions now existing or that may arise in the future against The Undersigned or Trust by way of aiding and abetting other actors. Take due heed and govern yourself accordingly. Any or all documents tendered to The Undersigned/Trust, lacking bona-fide ink signatures or dates per Title 18 U.S.C.A. § 513-514 are counterfeit security instruments causing you to be liable in your corporate and personal capacity by fraudulent conveyance now and forevermore. If and when you cause any injury and/or damages to the Undersigned or Trust, by violating any of the rights, constitutional rights, civil rights, privileges, immunities, or any terms herein, you agree to willingly, with no reservation of rights and defenses, at the written request of the Undersigned/Trust, surrender, including, but not limited to, any and all bonds, public and/or corporate insurance policies; and/or CAFR funds as needed to satisfy any and all claims as filed against you by the Undersigned or Trust. This applies to any and all Representatives, severally and individually of the "united States of America", the "government of the United States as created in the original Constitution for the united States of America, circa 1787", the "State of Wisconsin", i.e., "Republic of Wisconsin", or to your "<u>UNITED STATES CORPORATION</u>", also known as the corporate "UNITED STATES, "Corp. USA", "United States, Inc.", or by whatever name same may currently be known or be hereafter named, or any of its subdivisions including but not limited to local, state, federal, and/or international or multinational governments, Corporations, agencies, or sub-Corporations, and any de facto compact (Corporate) commercial STATES contracting therein, including the "STATE OF WISCONSIN", or by whatever name same may currently be known or be hereafter named, and the like.

This document cannot be retracted by any Representative, excluding the Undersigned on this registered document, for one hundred years from date on this legally binding **Statute Staple Security Instrument**.

ATTENTION:

Unless this is rebutted within the time limit contained herein, and the conditions of the rebuttal are met, you, or any Representative in any capacity of any agency, government, Corporation, or the like, agree to abide by this Contract anytime you interact with The Undersigned. This document will be on file in the public record. Your Failure to timely rebut the statements and warnings herein constitute your complete, tacit agreement with all statements and warnings contained herein. Your presumptions that the Undersigned/Trust is a "Corporate Fiction" or "Legal Entity" under the jurisdiction of the "Government of the United States" and/or "UNITED STATES Corporation", and that the Undersigned or trust is under the jurisdiction of the "UNITED STATES Corporation" are now and forever rebutted

Your failure to timely make rebuttal so leaves you in the position of accepting full corporate and personal responsibility for any and all liabilities for monetary damages, as indicated herein, that Undersigned or Trust incurs by any adversely affecting injuries caused by your overt, or covert actions, or the actions of any of your fellow public officers and agents in this or any other

relevant matters as described herein or related thereto in any manner whatsoever. You have Thirty (30) days, from the date of receipt of these documents by the Secretary of State's office, to respond and rebut the presumptions of any portion or this entire document/Contract, or you stand in total agreement to each and every statement made herein, by submitting to the Undersigned:
1) signed, certified, authenticated documents of the laws that rebut these declarations point by point
2) In written form with legal/lawful, verified, certified documentation in law, with copies of said law enclosed.
3) Parties making rebuttals to this agreement must print or type their full name and sign their rebuttal in blue ink.
4) Must be accompanied with a copy of proper identification for the person making the rebuttal, such as a driver license, passport or birth certificate, a copy of the person's badge and/or other identification that signifies the person's official capacity, and provide the following information:
    a. full legal name
    b. address;
    c. name of department, bureau, agency, or Corporation by which the person is employed or acts as a Representative
    d. supervisor's name and mailing address
5) certified copy of oath(s) of office if such is required by law;
6) if a member of the state bar, a certified copy of the person's bar card and license to practice law,
7) if the person is required by law to be bonded
    a. a certified copy of the person's official bond,
    b. name, address, and phone number of the bonding company;
8) if covered by a corporate insurance policy
    a. a certified copy of the insurance policy
    b. the name, address, and phone number of the insurance company
9) if a beneficiary of a CAFR
    a. a certified copy of the CAFR policy
    b. the name, address and phone number of the administrator.
10) This documentation must be provided on and For the Record under penalties of the law including perjury.

Note: Non-response and not acting on this notice can and most likely will result in the following crimes: 18 U.S.C. 911 impersonating a U.S. citizen, 18 U.S.C. 912, impersonating a public officer. Under 18 U.S.C. 3 and 4, you as the non-responder will be liable for misprision of felony and accessory after the fact in protecting the crimes that would result from inaction on your part. Partial response without rebuttal is agreement. Any points left unrebutted are points in agreement. Ignorance of the law is no excuse. Therefore, the Constitution places the burden of proof back upon the government, as required by the Administrative Procedures Act, 5 U.S.C. §556(d).

ALL OTHER CORPORATIONS not limited to: telephone companies, cable companies, utility companies, contractors, builders, maintenance personnel, investors, journeymen, inspectors, law enforcement officers, officers of the court, manufacturers, wholesalers retailers, and all others, including all persons natural or fictional, including, but not limited to corporations, limited liability companies, limited liability partnerships, limited and general partnerships, trusts, foundations, DBAs, and AKAs are bound by all paragraphs, terms, and conditions herein, regardless of the nature of limited liability corporation(s) or affiliations such as "DBA's," "AKA's," incorporations, or any types of businesses in commerce as deeded by this securities agreement and decree.

YOU ARE FINALLY NOTICED, having been given knowledge of the law and your personal financial liability in event of any violations of The Undersigned's rights and/or being. This **Statute Staple Securities Instrument** now in your hand constitutes timely and sufficient warning by good faith notice and grace regardless of your political affirmations

Additional Rights and Defenses – Twenty-Five sovereign "People" Magna Carta Grand Jury: In addition to any other rights or defenses that are afforded to The Undersigned by right and by this Contract, the Undersigned has the right to appeal to a "Twenty Five sovereign "People" Magna Carta Grand Jury" for the restoration of property, liberties, or rights of which The Undersigned has been dispossessed by an "Oppressing Government" or its Representatives. If The Undersigned shall have been dispossessed by the "united States of America", the "government of the United States", the "State of Wisconsin", or the "UNITED STATES Corporation", or any Representative thereof without a legal verdict of the Undersigned's Peers, of the Undersigned's property, liberties, or rights, even if such taking was by way of lien, levy, attachment, or garnishment, the Oppressing Government entity or Representative thereof shall immediately restore these things to the Undersigned. Should the Oppressing Government or Representative thereof fail to restore the property, liberties, or rights of which the Undersigned has been dispossessed, then the Undersigned may by right bring the matter before four of the sovereign "People" asking for relief from the transgressions of the Oppressing Government or Representative thereof The four sovereign "People shall petition the Oppressing Government for a redress of grievances, showing to the Oppressing Government its error, and asking the Oppressing Government to cause that error to be amended without delay. Should the Oppressing Government not amend that error within a term of forty (40) days from the time when the petition for redress of grievances is presented to the Oppressing Government, the four sovereign "People" shall refer the matter to the remainder of the "Twenty Five sovereign "People" Magna Carta Grand Jury" and they shall distrain and oppress the Oppressing Government and its Representative by taking their property and possessions in every way that they can, until amends shall have been made according to their judgment. Any citizen of the united States of America, the United States, or of the several States may swear to assist in carrying out the judgment of the "Twenty Five sovereign "People" Magna Carta Grand Jury", and with them any such citizen may take the property and possessions of the Oppressing Government. If any citizens be unwilling to swear to assist in carrying out the judgment of the "Twenty Five sovereign "People" Magna Carta Grand Jury", the "Twenty Five sovereign "People" Magna Carta Grand Jury" shall make them to swear by the mandate of the "Twenty Five sovereign "People" Magna Carta Grand Jury". At all times the decision of a majority of the "Twenty Five sovereign "People" Magna Carta Grand Jury" shall be considered binding and valid on the whole. And the aforesaid Twenty Five shall swear that they will faithfully observe all the foregoing, and will cause them to be observed to the extent of their power. The Oppressing Government or representative shall obtain nothing from any one, either through itself or through another, by which the powers of the "Twenty Five sovereign "People" Magna Carta Grand Jury" may be revoked or diminished. And if any such thing shall have been obtained, it shall be vain and invalid, and the offending government or reprehensive shall never make use of it either through itself or through another. The judgment of the "Twenty Five sovereign "People" Magna Carta Grand Jury", both by rule of law longtime standing and by the terms of this Contract, shall not be overturned by court, as there is no higher court in the realm.

NOTICE TO CLERK AND RECORDER

Pursuant to Title 18 U.S.C., chapter 101 § 2071(b), "Whoever, having the custody of any such record, proceeding, map, book, document, paper, or other thing, willfully and unlawfully conceals, removes, mutilates, obliterates, falsifies, or destroys the same, shall be fined under this title or imprisoned not more than three years, or both; and shall forfeit his office and shall be disqualified from holding any office under the United States."

NOTICE TO AGENT IS NOTICE TO PRINCIPAL AND NOTICE TO PRINCIPAL IS NOTICE TO AGENT

LS: _____
Londale-Quintae: Strickling,

WITNESSES

We, the undersigned witnesses, do hereby swear or affirm that it is the stated policy of Londale-Quintae: Strickling to present this "LEGAL NOTICE AND DEMAND" to all law enforcement officers, agents, or Representative of the "united States of America", the "government of the United States as created in the original Constitution for the united States of America, circa 1787", the "State of Wisconsin", i.e., "Republic of Wisconsin", or to your "UNITED STATES CORPORATION", also known as the corporate "UNITED STATES, "Corp. USA", "United States, Inc.", or by whatever name same may currently be known or be hereafter named, or any of its subdivisions including but not limited to local, state, federal, and/or international or multinational governments, Corporations, agencies, or sub-Corporations, and any de facto compact (Corporate) commercial STATES contracting therein, including the "STATE OF WISCONSIN", or by whatever name same may currently be known or be hereafter named, and the like, anytime that Secured Party has any interaction with them.

First Witness Signature
Date: 08-07-2019

Second Witness Signature
Date: 08-07-2019

Legal Notice & Demand

ATTACHMENTS 'A' - DEFINITIONS

1. **Abuse of Authority:** Means anyone who denies, withholds, refuses, deprives, limits, inhibits, counteracts, conceals, any right, benefit, protections, or privilege, as protected by the "Constitution for the united States of America", the Honorable "Bill of Rights, and/or the "Constitution of the State of Wisconsin." This includes arrest or detainment without documented evidence that a lawful crime has been committed by the Trustee/Secured Party/Bailee (hereafter Secured Party). This includes use of restraint devices on the Secured Party and/or physical abuse that makes any marks, scars, cuts, abrasions, or the like. This also includes denial of lawful Due Process, Habeas Corpus, Excessive Bail, Unlawful Arrest, Unlawful Detention, or the like, as outlined in this Contract.

2. **Abuse of Due Process:** Means any action against the Secured Party, when said action does not abide by all the rights and defenses contained in or represented by the "Constitution for the united States of America", the Honorable "Bill of Rights" and/or the "Constitution of the State of Wisconsin." This includes any charge, or claim, civil or criminal, or in admiralty, that is alleged or made by any Representative of the "government of the United States" or the "UNITED STATES Corporation"

3. **Agency, Entity, Department, Sub Division, Subsidiary, Contractor, Employee, Inspector, Investigator, Organization, Officer, Official, Agent, Branch of Government, Group, Authorized Representative, Policeman, Police Officer, Participant:** Means any person, Corporation, or entity of any kind, which works for, is compensated all or in part by, receives funds or collects funds for, contracts with, receives any benefit from, receives any privilege from, participates with, has allegiance to, or in any way has a relationship with, the "government of the United States" or the "UNITED STATES Corporation" or any of its subsidiaries, sub- Corporations, departments, or agencies, etc. The word "**Representative**" where used in this Contract, shall have the same meaning.

4. **Aiding and Abetting:** Means the efforts of any Representative of the "government of the United States" or the "UNITED STATES Corporation" or officer of the court to assist another of the same to hinder, coerce, restrict, resist, suppress, or deprive in any way, the Secured Party from receiving any and all rights, benefits, privileges, as provided by the Constitution for the united States of America, the Bill of Rights, and/or the "Constitution of the State of WI" or that would normally be offered to a citizen of the United States or of the State of Wisconsin. This also includes the provisions as provided in item #62 "**Racketeering**" and suppression of evidence

5. **Appellation:** means: A general term that introduces and specifies a particular term which may be used in addressing, greeting, calling out for, and making appeals of a particular living, breathing, flesh-and-blood man.

6. **Artificial Person:** Means a fictitious entity/trust that was created by the "government of the United States" and/or parents acting unknowingly in concert or the "UNITED STATES Corporation" for transacting in commerce. This artificial Man or Strawman is represented by the all capital letter name that appears to be spelled the same as the name of the Natural Man or Woman. When the Artificial Person is used in commerce by the Secured Party, it is a transmitting utility.

7. **Assault and Battery with Weapon:** Means any use of, threatened, or perceived use of any weapon, against Secured Party, by any Representative of the "government of the United States" or the "UNITED STATES Corporation" that creates an atmosphere of fear for the Secured Party. This includes non-lethal weapons, such as tazers, stun guns, mace, pepper spray, any chemical used to incapacitate, rubber bullets, shock force weapons, electronic weapon or any other type of weapon that may be used to control or to create fear. If a conflict arises about the events, the version told by the Secured Party will be accepted as truth and will not be contested.

8. **Assault and Battery without a Weapon:** Means the verbal abuse or physical contact, of any kind, upon the Secured Party without the express voluntary written consent of Secured Party. If a conflict arises about the facts involving the incident, the version as told by the Secured Party will be accepted as truth, without question, and will not be contested.

9. **Bill of Rights** Means, for the purposes of this Contract, the original "Bill of Rights" to the "Constitution for the united States of America" circa 1791.

10. **Clerk of the Public Record:** Means any clerk who records documents on the public record and who is employed by a city, county, state, municipality, federal government, international, multi-national, multijurisdictional Corporation.

11. **Coercion or Attempt to Coerce:** Means any attempt by any Representative of the "government of the United States" or the "UNITED STATES Corporation" to threaten, intimidate, deprive, conceal, or in any way prevent the Secured Party from receiving and/or enjoying any right, or privilege that is granted, outlined, or secured by the "Constitution for the united States of America" the Honorable "Bill of Rights", "Constitution of the State of Wisconsin ", or to knowingly allow or instruct another to do so

12. **Concealment:** Means withholding or keeping information that should normally be revealed, about property and/or rights from the Secured Party. This includes keeping evidence or law from a jury that could favorably alter the outcome of a case to the benefit of the Secured Party. No officer of any court or Representative of the "government of the United States" or the "UNITED STATES Corporation" may conceal any law and/or any evidence of any kind that is considered relevant by the Secured Party, and/or fail to disclose any law that benefits the Secured Party.

13. **Conduit:** means of transmitting and distributing energy and the effect/product of labor, such as goods and services, via the name, "LONDALE QUINTAE STRICKLING TRUST ", also known by any and all derivatives and variations in the spelling of said name with the exception of "Londale-Quintae: Strickling "

14. **Conspiracy:** Means the cooperation of two or more persons working together to, restrict, suppress, inhibit, or in any way deprive the Secured Party of any right, benefit, or privilege that would ordinarily be offered by the Constitution for the united States of America, the Bill of Rights, and/or "Constitution of the State of Wisconsin." and/or to a citizen of the United States or of the State of Wisconsin. This also includes the provisions in item #62 "**Racketeering**"

15. **Contract:** Means any agreement in writing that has been offered for review and acceptance by another party, wherein the offering party has ten (10) days or more, or as stipulated in the contract, to review and respond, accept or rebut, any provisions of the contract, as indicated

in the contract. Non Response on the part of the receiving party or agent of the receiving party will be a lawful offer and acceptance of all the terms and conditions contained in said contract. Rebuttal by the receiving party of any provision of the contract by any means other than those as are indicated in the contract will be non-response. Return of the contract unopened and/or without review will be acceptance of all conditions of said contract. Recording the contract with the clerk of court or any public records officer will be a lawful offer and notification and will be presentment to all officers of the court in that state or county. Notice to Agent is Notice to Principal and Notice to the Principal is notice to Agent.

16. **Corporate Capacity**: Means acting for, or on behalf of, a Corporation, or government entity, while under law or color of law.
17. **Corporate Fiction**: A Corporation, a creation of the law that does not actually exist in nature, like a natural man or woman; a legal entity that is false and not real, but which the law assumes to be true.
18. **Corporation**: Means any Representative, agency, sub-Corporation, contractor, or any person or entity that is employed by, receives or distributes funds for, receives any benefit or privilege from, or has any relationship of any kind with the "government of the United States" or the "UNITED STATES" Corporation".
19. **Constitution for the united States of America**: Means, for the purpose of this Contract, "The Constitution for the united States of America" circa 1787, as opposed to the "Constitution of the UNITED STATES" Corporation circa 1868.
20. **Counterfeiting Statute Staple Securities Instruments**: Means any attempt by any Representative of the "government of the United States" or the "UNITED STATES Corporation" to copy, duplicate, replicate any document that has "Statute Staple Securities Agreement" typed, printed, or hand written anywhere on the document, without the express written voluntary permission of the document's owner who is the Secured Party who filed said document in the public record, or is in possession of said document, or who is the maker of said document. If a dispute about permission to duplicate arises, the statements of the Secured Party will be accepted as fact without question and will not be contested.
21. **County or City**: Means any subdivision of any State of the "united States of America." This term excludes any jurisdiction, zone, or territory of the "UNITED STATES Corporation" unless described by the Secured Party in all CAPITAL letters. Any dispute over any errors contained in spelling or grammar will be resolved at the discretion of the Secured Party and will not be challenged by any Representative of the "UNITED STATES Corporation".
22. **Cruel and Unusual Punishment**: Means physical violence of any type or form that is used against a Secured Party that causes visible physical injury, i.e., marks, scrapes, scratches, bruises, abrasion, avulsions, fractures, sprains, restraint marks, dislocations, punctures, cuts, loss of blood, loss of body fluids, or any other type of physical stress to the body; or any chemically induced altered mental state of the Secured Party. This also includes any attempt to incarcerate, restrain, question, detain, withholding food when requested, withholding drink when requested, withholding medications as requested, withhold use of bathroom facilities and supplies when requested, withhold reading and writing materials, withholding communication with friends, family, legal counsel, and religious counsel, withholding proper clothing as needed for comfort, withholding blankets when requested, withholding hot and cold water for showers, withholding freedom when requested. This also includes ridicule, coercion, threats, verbal insults, rude and offensive language, veiled threats, or any other type of mental stress or anguish.
23. **Defacing**: Means the changing or altering the appearance of an item. This also includes changing or altering the meaning of laws, rights, property, documents, or any other thing that has value as determined by the Secured Party.
24. **Denial of Due Process**: Means any attempt by any officer of the court and or the "government of the United States" or the "UNITED STATES Corporation" to deny, deprive, restrict, prevent, or in any way inhibit the proper Due Process to any Secured Party as outlined in the "Constitution for the united States of America" the Honorable "Bill of Rights, and/or the "Constitution of the State of Wisconsin." Any public law, statute, regulation, ordinance, home rule, etc., that is incompatible with the Constitution for the united States of America", the Honorable "Bill of Rights", and/or the "Constitution of the State of Wisconsin", is null and void and will not be used in any action against any Secured Party.
25. **Deprivation of Rights or Property**: Means the concealment, keeping from, hiding, obstructing of any rights, property, privileges or immunities that are outlined or protected by the "Constitution for the united States of America", the Honorable "Bill of Rights, and/or the "Constitution of the State of Wisconsin."
26. **Derivative**: means coming from another; taken from something preceding; secondary; that which has not the origin in itself, but obtains existence from something foregoing and of a more primal and fundamental nature; anything derived from another.
27. **Destruction of Property**: Means any alteration, damage, deprivation, defacing, removing, changing, breaking, separating, removing parts from, erasing of files from, throwing, shooting, kicking, stomping, smashing, crushing, or the like of any property belonging to or in possession of the Secured Party or the Trust.
28. **Disrespect**: Means anything said or written to the Secured Party or Trust that Secured Party or Trust does not like, including body language, or anything that makes Secured Party or any reasonable man uncomfortable, or have fear.
29. **Encroachment**: Means to invade, intrude, or in any way prevent the Secured Party or Trust from enjoying the full and complete use of property, including the acts of trespass; impeding ingress or egress to the property of the Secured Party or Trust; or limiting the ability of the Secured Party or Trust to freely access, claim, hold, possess, use, convey, sell, rent, lease, barter, exchange, or in any way make full and unfettered use of property. This includes the placing or filing of an unlawful lien, levy, burden, charge, liability, garnishment, attachment or encumbrance against any and all property including wages, salaries, stocks, bonds, bank accounts (foreign or domestic), savings accounts, contents of safety deposit boxes, gold, silver, notes, insurance funds, annuities, retirement accounts, social security benefits, motor vehicles, automobiles, recreational vehicles, land, real estate, homes, structures, roads, driveways, personal property of any kind that is held by title, deed, contract, agreement (written or verbal), or is in possession of the Secured Party or Trust. This includes

but is not limited to, traffic stops, searches of vehicles, home invasion, confiscation of any lawful property owned by, in possession of, or under the control of the Secured Party or Trust.

30. **Ens Legis**: The term "*ens legis*" means a creature of the law; an artificial being, such as a Corporation, considered as deriving its existence entirely by the law, as contrasted with a natural person/natural man or woman.

31. **Excessive Bail**: Means any amount of bail set at an unreasonable rate as per the 8th amendment of the Constitution for the united States of America. This also means bail in excess of the amount of the fine, penalty, or penal sum that is associated with the alleged crime committed. This also means that if the Secured Party has lived in a community or has lived in one community or area for more than one year, provided that he has not recently moved within a year, works a regular job, or is a member of or involved with a church group, civic group, community enterprise, or can produce at least two affidavits from members of his community or area stating that he is involved with his community, he cannot be held without bail as a flight risk, or a threat to society. If the Secured Party can produce at least four (4) affidavits stating that he lives, works, and is involved in his community, or the prior community in which he lived, he must be released on his own recognizance without any bail required. This provision does not apply to anyone charged with rape, murder, or violent crimes against women, or children.

32. **Failure to Charge within Forty Eight (48) Hours**: Means any attempt by any Representative of the "government of the United States" or the "UNITED STATES Corporation" to delay, inhibit, prevent, or in any way stop a Secured Party from being lawfully charged by the court within forty eight (48) hours of arrest.

33. **Failure to Identify**: Means any time the Secured Party or Trust has interaction with any Representative of the "government of the United States" or the "UNITED STATES Corporation", the Representative must, upon request of the Secured Party or Trust, provide proper identification, written proof of authority, state what his business is with the Secured Party, complete a public servants questionnaire in advance of arrest or detention, provide documentation properly identifying the officer or respondents superior's name and contact information, and any other relevant information as requested by the Secured Party. The officer may not detain the Secured Party for more than ten (10) minutes while he obtains this information.

34. **Failure to Respond**: Means any attempt by any Representative of the "government of the United States" or the "UNITED STATES Corporation" to ignore, inhibit, withhold, delay, or deny a request for information from a Secured Party or Trust.

35. **False Imprisonment**: Means any attempt by any Representative of the "government of the United States" or the "UNITED STATES Corporation" to incarcerate any Secured Party against his will and/or against any and all protections of the laws and provisions of the "Constitution for the united States of America", the Honorable "Bill of Rights, and/or the "Constitution of the State of Wisconsin".

36. **Federal Zone**: See - "**Jurisdiction of the "Government of the United States" and of the "United States Corporation"**"

37. **Freedom of Speech**: Means the right to speak open and plainly without the fear of reprisal. This includes the right of the Secured Party to speak at hearings and trials, before magistrates, judges, officers of the court, Representatives, or the like, of the "government of the United States" or the "UNITED STATES Corporation". It also means that no attempt to suppress this right will be made by any officer of the court, Representatives, or the like of the "government of the United States" or the "UNITED STATES Corporation". No judge or officer of any court or tribunal will threaten contempt of court for free speech by any Secured Party.

38. **Government of the United States**: The term "government of the United States", when used in this Contract, means the government that was originally established in the "Constitution for the united States of America" adopted in 1787, and does not include any "imposter government" known by any name whatsoever, no matter how similar in spelling the name of any such "imposter government" may appear to be to the spelling of the name of the constitutionally authorized "government of the United States". It is to be noted that the term "United States" as used here is "plural" and not "singular" in number, as is the name "UNITED STATES" used by the "imposter government" (i.e., "UNITED STATES Corporation") now *acting* as the "government of the United States".

39. **Hold-harmless and Indemnity Agreement**: means Hold-harmless and Indemnity Agreement No. 07111983-LQS-HHIA. This Agreement may be amended and modified in accordance with the Declaration of Trust.

40. **Ignore**: Means to refuse or in any way to deny a lawful request for an officer to complete legal documents that will provide information when requested by the Secured Party or Trust.

41. **Illegal Arrest**: Means same as below item #84, "**Unlawful Arrest**".

42. **Personal Capacity**: Means acting on one's behalf, in one's individual capacity, to do a thing. A Representative acting under law or color of law and *ultra vires* of the Representative's official capacity as assigned by the law, or acting in violation of his/her oath(s) of office take on personal liability.

43. **Interpretation**: Means if any conflict arises concerning the definition of any of the terms and or conditions of this Contract, the conflict concerning the meaning of the term or condition will be decided by the Secured Party. Secured Party's decision will be final and not subject to review or argument. No liability or penalty will be incurred by the Secured Party due to his interpretation of such terms and or conditions.

44. **Interstate Detainer**: Means the same as unlawful detainer as when involving the Secured Party and involving more than one Representative, agency or STATE of the "government of the United States" or the "UNITED STATES Corporation", or any Representative who has any agreement with, contract with, or permission to act on behalf of any municipal Corporation of the "government of the United States" or the "UNITED STATES Corporation" or any subsidiary or sub-Corporation thereof.

45. **Jurisdiction of the "government of the United States" and of the "United States Corporation"** (If indeed the later has any jurisdiction at all.): The constitutionally authorized "government of the United States" is recognized by the Secured Party as having exclusive legislative jurisdiction only over the following geographic areas: 1. The District of Columbia, as authorized by Article 1, Section 8, Clause 17 of the Constitution for the united States of America; 2. Federal enclaves within the States, such as land, property or buildings which the Government of the united States of America has purchased by the consent of the legislatures of the States for purposes of erecting

forts, magazines, arsenals, dock-yards, and other needful buildings, as authorized by Article 1, Section 8, Clause 17 of the Constitution for the united States of America; and 3. Territories and possessions belonging to the Government of the United States, as authorized by Article 4, Section 3, Clause 2 of the Constitution for the united States of America. The imposter government - "UNITED STATES Corporation" - while having no real jurisdiction, as no jurisdiction has been lawfully granted, can nevertheless have no claim, even under color of law, to exercise jurisdiction except in those areas where the constitutionally authorized "Government of the United States" has been granted jurisdiction by the sovereign people. The area just described over which the "Government of the United States" lawfully" exercises jurisdiction is also referred to as the "Federal Zone", and all private property held by the Secured Party, which properties are located outside of the Federal Zone are therefore outside of the jurisdictions of the "Government of the United States" and the "UNITED STATES Corporation". Additionally, the constitutionally authorized "Government of the United States" is recognized by the Secured Party as having jurisdiction only as to those matters which the sovereign people, through their several State governments gave to the "Government of the United States", which powers are exclusive as to the powers not granted by the sovereign people through their several State governments and powers reserved to the States by the 10th Amendment to the Constitution for the united States of America. These are the facts and may be presented in any court by affidavit of the Secured Party, where any property or property interest belonging to Secured Party or Trust is involved in any interaction with the "Government of the United States" or the "UNITED STATES Corporation" or any of its Representatives, as outlined in this Contract.

46. **Juristic person:** means an abstract, legal entity, ens legis, such as a corporation, created by construct of law and considered as possessing certain legal rights and duties of a human being; and imaginary entity such as **TRUST**, i.e. "LONDALE QUINTAE STRICKLING TRUST " which, on the basis of legal reasoning, is legally treated as a human being for the purpose of conducting commercial activity for the benefit of a biological, living being, such as Secured Party/Trustee/Beneficiaries. "From the earliest of times the law; has enforced rights and exacted liabilities by utilizing a corporate concept - by recognizing that is, juristic persons other than human beings. The theories by which this mode of legal operation has developed, has been justified, qualified, and defined are the subject matter of a very sizeable library. the historic roots of a particular society, economic pressures, philosophic notions, all have had their share in the law's response to ways of men in carrying on their affairs through what is now the familiar device of the corporation— Attribution of legal rights and duties to a juristic person other then man is necessarily a metaphorical process. And none the worse for it. No doubt, "Metaphors in law are to be narrowly watched". Cardozo, J., in Berkley v. Third Avenue R. Co., 244 N.Y 84, 94. "But all instruments of thought should be narrowly watched lest they be abused and fail in their service to reason". See U.S. v. SCOPHONY CORP OF AMERICA, 333 U.S. '795; 68 S.Ct. 855; 1948 UTsTl Observation: A person has a property right in the use of his or her name which a person may transfer or assign. Gracy v. Maddin, 769 S.W. 2nd 497 (Tenn. Ct. App. 1989).

47. **Lawful 4th Amendment Warrant** Means a warrant that follows the provisions of the fourth amendment to the original "Constitution for the united States of America." This warrant must not deter from the exact procedures as outlined by the Fourth Amendment.

48. **Legal Counsel:** Means anyone that the Secured Party or Trust chooses to have as legal assistance of counsel, whether counsel is licensed or not, or members of the Bar Association. Counsel may assist, represent, speak on behalf of, write cases for, or perform any act in or out of court for the Secured party or Trust without any hindrance, threat, prosecution, charge, repercussion from any officer of the court, or Representative of the "government of the United States" or the "UNITED STATES Corporation", or any Representative thereof.

49. **Legal Status:** Means the two classes of Natural Men and Women recognized in the Constitution for the united States of America – "People" and "Persons". Legal Status in the united States of America defines the rights, duties, capacities, incapacities, privileges, and immunities assigned to each legally recognized class of natural persons. Legal Status also determines to a large degree the type of "Citizenship" to which each class legally recognized class of natural persons is assigned. See definitions for "People" and "Persons" below.

50. **Living, breathing, flesh-and-blood man:** means the Trustee "Londale-Quintae: Strickling" a sentient, living being, as distinguished from an artificial entity, juristic corporation, partnership, association, and the like. "There. every man is independent of all laws, except those prescribed by nature. He is not bound by any institution formed by his fellowmen without he consent." CRUDEN v. NEALE, 2 N.C. 338 (1796) 2 S E 70.

51. **Natural Man or Woman:** Means a sentient, flesh and blood, living, breathing, biological man or woman, created by God, as represented by the Upper and Lower Case Name, including "Natural Man or Woman," or "Real Man," or "Real Woman," or "Real Man/Woman." This is not to be confused with the Fictitious Legal Entity that was created by the Government/Parents that is represented by the All Capital Letter Name.

52. **Natural Man or Woman Secured Party:** Means any flesh and blood, living, breathing Man or Woman, created by God, who notifies any Representative of the "government of the United States" or the "UNITED STATES Corporation", verbally or in writing, that he is not a Strawman, Vessel in Commerce, Corporate Fiction, Legal Entity, ens legis, or Transmitting Utility, of, for, by, to the "united States of America", the "government of the United States", the "State of Wisconsin", i.e., "Republic of Wisconsin", or to the "UNITED STATES Corporation". This is not to be confused with the Fictitious Legal Entity that was created by the Government/Parents and is represented by LONDALE QUINTAE STRICKLING TRUST. Any attempt to notify any Representative of the status of the Secured Party will be sufficient notice. Sufficient notice will be determined by oath, statement, or affidavit by the Secured Party; and the validity of such will not be challenged by any officer of the court.

53. **Non obstante:** means words anciently used in public and private instruments with the intent of precluding, in advance, any interpretation other than certain declared objects and/or purposes.

54. **Obstruction of Justice:** Means any attempt by any officer of the court or Representative of any agency that represents the "government of the United States" or the "UNITED STATES Corporation", or any of its subdivisions, agencies, contractors, etc., to deprive, hinder, conceal, coerce, threaten the Secured Party or Trust in an attempt to prevent his any and every opportunity to legally/lawfully defend him/herself by attempting to produce and file lawful documents, and or testimony, to officers, judges, magistrates, the court, clerk of court,

or Representatives, in order to settle any legal/lawful controversy. This also includes any attempt by a judge or officer of the court from hindering the Secured Party or Trust from filing, admitting, presenting, discussing, questioning, or using any evidence, document, paper, photographs, audio and/or video recordings, or any other type of evidence that they desire to submit as evidence in any type of court proceeding. The determination of what is evidence and what will be admitted is to be solely determined by the Secured Party or Trust. Any evidence will be tried on merits of the lawful content and validity. Any judge or officer of the court who attempts to suppress or dismiss legal or lawful evidence will voluntarily surrender all bonds, insurance, property, CAFR funds, corporate property, bank accounts, and savings accounts of value to the Secured Party upon written demand and surrender all rights to and defenses against said property. This also includes evidence that is supported by case law. This includes attempts by any officer of the court from making motions, order such as Gag Orders or any other means of keeping information suppressed from the public or the official record. The determination of whether the acts of the court are an attempt to suppress evidence will be solely determined by the Secured Party. This also includes the provision as indicated in item #62 "**Racketeering**"

55. **Oppressing Government**: Means any Government or Representative thereof that shall have transgressed against Secured Party or Trust or any of Secured Party's or Trust's property, rights, privileges, capacities, or immunities in any respect.
56. **Peers**: Means the same as the definition of a Secured Party.
57. **People**: The "People" are those natural men and women who hold the sovereignty in joint tenancy in the united States of America and the several States, by virtue of the Treaty of Peace of 1783, signed by His Most Royal and Dread Sovereign Majesty, King George the 3rd and its two addendums signed by the then Kings of Spain and France. The "People" are those who were the free inhabitants in the several States and their posterity (paupers, vagabonds and fugitives from justice excepted), who ordained and established the "Constitution for the united States of America" in 1787 and the Bill of Rights of 1791, for themselves and their posterity, and who established the constitutions for the several states, reserving unto themselves and their posterity the sovereignty of both the united States of America and the several states. The "People" are not citizens of or subject to the jurisdiction of the "government of the United States", as created in the original "Constitution for the united States of America", circa 1787, or to your "UNITED STATES Corporation", also known as the corporate "UNITED STATES, "Corp. USA", "United States, Inc.", or by whatever name same may currently be known or be hereafter named, or any of its subdivisions including but not limited to local, state, federal, and/or international or multinational governments, Corporations, agencies, or sub-Corporations, and any de facto compact (Corporate) commercial STATES contracting therein, including the "STATE OF WISCONSIN", or by whatever name same may currently be known or be hereafter named, and the like. The "People" are citizens first of the State in which they reside, and second of the united States of America.
58. **Person**: The word "Person", when used in this Contract and written in upper and lower case letters shall mean a natural man or woman, and not an incorporeal person. Further, a "Person" is distinguished from a "People", in that the "People", hold the sovereignty in the united States of America (see "People" #57), and the "Persons" derive all of their rights and privileges from the "People", through the Constitution for the united States of America and the Constitutions for the several States. The "Persons" are identified in the Constitution for the united States, first at Article 1, Section 9, Clause 1, their rights and privileges and defenses and protections are defined at Amendment Five of the Bill of Rights, and their duties and citizenship status are defined at Amendment Fourteen of the Constitution for the united States of America.
59. **Presumption**: Means legal assumption or inference that places the burden of proof or burden of production on the other party, but never on the Secured Party or Trust. No presumption shall prevail against the Secured Party or Trust without lawful, documented evidence that supports the presumption which is certified by the officers of the court, on and for the record, under penalty of perjury.
60. **Public Record**: Means any record or document placed into the public by the Secured Party. For example, when this document is recorded at a Register of Deeds office or Secretary of States, it becomes a public record.
61. **Purchase Price**: Means the new replacement costs of items of property at the time of replacement. This includes locating, packing, shipping, handling, delivery, set up, installation, and any other fee associated with total replacement of property.
62. **Racketeering**: Means any attempt by any two or more officers of "government of the United States" or the "UNITED STATES Corporation", to restrict, suppress, coerce, manipulate, inhibit, or in any way deprive the Secured Party from receiving every right, benefit, or privilege or exercising every immunity that is outlined by the Constitution for the united States of America, the Honorable "Bill of Rights, and/or the "Constitution of the State of Wisconsin." This also includes any effort by the officers of the court or any Representative of "government of the United States" or the "UNITED STATES Corporation", to hinder in any way the introduction of evidence, law, facts, affidavits, statements, witness testimony, or any information that is considered relevant by the Secured Party or Trust, or any attempt to prevent a jury from hearing this evidence. This also includes any attempt to prevent this evidence from being heard in a public forum and before any and all members of the general public, as many as can be accommodated by the main courtroom. All hearings, tribunals, or trials will be held in a public place; and any and all members of the general public will be allowed to attend, without restriction. This also includes questioning and/or interrogation by police officers before, during, and after an arrest.
63. **Reckless Endangerment**: Means any attempt by any officer of the court or Representative of "government of the United States" or the "UNITED STATES Corporation", as defined herein, to endanger, attempt, or threaten to attempt to endanger the life or property of the Secured Party or Trust. This includes dangerous driving in a car, use or threatened use of lethal or non-lethal weapons or chemicals, improper use of restraint devices, use of restraint devices on a non-combative Secured Party. If a conflict arises as to whether or not reckless endangerment has occurred, the version of the Secured Party will be considered as truth.
64. **Representative**: Means any agent, agency, department, officer, investigator, subsidiary, sub-Corporation, contractor, employee, inspector, individual or Corporation that has any affiliation, association, collects or distributes funds for, does any task for, receives any benefit or privilege from, etc., of or for "government of the United States" or the "UNITED STATES Corporation", or anyone, or anything that represents the interests of, or is being funded by, or receives funds from, or has any attachment to "government of the United States" or the "UNITED STATES Corporation", or any of their Representatives, sub divisions or sub-Corporations.

65. **Rights and Defenses**: Means Secured Party's or Trusts legal and/or lawful right and/or ability to defend himself/ herself in any action. Upon agreement, the defendant in an action may give up his right to defend himself/herself in a given action. This includes tacit agreement or agreement by default; and the Secured Party is never the defendant.
66. **Right to Speedy Trial**: Means trial will commence within 90 days of the date of arrest.
67. **Right to Travel**: Means the right to freely move about and/or control any type of craft by whatever means, via land, sea, or air, without any interference by any Representative of "government of the United States" or the "UNITED STATES Corporation", that in any manner willfully causes adverse effects or damages upon the Secured Party or Trust by an arrest, inhibition, detainment, restraint, deprivation or prevention.
68. **Secured Party**: In this Contract, the term "Secured Party", means a "Trustee/Secured Party Creditor/Bailee", which means Londale-Quintae: Strickling, a natural, living, Breathing flesh-and-blood man or sentient being as against a juristic person created by legal construction and/or the appointment declared under declaration of trust appointing another or additional "Trustee/Secured Party Creditor/Bailee" as stated therein.
69. **Sentient, living being** means the Trustee "Londale-Quintae: Strickling" a living, breathing, flesh-and-blood man, as distinguished from an abstract legal construct such as an artificial entity, juristic person, corporation, partnership, association, and the like.
70. **State**: The word "State", which is distinguished in this Contract by being written in upper and lower case letters, means any of the fifty independent sovereign nations, states and republics which make up the Union and are commonly referred to and known as states of the "united States of America" (For example: the "State of Wisconsin", i.e., "Republic of Wisconsin"), which use of the word "State" is not the same as a "STATE" of the "UNITED STATES Corporation" and any such "State" is not a creation or subdivision thereof, and is not subject to the jurisdiction thereof.
71. **STATE**: The word "STATE", which is distinguished in this Contract by being written in all upper case letters, means any of the de facto compact (Corporate) commercial states contracting within the "UNITED STATES Corporation", also known as the corporate "UNITED STATES, "Corp. USA", "United States, Inc.", or by whatever name same may currently be known or be hereafter named, by way of example, including, but not limited to the "STATE OF WISCONSIN", or by whatever name same may currently be known or be hereafter named. STATES are a part of and subject to the jurisdiction of the "UNITED STATES Corporation", and are not States of the "united States of America" As a condition of this Contract, the Secured Party will determine 1. Whether or not any State is a part of the "UNITED STATES Corporation", and 2. Whether the alleged offense occurred within the limits of the "UNITED STATES Corporation". A violation of this provision will be #87 Unlawful Determination and punishable as indicated by this Contract.
72. **Statute Staple Securities Instrument**: Means a registered bond, statute, which establishes a procedure for settlement of commercial debt or obligation of record. This also establishes the law as it relates to the Secured Party.
73. **Strawman**: In this documentation the term "strawman" means the Debtor, i.e., LONDALE QUINTAE STRICKLING, also known as LONDALE QUINTAE STRICKLING TRUST or simply Trust or TRUST and any and all variations and derivatives of the spelling of said name except Londale-Quintae: Strickling; a front, a third party who is put up in name only for participating in a transaction. The "strawman" is synonymous with # 76. "Transmitting Utility"
74. **The Placing or Filing of an Unlawful Lien, Levy, Burden, Charge, Liability, Garnishment, Encumbrance, or Attachment**: Means any attempt by any Representative of "government of the United States" or the "UNITED STATES Corporation", to place a lien, levy, garnishment, or attachment on the property or collateral of the Secured Party or Trust. Any such Representative must first prove his authority to do so by lawfully documented evidence, furnishing all documents, forms, and papers as necessary to prove his authority to do so to a neutral Three (3) Notary Panel, hereinafter referenced as The Panel, selected by the Secured Party or Trust. Said Representative must guarantee in writing that the Representative signing said documents will be personally liable for any damage(s) due to his unlawful and/or illegal actions. He must supply bonds or other lawful funds to be held in trust by The Panel until The Panel determines if any actions of the Representative have violated any laws or caused damage to the Secured Party or Trust. The Panel will have the sole power to determine if any damage(s) has occurred and will release the funds according to The Panel's adjudication. The decision of The Panel will be final with no recourse. The surety bonds and/or funds held in escrow by The Panel must be at least four (4) times the estimated value of the property that is liened, levied, garnished, or attached. The assessment of value will be recorded via affidavit by the Secured Party and delivered to The Panel. The Panel's determination and the assessment thereof will be accepted as truth without question or recourse. Said Representative agrees to surrender, including, but not limited to, any and all surety bonds, public and/or corporate insurance policies, CAFR funds, or corporate property as needed to satisfy any and all claims and/or assessments as filed against said Representative by the Secured Party. Said Representative agrees that any and all property or collateral with a current or existing lien will remain in the custody and control of the Secured Party until such time as a determination has been made by a jury of twelve of the Secured Party's Peers as defined herein. In the event that a jury of twelve of the Secured Party's Peers cannot be convened or has not been convened within sixty (60) days from the date of the order of the lien, levy, attachment, or garnishment, any action against the Secured Party or Trust shall be dismissed with prejudice; and every lien, levy, attachment, or garnishment shall be released within ten (10) days and all property rights restored, unencumbered. The Representative who has authorized said lien, levy, attachment, or garnishment agrees to surrender any and all surety bonds, public and/or corporate insurance policies, CAFR funds, or corporate property as needed to satisfy any and all claims and/or assessments as filed against said Representative.
75. **Trespassing/Trespass**: Means the entry into, or onto the domain, property, residence, area, location, grounds, dwellings, buildings, barns, sheds, caves, structures, lands, storage areas, tunnels, automobiles, trucks, safe houses, underground shelters, automobiles, motor vehicles, recreational vehicles, boats, planes, trains, ships, containers, vans, heavy equipment, farm implements, culverts, driveways, trees, yards, real property, real estate, land, etc., of the Secured Party without Secured Party's express written permission, or without a lawfully executed

fourth (4th) amendment warrant, and any and all Representatives of "government of the United States" or the "UNITED STATES Corporation", will fully and completely observe any and all protections as outlined in the Constitution for the united States of America, the Honorable "Bill of Rights, and/or the "Constitution of the State of Wisconsin." Any personal property that is damaged, lost, stolen, or misplaced, etc., will be recoverable as indicated in the Legal Notice and Demand document. Secured Party solemnly swears and affirms that Secured Party does not have any illegal contraband on Secured Party or Trusts property; Secured Party has never had any illegal contraband on or around my property and never will. Secured Party simply does not allow it on Secured Party's or Trusts property. Any contraband if it is found on said property will have been introduced by the officers or agents during time of trespass. Contraband or illegal items if they are found in a search do not belong to Secured Party or Trust and may not be used in any attempt in any claim against me. Any and all Representatives of the "government of the United States" or the "UNITED STATES Corporation", will be held individually and personally liable for the full amount of damages as outlined in this Notice and Demand document for trespassing.

76. **Transmitting Utility**: the term "Transmitting Utility "LONDALE QUINTAE STRICKLING, also known as LONDALE QUINTAE STRICKLING TRUST ", and any and all derivatives and variations in the spelling of said name except Londale-Quintae: Strickling.
77. **TRUST**: means "LONDALE QUINTAE STRICKLING TRUST " also known by any and all derivatives and variations in the spelling of said name with the exception of "Londale-Quintae: Strickling". this is a copyrighted entity with all rights reserved.
78. **Trustee**: means "Londale-Quintae: Strickling"
79. **UCC**: Herein the term "UCC" means Uniform Commercial code.
80. **Unalienable Rights (Inalienable Rights)**: Means Natural Rights given by God as acknowledged by the Law of Nations and incorporated into the "Bill of Rights," of the Constitution of the State of Wisconsin such as, but not limited to right of enjoying and defending their lives and liberties; of acquiring, possessing and protecting property; and of seeking and obtaining their safety and happiness.
81. **Unfounded Accusations**: Means any accusation, charge, or claim, civil or criminal, or in admiralty that is alleged or made by any Representative of the "government of the United States" or the "UNITED STATES Corporation", as defined herein, that is not proven by written documented evidence presented under oath and penalty of perjury by an authorized Representative of the "government of the United States" or the "UNITED STATES Corporation". The accuser has eight (8) hours to provide said documents to be reviewed and in possession of the Secured Party; and failure to do so will be unfounded accusation and subject to the penalties contained herein.
82. **UNITED STATES Corporation**: "UNITED STATES Corporation" means the corporate "UNITED STATES", "Corp. USA", "United States, Inc.", or by whatever name it may currently be known or be hereafter named, (exclusive of the "united States of America" and the "government of the United States as created in the original Constitution for the united States of America, circa 1787"), or any of its agencies, or sub-Corporations, including but not limited to any de facto compact (Corporate) commercial states contracting therein, including, but not limited to the "STATE OF WISCONSIN", or by whatever name it may currently be known or be hereafter named (Exclusive of the "State of Wisconsin", i.e., "Republic of Wisconsin")
83. **united States of America**: The term "united States of America", when used in this Contract is distinguished by being written in upper and lower case letters, except that the first letter of the first word, i.e., "united" is a lower case letter, and means that union of independent sovereign nations, states and republics, which as colonies of Great Britain and having declared their independence from Great Britain in The Declaration of Independence adopted July 4, 1776, and having won their independence from Great Britain in the American Revolutionary War, and thereafter having gained recognition as independent sovereign nations, states and republics in international law by the Treaty of Peace of 1783, signed by His Most Royal and Dread Sovereign Majesty, King George the 3rd and its two addendums signed by the then Kings of Spain and France, and which independent sovereign nations and states did adopt the "Articles of Confederation" of 1778 and thereafter adopted the "Constitution for the united States of America" in 1787. The word "united States of America", when used in this Contract, does not include the UNITED STATES Corporation, as that term is defined herein.
84. **Unlawful Arrest**: Means restricting the Secured Party's right to move about freely without the proper use of a lawful 4th amendment warrant signed by a judge of "Competent Jurisdiction" while under oath. This includes unnecessary use of restraint devices, traffic stops, raids, or any other type of interaction, when an officer is presented with and ignores a "Notice and Demand." "Public Servants Questionnaire," "Right to Travel" Documents, or other documents notifying the officer of the lawful rights of the Secured Party created by God, who is not to be confused with the Corporate Fiction "Strawman" which was created by the STATE. This includes arrest when the Secured Party is incarcerated for refusing to sign any citation, arrest due to contempt of court when he or she is not violent or a physical threat to the court, arrest by Internal Revenue Service for failure to produce books, records, or other documents, arrest and refusal of Habeas Corpus, arrest for conspiracy of any kind without lawfully documented affidavits from at least two (2) eye witnesses, signed under oath and penalty of perjury.
85. **Unlawful Detainer**: Means any attempt by any officer of the court or Representative of the "government of the United States" or the "UNITED STATES Corporation" to arrest, check, hinder, delay, possess, hold, keep in custody, restrain, retard, stop, withhold the Secured Party without affording him every protection as outlined by the "Constitution for the united States of America", the Honorable "Bill of Rights, and/or the "Constitution of the State of Wisconsin." Any public law, statute, regulation, ordinance or the like will be null and void and will not be used in any action in which the Secured Party is involved.
86. **Unlawful Detention**: Means restraining the Secured Party's freedom of movement, and/or Right to Travel, against his will for more than sixty (60) seconds without a properly authorized lawful 4th amendment warrant signed by a judge of competent jurisdiction while under oath. This includes routine traffic stops, raids, random identification checks, security checks, only after the Representative has been notified by the Secured Party of his status and after the officer has been given documents to prove said status, along with up to ten (10) minutes for officer to examine said documents.

87. **Unlawful Determination:** Means any statement, speech, gesture, writing, presentment, or the like that suggests an idea that negatively represents the character, actions, plans, procedures, customs, ways of the Secured Party or Trust, or group of Secured Parties, that is not proven by documented authorized certified evidence, on and for the record under penalty of perjury. This includes off color statements, accusations, or remarks by a judge or other officer of the court and any other Representative of the "government of the United States" or the "UNITED STATES Corporation".
88. **Unlawful Distraint.** Means seizure or taking of any property that is lawfully owned or in possession of the Secured Party or Trust that Secured Party Represents without proper probable cause, and/or due process, and lawful 4th amendment warrant. This includes any seizure by any Representative, in any capacity, or relationship with the "government of the United States" or the "UNITED STATES Corporation" or any of its agencies, contractors, subdivisions, subsidiaries, or the like.
89. **Unlawful Restraint:** Means any action by any Representative to prevent, coerce, intimidate, hinder, or in any way limit the right of the Secured Party or Trust from any type of freedom of legal/ lawful speech, travel, movement, action, gesture, writing, utterance, or enjoyment of any right or privilege that is commonly enjoyed by any citizen of the United States or of the State of Wisconsin.
90. **US Dollars:** Means the currently recognized medium of exchange as used by the general public at the time of offense, at par value, equal to one ounce silver dollar equivalent per each dollar unit, as represented in a claim. All claims and damages will be paid at par value as indicated. Par value will be established by written law or the value established by the US MINT for the purchase of an official one troy ounce 99.999% Pure Silver Coin, whichever is higher at the time of the offense.
91. **Verbal Abuse:** Means the use of offensive, and /or threatening verbal words, body language, and nonverbal gestures or actions by any representative of the "government of the United States" or the "UNITED STATES Corporation", as defined herein, upon the Secured Party. If a controversy arises about an incident, the version told by the Secured Party will be accepted as truth and will not be contested.
92. **Vessel in Commerce**: "vessel in commerce" means the strawman, LONDALE QUINTAE STRICKLING© TRUST, and any and all derivatives and variations in the spelling of said name except Londale-Quintae: Strickling, a transmitting utility, an all-capital letter name representing the Strawman/Trust entity/Ens Legis for the use in commerce by which the Trustee/Secured Party can participate in commerce, and appear in court.
93. **Victim:** Means the Secured Party or Trust who has received direct damages to themselves or their property as the result of an unlawful or illegal act by another.
94. **Victimless Laws:** Means any law that is passed or presumed to be passed that creates a violation of law where no Natural Man or Woman has been damaged. This includes any statute, ordinance, regulation, policy, or color of law provision. These types of laws will not be used in any action, of any kind, against any Natural Man or Woman or the property thereof.
95. **Willingly:** Means that a Secured Party is in full knowledge, understanding, agreement, and full consent, at all times, without fear of reprisal, threat, or coercion, during any interaction in which he is involved with any Representative of any court or Corporation, including incorporated governments.
96. **Written or Verbal Agreement:** Means any agreement entered into by the Secured Party or Trust, written or verbal. Any question of any contract will be resolved by an affidavit from the Secured Party or Secured Party on Behalf of Trust. Secured Party's affidavit whether in behalf of the Secured Party or the Trust, will be considered fact in any action or dispute, without question of any Representative of any Corporation, including incorporated governments.

Public Servant Questionnaire

This questionnaire must be filled-out by any public servant before s/he can ask any question of Londale-Quintae: Strickling, Trustee/Secured Party/Bailee. This Questionnaire is not specific to you, this is the general policy and procedure of the aforementioned private man with all public Servants in any type of public relations. This Questionnaire is provided authorized under Federal law, including the Privacy Act, 5 U.S.C. 552a, 88 Stat. 1896, et seq., 1974, as well as applicable state laws. This is not a failure to cooperate but rather provision to establish the capacity in which we are contracting as well as open and fair dealing under the Good Faith Oxford, Clean Hands, and Fair Dealings Doctrines. A blank copy of this documentation is also on record with the Secretary of State as a matter of public record under Necessity as a matter of established policy and procedure.

1. Public servant's full legal name: _____
2. Public servant's residence address: _____
3. Name of agency: _____
4. ID number: _____
5. Badge Number: _____
6. Bonding agency and number: _____
7. Full legal name of supervisor and office address: _____
8. Will you as a public servant uphold the constitution of the United States? ☐ Yes ☐ No
9. Will you as a public servant furnish a copy of the law or regulation that authorizes the action being taken or information requested in this case? ☐ Yes ☐ No
10. Will you as a public servant provide in writing, that portion of the law authorizing the questions asked? ☐ Yes ☐ No
11. Are answers to your questions voluntary or mandatory? ☐ Voluntary ☐ Mandatory
12. What will be the effect upon me if I should not choose to answer any or all of these questions? _____
13. Are the questions being asked based upon a specific law or regulation, or are they a discovery process? ☐ Law/Regulation ☐ Discovery Process
14. If based on a specific law or regulation, please state: _____
15. What other uses may be made of this information? _____
16. What other agencies may have access to this information? _____
17. Name of person in government requesting this information: _____
18. Is this investigation general or special? ☐ General ☐ Special
    Note: by 'general,' it means any kind of blanket investigations in which a number of persons are involved because of geography, type of business income, etc. By 'special,' it means any investigation of an individual nature in which others are not involved.
19. Have you consulted, questioned, interviewed, or received information from any third party relating to this matter? ☐ Yes ☐ No
20. If yes, give identity of all such third parties: 1) _____
    (Use back of sheet if more area is needed.) 2) _____
21. Do you reasonably anticipate either a civil or criminal action to be initiated or pursued based upon any of the information, which you seek? ☐ Yes ☐ No
22. Is there a file of records, information, or correspondence relating to me being maintained by this agency? ☐ Yes ☐ No
23. Is this agency using information on me, which was supplied by another agency or government source? ☐ Yes ☐ No
24. Will the public servant guarantee that no department (other than the one by which he is employed) will use the information in these files? ☐ Yes ☐ No

I hereby sign and affirm under the penalty of perjury that the answers supplied herein are true and correct in every particular.

_____
Signature of Public Servant

Would you like a copy of this completed Questionnaire to be provided to the address you listed above? ☐ Yes ☐ No

Notice: If any person or agency receives any request for information relating to the aforesaid, the aforesaid must be advised in writing before releasing such information. Failure to do so may subject you to possible civil or criminal action as provided by this act and/or other applicable law(s).

Public Servants Questionnaire   Page 1 of 1   Form No.: 07111983-LQS-PSQLND

State of Wisconsin

Department of Financial Institutions

Endorsement

DECLARATION - DOMESTIC COMMON LAW TRUST - FORM 702

LONDALE QUINTAE STRICKLING

Received Date: 6/22/2023   Filed Date: 6/23/2023

Filing Fee: $50.00
Expedited Fee: $25.00   Entity ID#: L078038
Total Fee: $75.00

EFFECTIVE 6/23/2023

MILWAUKEE COUNTY

DECLARATION OF TRUST
AN IRREVOCABLE TRUST ORGANIZATION

THIS declaration of trust made this day between the undersigned parties, known hereinafter as the "**Creator**" and the "**Trustee**" agree to wit:

1. Creator herein offers for consideration to create an organization under common law having a fixed number of certificates which evidence a right of distribution, commonly known as an Irrevocable Trust Organization or Unincorporated Business Organization, and
2. Trustee herein agrees to the exchange, in trade, good and valuable consideration for certificates of the newly created organization, LONDALE QUINTAE STRICKLING Trust.

THEREFORE, the parties mutually agree, promise and covenant as follows:

CONSIDERATION:
a. Trustee herein agrees to bargain, exchange, assign, convey and deliver to this organization or its appointed Trustee
b. Immediately upon execution of this agreement, Creator agrees to appoint a Trustee having authority to carry out the exchange and hold and administer the consideration received.
c. This initial exchange, a description of the consideration, whether personal and/or real property, and the number of certificates issued, shall be documented in the minutes of the organization.
d. Both parties herein contract to perform, and agree that this exchange is not a sale or a gift, but an equal-in-value exchange.

ADMINISTERED AS TRUST ESTATE:
a. Assets of this organization shall be deemed, for administrative purposes, a trust estate and the consideration received from Trustee shall be deemed the initial corpus.
b. Any additional property received from any future Trustee or any party shall be deemed an addition to corpus.
c. Any persons may add property of any character to the trust estate at any time by gift, grant, conveyance, exchange, insurance proceeds, assignment, will or any other method so long as the property and method of transfer is approved by the Trustee(s).
d. All assets belonging to the trust estate shall be listed on Schedule "A", or an addendum to Schedule "A", and administered as provided herein.

IRREVOCABLE AGREEMENT:
a. The parties herein agree that this contract and declaration, including all trust provisions contained herein, shall be irrevocable.
b. Trustee irrevocably relinquishes all rights to the property exchanged into this organization.
c. Neither Creator nor Trustee nor any certificate holder shall have any right to revoke or amend this contract and declaration.
d. Amendments may only be made by unanimous approval of the Board of Trustees as provided herein. Further, the board of Trustees shall have exclusive power to construe and determine the meaning and intent of this contract and declaration.

APPOINTMENT OF TRUSTEE:
Upon execution of this contract and declaration, Creator shall appoint a Trustee, known hereinafter as the "first" Trustee, to administer this organization as provided herein. The first Trustee shall provide Creator a written acceptance of the appointment, which shall be made a part of the permanent records.

BOARD OF TRUSTEES:
a. The first Trustee, upon acceptance of the appointment, may thereafter appoint a second Trustee.
b. They in turn may jointly appoint one or more additional Trustees and may designate successors.
c. Trustees shall collectively act by authority of this contract and the trust provisions contained herein as a Board of Trustees for the purpose of holding and administering company assets for the benefit of certificate holders.
d. All members of the Board of Trustees shall serve without bonds.

DECLARATION OF TRUST
AN IRREVOCABLE TRUST ORGANIZATION

DISCRETIONARY POWERS:
    a. The parties herein agree that the Board of Trustees shall have absolute and sole discretionary power over this organization, its assets and earnings therefrom.
    b. The Board shall have authority to:
        I. Determine what shall constitute principal and earnings,
        II. how such assets shall be allocated, and
        III. shall have absolute authority to determine if and when distributions of principal or earnings will be made to certificate holders.

ACCEPTANCE BY TRUSTEES:
The first Trustee, and all subsequent Trustees and successor Trustees, by accepting the appointment as Trustee of this organization causes all present and future Trustees to agree to the following:
    a. They accept the initial gift or conveyance of property on behalf of the organization and acknowledge the delivery of all property specified on Schedule "A".
    b. They agree to conduct the organization's affairs in good faith, in conformity with the terms and conditions set forth in this contract and its inherent trust provisions.
    c. They agree to exercise their best judgment and discretion to conserve and improve the property of the trust estate in accordance with decisions of the Board of Trustees as set forth in the organization's minutes.
    d. They agree, upon final liquidation of the trust estate, to distribute the assets to the existing certificate holders as their contingent rights may appear.

ADMINISTRATIVE PROVISIONS:
Trustees, and their successors, may hold administrative offices within the organization, and may singularly or collectively exercise authority granted by the Board of Trustees in the management of company affairs. They are herein authorized to exclusively manage, administer and control the trust estate without the consent of certificate holders. The following specific terms and conditions apply:
    a. The Board of Trustees shall be at least one (1) in number, and may be increased as deemed necessary in the manner set forth above.
    b. A Trustee may resign or be removed from the Board, with or without cause, by a resolution of the Board of Trustees determined by a majority vote.
    c. In the event of death, removal from the Board, or resignation of a Trustee, the vacant position shall be filled by a successor Trustee, if pre-appointed, or the remaining Board of Trustees may appoint a successor by unanimous vote. Should the entire Board of Trustees become vacant, the trust will make full distribution to the beneficiaries.
    d. The signing and acknowledging of this contract by any Trustee or Trustees shall constitute Trustees' collective acceptance of this contract and its trust provisions and Trustees' acknowledgment that **this organization's property and assets are vested in fee simple in the trust estate without any further act or conveyance by the Board of Trustees.** Trustees as discretionary fiduciaries shall hold legal and equitable title to all assets.
    e. The Board of Trustees may provide for meetings at stated intervals without notice, and special meetings may be called at any time by one or more Trustees upon three day's written notice. At any regular or special meeting, a majority of Trustees shall constitute a quorum for conducting business, provided affirmative action may only be had upon a majority vote of Trustees, whether present or absent, except that in a special meeting called for a special purpose the majority present may affirmatively act in emergency matters. A telephone or fax vote shall be a valid vote.
    f. Any resolution of the Board of Trustees shall be deemed within the Board's power so long as the resolution is not inconsistent with this organizational document and any amendments thereto.
    g. Trustees shall be controlled by this document as amended and future resolutions of the Board of Trustees. All meetings and resolutions shall be recorded in a company minute book.
    h. Trustees shall keep proper records and accounts as the Board of Trustees deems necessary for the proper

DECLARATION OF TRUST
AN IRREVOCABLE TRUST ORGANIZATION

management of the trust estate.

i. Trustees shall not be required to individually assume liability for loss of company assets while acting in good faith on behalf of the organization, or for any act or omission of any other Trustees, agents or employees. They shall, however, be liable for their own breach of good faith. If a Trustee shall for any reason suffer a personal loss while providing good faith service to the trust, the Trustee shall be reimbursed for such loss from the trust estate further reimbursement may be documented in agreement with the trust.

j. The Board of Trustees, at the expiration of the term as set forth herein, shall wind up company affairs and terminate the company operations, making final distribution as provided. If the organization was recorded publicly, Trustees shall file with the Recorder a notice of termination; and Trustees, thereupon, shall automatically be discharged, provided final administration and distribution was made in accordance with the terms and conditions of this agreement. Otherwise, a court of equity may be invoked to review and correct any tort or error, if necessary.

k. When there are no longer trustees and beneficiaries the Manager will have the right to dissolve the trust by following the procedures in "J".

l. Any Affidavits for Public Notice, Declarations, and Honorable Clarifications, not limited to any Corporeal and/or Incorporeal Hereditaments concerning any conveyance included in the Security Agreement, and/or Authenticated foreign document(s) is under the Hague Convention, 5 October, 1961.

TRUSTEE POWERS:

Trustees shall have general common law powers over the company and the trust estate herein, and may do anything any citizen may lawfully do in any state or country. Specifically, but not by way of limitation, they shall have all rights, authority and power as follows:

a. To compromise or abandon any claims arising out of, in favor of, or against the company and its trust estate, and Trustees' good faith decision in that regard shall be binding and conclusive on all parties.

b. To manage, invest and reinvest the trust estate, or any part thereof, in any kind of property or venture which men of prudence, discretion and intelligence consider for their own account, without being restricted to investments which are ordinarily permitted by law or customarily used for trust funds, and without restrictions as to the duration of this organization. Specifically included, but not by way of limitation, are real estate, collectables, gems, art works, precious metals, corporate obligations of every kind, preferred and common stock, commodities, mutual funds and trust funds.

c. To open, maintain and close bank and thrift accounts of every kind, and conduct all monetary affairs of this trust.

d. To sell at public or private sale for cash, credit, or cash and credit, and upon such terms and conditions as Trustees may deem proper.

e. To sell, grant, convey, mortgage, option, rent, lease or pledge all trust estate assets, real, personal or mixed, in such manner as deemed appropriate and nondestructive to the general welfare of the trust.

f. To borrow on or encumber the trust estate without restriction and to make loans with or without security. All borrowed funds shall immediately become a part of the trust estate.

g. To allocate capital gains and/or dividends to trust principal as may be deemed appropriate or advantageous to the trust estate.

h. To register company property in the name of the company, a fictitious trade name of the company, a Trustee or nominee so long as company ownership of such property can be clearly demonstrated.

i. To make distributions in cash or in kind and to assign values to such property according to Trustees' best judgment.

j. To accept additions to the trust estate by deed, will, assignment, exchange, gift, grant, insurance proceeds or any other methods deemed acceptable to Trustees. Trustees are further authorized to honor any buy-sell agreements extant as to any property or interest held in trust.

k. To elect and remunerate officers from the Board or elsewhere as deemed appropriate or expedient. To hire and remunerate employees, agents or contractors. To incur and pay the ordinary and necessary expenses of administration, including, but not limited to, legal fees, accountant's fees, Trustee fees, brokerage fees, consulting fees and the like, and to allocate all the expenses and receipts between principal and income as

DECLARATION OF TRUST
AN IRREVOCABLE TRUST ORGANIZATION

Trustees shall deem proper.

l. To give proxies, to deposit securities with and transfer title to committees representing securities holders and to participate in voting trusts, reorganizations and other transactions involving the common interest of security holders.

m. To open margin accounts with securities firms and commodities traders and to buy, write or trade in options, commodities, and to make short sales. Trustees shall be empowered to hold securities in their own names, the name of a nominee, in street name, or unregistered in such condition that ownership will pass. Trustees shall incur no liability to the company for any loss. The Trust shall indemnify the trustee from all liability. Further, any securities firm or commodities traders may rely on this document and the trust provisions herein in respect of a Trustee's authority without making further inquiry.

n. Trustees are expressly authorized to hold, manage and operate any company property, or business or enterprise. The profits and losses, if any therefrom, shall be chargeable respectively to the trust estate.

o. Trustees are authorized to pay all taxes out of the trust estate, and have complete discretion, power and authority to make any decisions or elections that would effectively minimize such taxes if any taxes are eligible to be levied.

p. Trustees may expressly delegate one or more of their powers to any other person or persons as may be deemed expedient for the management of company affairs, and may revoke such delegation at any time by written notice delivered to such persons.

q. Trustees, by a majority vote, may change the domicile of the company with or without cause if they deem such change will protect or benefit the trust estate.

r. Trustees, by unanimous vote, may make amendments to this contract and declaration and take such other consequential actions as they deem necessary or appropriate to protect the integrity of the organization and to insure the organization will continue to function and be administered in the best interest of certificate holders and in the manner intended.

s. Trustees, by majority vote, may at any time and at their sole discretion wind up company affairs, terminate this organization and make distributions of the trust estate to certificate holders as provided herein.

RIGHT TO DISTRIBUTION:

Trustees have discretionary powers to make distributions from this organization without regard to equality of certificate holders except for final liquidation. Notwithstanding, a right to any distribution from this organization shall be evidenced by the holding of one or more certificates, and the following provisions respecting such certificates shall remain in full force and be carefully observed by Trustees, certificate holders, and interested third parties at all times:

a. Trustees shall be authorized to issue one hundred (100) certificate units (hereinafter called TCUs or certificates), representing 100% of the rights to distribution from the organization's trust estate. Trustees shall not issue TCUs in excess of that number. The TCUs shall have no par value, and Trustees shall not place any nominal value on TCUs at any time. TCUs are non-assessable, nontaxable, nonnegotiable and limited in transferability. The lawful possessor shall be construed the true and lawful owner thereof. Creator herein may own TCUs. No person having or controlling a majority vote on the Board of Trustees, however, shall have or possess any rights to distribution from the trust estate.

b. Trustees are authorized to receive property into the trust estate in exchange for a negotiated number of TCUs. The party exchanging the property shall be deemed to be a Trustee. All owners of TCUs shall be identified on a Registry of Trust Certificate Units, kept in the company minute book. Ownership of TCUs shall not entitle the holder to any legal or equitable title in the company or the trust estate, nor to any undivided interest therein, nor management thereof.

c. TCUs shall be immune from seizure by any creditor of the lawful owner.

d. Death, insolvency or bankruptcy of any TCU holder, or the transfer of his TCUs by gift, exchange or sale, shall not operate as dissolution of this organization or its operation or business; nor shall such events entitle his creditors, heirs or legal representatives to demand any partition or division of the trust estate or any special accounting. Death of a TCU holder shall terminate his or her rights under the TCU and said rights may not thereafter pass by probate or operation of law to any heir or legatee, but shall revert to the Board

DECLARATION OF TRUST
AN IRREVOCABLE TRUST ORGANIZATION

of Trustees to be reissued as determined by an action of the Board.

e. TCUs may be surrendered to or transferred back to the organization subject to the approval of the Board of Trustees, but may not otherwise be pledged, assigned, hypothecated or transferred by a TCU holder without the consent of a majority in interest of all other current TCU holders. Should a TCU holder transfer or surrender his TCUs to the organization, the Board of Trustees may, at its sole discretion assign, convey or exchange said TCUs to any other person(s) or entities upon approval of the Board. If any TCU holder contests, in any court of law, the validity of this organization or any provision herein, or the authority of Trustees, that TCU holder's certificates shall revert back to the Board of Trustees and may be reissued to other parties at the discretion of the Board.

NEGOTIATION AND EXCHANGE:
The Trustee is herein authorized to bargain, exchange, trade or sell certificates to a willing Trustee upon board approval at the initial Board of Trustees' meeting or any time thereafter.

NOTICE TO THIRD PARTIES:
Notice is hereby given to all persons, companies or corporations extending credit to, contracting with or having claims against this organization or its Trustees, that they must look only to the funds and property of the organization for payment or for settlement of their damages, accounts receivable or claims. Trustees, officers or agents of this organization are not personally liable for the organization's obligations.

COPIES AS ORIGINALS:
A copy of this organizational document bearing the seal or signature of a Trustee, or a copy certified by a Notary Public as a correct copy, shall be relied upon as an original document and shall have the full force and effect of the original document in every respect.

PURPOSE AND INTENT OF THIS AGREEMENT:
This contract with trust provisions is intended to create a common law contractual company, (also known as an Unincorporated Business Organization) for receiving, conveying or holding property in fee simple, and for providing prudent management of such property, and for conducting any legitimate business through appointed Trustees for the benefit of certificate holders. Trustees shall hold both legal and equitable title to the trust estate, and shall act solely within their powers as provided herein and within their common law rights and immunities. The administration of this organization shall be amenable to Common Law regulation and under the protection of the Bill of Rights as well as Declaration of Independence, although Trustees can seek relief in any court or venue they may choose or deem necessary. If any provision herein is unenforceable, the remaining provisions shall nevertheless be carried into effect. Nothing herein contained shall be construed as intent to evade or contravene any law, nor to delegate to Trustees any special power belonging exclusively to a statutory company, franchise or incorporation, but rather in equity create an equal playing field.

COMMON LAW ORGANIZATION:
Creator expressly declares this to be an organization founded upon the freedoms and rights inherent in the common law of the Republic of the United States of America, and all references herein to the United States shall be construed to refer to the Continental United States of America in its original context as set forth in the Constitution of the United States, the original Bill of Rights and the state constitutions of the several sovereign states comprising the union of the United States of America. This organization, then, is created under the common law of contracts, protected by Article I, Sec. 10, Para. 1 of the Constitution of the United States. It is, therefore, not created under the statutes of any U.S. state, and does not depend upon any statute for its existence. It is not a partnership or corporation or statutory trust, but a separate legal entity having its own common law identity.

LEGAL DOMICILE:
This organization shall be domiciled in the state where it conducts its principal business. Notwithstanding, Creator herein provides that upon a majority vote of the Board of Trustees this organization may be moved to, and

DECLARATION OF TRUST
AN IRREVOCABLE TRUST ORGANIZATION

administered in, any state or territory of the United States of America, or in any English common law foreign jurisdiction.

PRIVACY:

This organizational document and all company business shall be kept private, protected by the Privacy Act of 1974, 5 USC 552(a), the Fourth and Fifth Amendments to the Constitution of the United States, and the common law privacy rights available in the United States of America and every other applicable jurisdiction.

TERM OF YEARS:

This organization, unless terminated earlier as provided herein, shall continue for a term of 100 (one-hundred) years. The life of the company may, however, be extended for additional 25-year terms, subject to a unanimous affirmative vote of the Board of Trustees at least ninety days prior to each termination date. At dissolution, the trust estate shall be distributed on a pro-rata basis to the then existing certificate holders.

COMPANY NAME:

This organization shall be named as shown on page one of this contract and declaration. This shall be deemed the company name. Company business shall be conducted under this name, or under one or more fictitious trade names, or in the name of a Trustee or nominee determined at the sole discretion of the Board of Trustees.

IN WITNESS WHEREOF:

Creator and Trustee execute this contract and declaration in recognition of the delivery and acceptance of the property named herein, and in recognition of the powers and duties imparted to Trustees of this organization. They assent to all the terms and conditions set forth herein, and declare that the effective date of this organizational document is infra.

JURAT

In compliance with Title 28 U.S.C. § 1746(1), and executed WITHOUT THE UNITED STATES, we affirm under the penalties of perjury, and to the laws of the De Jure united States of America, that the foregoing is true, correct, and complete to the best of my belief and informed knowledge. And Further the Deponent Saith Not. I now affix my Signature and Official Seal to the above Document with EXPLICIT RESERVATION OF ALL OUR UNALIENABLE RIGHTS, WITHOUT PREJUDICE TO ANY OF THOSE RIGHTS, in compliance with UCC § 1-308:

This agreement is entered into and executed willingly, knowingly and voluntarily by each party in good faith, and shall endeavor to execute the promises, terms and conditions herein with diligence and in the best interest of the other party this August 7, 2019 A.D.

Executed at the following address: 7526 W FONDDULAC
MILWAUKEE WI 53218

Creator	Trustee
Signature of Creator	Signature of Trustee
Address: Londale-Quintae: Strickling c/o 8663 North 60th Street Milwaukee Wisconsin [53223]	Address: Paula Renee Bullocks 8663 North 60th Street Milwaukee Wisconsin 53223

WITNESSES

We the undersigned Witnesses hereby STAND and Attest that the fore signed, signed this document on the date listed supra, of their own Free Will, as witnessed by Our Signatures below:

DECLARATION OF TRUST
AN IRREVOCABLE TRUST ORGANIZATION

First Witness Signature: _____
Address: 8865 N 60TH STREET
MILWAUKEE, WI 53223

Second Witness Signature: Marshella Mushell
Address: 4725 N. 29th St.
Milwaukee, WI 53206

5. The original Declaration of Trust, or a true copy of the declaration and all amendments are attached as **EXHIBIT A**. (The statement is to be **signed by all the Trustees** of the Common Law Trust. It may be executed in counterparts, if necessary).

6. TRUSTEES printed names and addresses:	Signature:
I)	I)
II)	II)
III)	III)
IV)	IV)
V)	V)

FILING FEE - $50.00, or more. Remit an additional fee computed at the rate of $1.00 for each $1,000 of beneficial certificates sold or offered for sale in Wisconsin. Such additional fee on beneficial shares sold or offered for sale in Wisconsin may be collected incidental to the filing of the trust's annual report with the department.

RECORDING WITH COUNTY REGISTER OF DEEDS – After the Declaration of Trust has been filed with the Department of Financial Institutions, a certified copy of the instrument will be returned to the submitter for them to record, within 30 days, with the Register of Deeds of the county within which the trust has its principal office or place of business in Wisconsin.

ANNUAL REPORT – The trust is obliged to file an annual report with the department, due March 31. Annual report forms are mailed in January to the trust's principal office on record with the department.

CERTIFICATE OF AUTHORIZATION
TO DO BUSINESS IN PUERTO RICO

I, Omar J. Marrero Díaz, Secretary of State of the Government of Puerto Rico;

CERTIFY: That **LONDALE QUINTAE STRICKLING TRUST**, register number **502574**, is a **Foreign - NON US For Profit Trust** organized under the laws of United States Minor Outlying Islands duly authorized to do business in Puerto Rico on this **16th of February, 2023 at 04:29 PM**.

IN WITNESS WHEREOF, the undersigned by virtue of the authority vested by law, hereby issues this certificate and affixes the Great Seal of the Government of Puerto Rico, in the City of San Juan, Puerto Rico, today, **February 16, 2023**.

Omar J. Marrero Díaz
Secretary of State

CERTIFICATE OF AUTHORIZATION
TO DO BUSINESS IN PUERTO RICO

I, Omar J. Marrero Díaz, **Secretary of State** of the Government of Puerto Rico;

CERTIFY: That **KABIR ELOHIM ISREAL- TRUST**, register number **501560**, is a **Foreign - NON US For Profit Trust** organized under the laws of United States Minor Outlying Islands duly authorized to do business in Puerto Rico on this **1st of February, 2023 at 10:19 PM**.

IN WITNESS WHEREOF, the undersigned by virtue of the authority vested by law, hereby issues this certificate and affixes the Great Seal of the Government of Puerto Rico, in the City of San Juan, Puerto Rico, today, **February 1, 2023.**

Omar J. Marrero Díaz
Secretary of State

28159410 - $150.00

Wisconsin Department of Financial Institutions
Strengthening Wisconsin's Financial Future

Corporations Bureau

Form 521 - Foreign Limited Liability Company Registration Statement

Entity Name

Name of the Foreign Limited Liability Company: LONDALE QUINTAE STRICKLING LLC

Fictitious Name

Legal Name: LONDALE QUINTAE STRICKLING LLC

If the company's name does not satisfy s. 183.0112, Wis. Stats., the foreign limited liability company may obtain a certificate of registration to transact business in Wisconsin under a fictitious name that is available and that satisfies s. 183.0112.

Enter a Fictitious Name to operate under in Wisconsin: Londale Quintae Strickling

Formation

Formed under the laws of: PUERTO RICO

Registered Agent

Registered Agent Name: Kabir-Elohim Isreal LLC
Name of Entity:
Street Address: P.O. Box
Street Address Line 2: 101002
City: Milwaukee
State: WI
Zip: 00000
Registered Email Address: KabirIsreal@yahoo.com

Principal Office

Street Address: 220 Calle Manuel Domenech PMB 2059
Street Address Line 2:
City: San Jan
State: Puerto Rico
Zip: 00918
Country: Puerto Rico

Statements

Has the company transacted business in Wisconsin without holding a certificate of registration? No

In what year did the Foreign LLC begin transacting business in

Wisconsin?:

Signature

I certify that the applicant is a foreign limited liability company:	Yes
Title:	Registered agent
Date:	03/15/2023
I understand that checking this box constitutes a legal signature:	Yes
Signature:	All Rights Reserved Kabir-Elohim Isreal

Delayed Effective Date (Optional)

This document will be effective on the date it is received by the department unless a delayed (future) date is included here.

(Optional) This document has a delayed effective date of:

Contact Information

You are required to provide a valid email address, as we will email you a copy of your filing along with the Certificate.

Name:	Kabir-Elohim Isreal
Street Address:	C/o P.O.Box 101002
City:	Milwaukee
State:	Wisconsin
Postal Code:	00000
Country:	United States
Phone Number:	8728221849
Email:	trueking7@yahoo.com

Endorsement

	FILED
Received Date:	03/31/2023

Recording requested by:

LONDALE QUINTAE STRICKLING©

Return to:

LONDALE QUINTAE SRTICKLING©

7526 W FOND DU LAC AVE

MILWAUKEE, WISCONSIN, 53218

And

Name: Londale Quintae Strickling

Address: 8663 N 60th Street

Milwaukee, Wisconsin, [53223]

Phone Number: 414-484-0160 Document

prepared by:

Londale-Quintae: Strickling
with
LONDALE QUINTAE SRTICKLING©

DOC. # 10909499
RECORDED:
09/23/2019 11:53 AM
ISRAEL RAMON
REGISTER OF DEEDS
MILWAUKEE COUNTY, WI
AMOUNT: 30.00

DURABLE POWER OF ATTORNEY

1. **APPOINTMENT OF MY AGENT.** I, LONDALE QUINTAE STRICKLING© (hereinafter referred to as ("**Principal**"), hereby execute this Durable Power of Attorney appointing the following named individual as my "**Agent**" (also known as Attorney-in-Fact):

    Name: Londale-Quintae: Strickling

    Address: 8663 N 60th Street

    Milwaukee, Wisconsin, 53223

    Phone Number: 414-484-0160

2. **EFFECTIVENESS.** This shall be effective from when I sign it. The authority of my Agent, when effective, shall not terminate or be void or voidable if I am or become disabled or in the event of later uncertainty as to whether I am dead or alive.

3. **AGENT AS FIDUCIARY.** I give my Agent the powers specified in this Durable Power of Attorney with the understanding that they will be exercised for my benefit, on my behalf, and solely in a fiduciary capacity.

4. **GENERAL AUTHORITY TO ACT.** I hereby grant my Agent, including any Successors or CoAgents, the general authority to act on my behalf in the following subjects: **(INITIAL ALL POWERS THAT APPLY)**

   a. ____ Real property

   b. ____ Tangible personal property

   c. ____ Stocks and bonds

   d. ____ Commodities and options

   e. ____ Banks and financial institutions

   f. ____ Operation of entity or business

   g. ____ Insurance and annuities

   h. ____ Estates, trusts, and other beneficial interests

   i. ____ Claims and litigation

   j. ____ Personal and family maintenance

   k. ____ Benefits from governmental programs and civil or military service

   l. ____ Retirement plans

   m. ____ Taxes

   n. ____ Gifts

5. **SPECIFIC ACTS AUTHORIZED.** In addition to the general powers authorized above, I specifically authorize my Agent to perform the following acts: **(INITIAL ALL POWERS THAT APPLY)**

   a. _____ Create or amend designations of rights of survivorship

   b. _____ Create or amend designations of Beneficiaries

   c. _____ Delegate or otherwise authorize another person to exercise the powers delegated to the Agent under this instrument

   d. _____ Waive Principal's right to be a Beneficiary of a joint and survivor annuity, including a survivor benefit under a retirement plan

   e. _____ Exercise fiduciary powers validly delegated by Principal

   f. _____ Disclaim, refuse, or release an interest in property or a power of appointment

   g. _____ Trusts. LONDALE QUINTAE STRICKLING exists and operates under foreign jurisdiction lawfully enforced by 26 U.S.C. 7701(a)(31); 8 U.S.C. 1101(e)(14); 28 U.S.C. 1603(b)(3) and is herein lawfully declared as such. I, LONDALE QUINTAE STRICKLING, give my Agent the power to take all actions that my Agent considers necessary or desirable with respect to any and all trusts that exist in regards to the name LONDALE QUINTAE STRICKLING when this power is executed or that are established thereafter, including the following powers: to establish or manage trusts in the name of LONDALE QUINTAE STRICKLING or under the creation, control authority and management of aforementioned name. As well as trusts for the benefit of my spouse, partner, children, grandchildren, and parents; to contribute or transfer assets to any trust in which I have an interest; and to exercise any power I may have as an individual, other than as a trust beneficiary, such as borrowing trust assets, amending or revoking trust agreements, and voting shares of stock, but subject to the limitation that any trust I have created may be modified or revoked by my Agent only if expressly permitted by the trust instrument. Londale-Quintae-Strickling, also referred to as "Londale Quintae Strickling" Vi Coactus, is LONDALE QUINTAE STRICKLING and is therefore is a representative under foreign jurisdiction. This section must not be construed as limiting the authority of my Agent to exercise any power, with respect to trusts, that I may hold in a fiduciary capacity or as a trust beneficiary, to the extent that such authority is specifically given elsewhere in this instrument.

   h. _____ Pets. I give my Agent the power to house, or arrange for the housing, support, and maintenance of any animals that I own or have custody of and to pay reasonable boarding, kenneling, and veterinary fees for such animals.

   i. _____ Funeral and Burial Arrangements. I give my Agent the power to arrange for my funeral or other memorial service and for burial or cremation of my remains, including the purchase of a burial plot or other place for interment of my remains or ashes, as directed by my Agent under my advance healthcare directive, for which payments my Agent is hereby released from any and all liability.

j. _____ **After-Acquired Property.** The powers granted to my Agent in this instrument are exercisable equally with respect to interests in property I own when this instrument is executed and after-acquired property interests, wherever the property is located, and whether or not the powers are exercised or the Durable Power of Attorney is executed in the same state.

k. _____ **Gifts to Agent.** Notwithstanding any other provision in this Durable Power of Attorney, my Agent may make gifts in amounts not to exceed the annual federal gift tax exclusion to him or herself but only if my Agent is in need of funds to meet the reasonable expenses of the following: support in accordance with my Agent's accustomed manner of living; medical, dental, hospital, and nursing services, and other costs relating to the health care of my Agent; and my Agent's education.

l. _____ **Nominating a Conservator.** If proceedings are initiated for the appointment of a Conservator of my person or my estate or both, I authorize my Agent to nominate whomever he or she believes is appropriate as Conservator of my person or my estate or both, including appointing him or herself. I authorize my Agent to waive the requirement of a bond for any person appointed, if he or she believes a waiver is appropriate.

m. _____ **Other Matters, Alter Ego, Incidental Powers.** Except for those actions that conflict with or are limited by another provision of this Durable Power of Attorney, I give my Agent the power to act as my alter ego with respect to all matters and affairs that are not included in the other provisions of this power, to the extent that a principal can act through an agent. This section does not authorize my Agent to make healthcare decisions.

In connection with the exercise of any of the powers described in the preceding sections, I give my Agent full authority, to the extent that a principal can act through an agent, to take all actions that he or she believes necessary, proper, or convenient, to the extent that I could take these actions myself, including, without limitation, the power to prepare, execute, and file documents and maintain records; to enter into contracts; to hire, discharge, and pay reasonable compensation to attorneys, accountants, expert witnesses, or other assistants; to engage in litigation regarding a claim in favor of or against me; and to execute, acknowledge, seal, and deliver any instrument.

n. _____ **Restrictions on Property Management Powers.** Notwithstanding any other provision in this Durable Power of Attorney, my Agent does not have any of the following powers related to property management: to use my property to discharge the legal obligations of my Agent, including but not limited to the support of the dependents of my Agent, except for those dependents to whom I also, along with my Agent, owe a duty of support; to exercise any incident of ownership over any insurance policy that I own and that insures the life of my Agent; or to exercise powers of a trustee under an irrevocable trust of which my Agent is the settler and of which I am a trustee.

o. _____ **Beneficial Use.** If my Agent is not my ancestor, descendant, or spouse, my Agent MAY use my property to Agent's own benefit and/or for supporting someone to whom Agent owes a support obligation.

6. **SPECIAL INSTRUCTIONS.** My special instructions are as follows: The agent shall go by the appellation of Kabir Elohim Isreal when representing the principal.

7. **NOMINATION OF A GUARDIAN OR CONSERVATOR (OPTIONAL).** If a Conservator or Guardian of my person or estate needs to be appointed for me by a court: (INITIAL)

   a. _____ I nominate Londale Quintae Srtickling.   First Choice: Londale-Quintae: Strickilng
   Address: 8663 N. 60th Street   Milwaukee, Wisconsin, [53223]   Phone Number: 414-484-0160

8. **AMPLIFYING POWERS**

   a. **Compensation**

      i. My Agent will be entitled to reasonable compensation for services rendered as Agent under this Durable Power of Attorney. Factors that should be considered in determining the amount of compensation are as follows:

         A. The time expended by my Agent

         B. The value of the property over which my Agent exercises control and management

         C. The complexity of the transactions entered into by my Agent

      ii. My Agent may pay the compensation from my assets once each week, and must keep records of the services performed, the time spent in performing them, and the date and amount of each payment.

   b. **Reimbursement for Costs and Expenses.** My Agent will be entitled to reimbursement from my property for expenditures properly made in performing the services conferred by me in this instrument. My Agent must keep records of any such expenditures and reimbursements.

   c. **Reliance by Third Parties.** To induce third parties to rely on the provisions of this instrument, I, for myself and on behalf of my heirs, successors, and assigns, hereby waive any privilege that may attach to information requested by my Agent in the exercise of any of the powers described in this instrument. Moreover, on behalf of my heirs, successors, and assigns, I hereby agree to hold harmless any third party who acts in reliance on this power for damages or liability incurred as a result of that reliance.

d. **Ratification.** I ratify and confirm all that my Agent does or causes to be done under the authority granted in this instrument. All contracts, promissory notes, checks, or other bills of exchange, drafts, other obligations, stock powers, instruments, and other documents signed, endorsed, drawn, accepted, made, executed, or delivered by my Agent will bind me, my estate, my heirs, successors, and assigns.

e. **Exculpation of Agent.** My Agent will not be liable to me or any of my successors in interest for any action taken or not taken in good faith, but will be liable for any willful misconduct or gross negligence.

f. **Revocation and Amendment.** I revoke any and all Durable Powers of Attorney that I have executed before executing this Durable Power of Attorney. I retain the right to revoke or amend this Durable Power of Attorney and to substitute other agents in place of my Agent. Amendments to this Durable Power of Attorney must be made in writing by me personally. They must be attached to the original of this document and, if the original is recorded, must be recorded in the same county or counties as the original, although failure to record any amendment will not alter its affect.

9. **GENERAL PROVISIONS**

   a. **Signature of Agent.** My Agent must use the following form when signing on my behalf pursuant to this Durable Power of Attorney: [Principal] by [Agent], Agent of the Principal.

   b. **Severability.** If any of the provisions of this instrument are found to be invalid for any reason, that invalidity will not affect any of the other provisions of this power, and all invalid provisions will be wholly disregarded.

   c. **Governing Law.** This Agreement shall be governed, construed, and enforced in accordance with the laws of the State of Wisconsin, without regard to its conflict of laws rules.

   d. **Reliance on This Durable Power of Attorney.** Any person, including my Agent, may act in reliance upon the validity of this Durable Power of Attorney or a copy of it unless that person knows it has terminated or is no longer valid.

This Durable Power of Attorney is executed by me on 9/19/19, in Wisconsin.

Name: LONDALE QUINTAE STRICKLING©

Signature: _____

NOTICE TO PERSON ACCEPTING THE APPOINTMENT AS ATTORNEY-IN-FACT

By acting or agreeing to act as Agent (also known as Attorney-in-Fact) under this Power of Attorney, you assume the fiduciary and other legal responsibilities of an agent. These responsibilities include the following:

1. The legal duty to act solely in the interest of Principal and to avoid conflicts of interest

2. The legal duty to keep Principal's property separate and distinct from any other property owned or controlled by you

You may not transfer Principal's property to yourself without full and adequate consideration or accept a gift of Principal's property unless this Power of Attorney specifically authorizes you to transfer property to yourself or accept a gift of Principal's property. If you transfer Principal's property to yourself without specific authorization in the Power of Attorney, you may be prosecuted for fraud and/or embezzlement. If Principal is 65 years of age or older at the time that the property is transferred to you without authority, you may also be prosecuted for elder abuse. In addition to criminal prosecution, you may also be sued in civil court.

You must stop acting on behalf of Principal if you learn of any event that terminates this Power of Attorney or your authority under this Power of Attorney; for example, the death of Principal; Principal's revocation of this Power of Attorney or your authority; or, if you are married to Principal, a legal action is filed with a court to end your marriage, or for your legal separation, unless the Special Instructions in this Power of Attorney state that such an action will not terminate your authority.

If there is anything about this document or your duties that you do not understand, you should seek legal advice.

I have read the foregoing notice and I understand the legal and fiduciary duties that I assume by acting or agreeing to act as Agent (Attorney-in-Fact) under the terms of this Power of Attorney.

ACCEPTANCE BY AGENT

Name: Londale Quintae Strickling

Signature: _____ Dated: 9/8/19

NOTARY ACKNOWLEDGMENT

State of Wisconsin SS. County of Milwaukee

On 9/19/19 (date), Londale Strickling ( ), personally appeared before me who proved to me on the basis of satisfactory evidence to be the persons whose names are subscribed to within this indenture, and acknowledged to me that this indenture was executed the same in authorized capacities, and that by the signature(s) on the instrument the person(s), or the entity upon behalf of which the person(s) acted, executed the instrument.

I certify under PENALTY OF PERJURY that the foregoing paragraph is true and correct.

WITNESS my hand and official seal.

Printed Notary Name: Yashiria E. Gonzalez Morales

Commission Expires: 5/17/21

Notary Signature: _____ Affix Seal:

YASHIRIA E. GONZALEZ MORALES
Notary Public
State of Wisconsin

STATEMENT OF WITNESS

I declare under penalty of perjury 1) that the individual who signed or acknowledged this Durable Power of Attorney is personally known to me, or that the individual's identity was proven to me by convincing evidence; 2) that the individual signed or acknowledged this Durable Power of Attorney in my presence; 3) that the individual appears to be of sound mind and under no duress, fraud, or undue influence; and 4) that I am not a person appointed as Agent by this Durable Power of Attorney.

FIRST WITNESS

Name: _____ Paula Bullocks

Signature: _____ Dated: 9-17-19

SECOND WITNESS

Name: Deann T. Allen

Signature: _____ Dated: 09/19/2029

State of Wisconsin
Department of Transportation

LONDALE Q STRICLKING   Date Of Birth: 07/11/1983
DL/ID: S362-5358-3251-05

Drivers License Information

> Our records indicate that you are no longer a Wisconsin resident.

Driver license status results as of Sat Dec 31 00:15:10 CST 2022

Driver License
(expiration date: 07/11/2026)

Real ID Compliant:
No
Issuance date:
07/11/2018
Classes:
D - Valid (Moved out of State)

Disclaimer: Correspondence from DMV supersedes information displayed in this application. If the information displayed contradicts other information communicated to you by DMV, please contact Wisconsin DMV email service.

Exit   Print

Certified Mail Receipt Number ___7021 1970 0002 2925 5129___

MILWAUKEE CIRCUIT COURT
901 N 9th STREET
MILWAUKEE WISCONSIN 53233

RECEIVED JUN 0 5 2023
Office of District Attorney
Milwaukee, WI 53233

From: Kabir Elohim Isreal
Secured Party Creditor Filing #P19007796-6, #P19008387-8 and #20210215000594-1
Power of Attorney 10909499
On Behalf of: LONDALE QUINTAE STRICKLING©
Case# 2023CF001349

COMMERCIAL OFFER FOR PRESENT SALE

RE: To Prosecuting agency attorney: Piotrowski, Owen M
This Document is a Contract according to:
UCC 2-204 A *contract* for sale of goods may be *made in any manner sufficient to show agreement*, including conduct by both parties which recognizes the existence of such a contract.

UCC 2-205 *An offer* by a merchant to buy or sell goods *in a signed writing* which by its terms gives assurance that it will be held open *is not revocable, for lack of consideration, during the time stated*.

WI ST § 402.204. Formation in general
UCC 2-106 *In this Article unless the context otherwise requires* "contract" *and* "agreement" *are limited to those relating to the present or future sale of goods.* "Contract for sale" *includes both a present sale of goods and a contract to sell goods at a future time. A* "sale" *consists in the passing of title from the seller to the buyer for a price (Section 2-401). A* "present sale" *means a sale which is accomplished by the making of the contract.* (2) *Goods or conduct including any part of a performance are* "conforming" *or conform to the contract when they are in accordance with the obligations under the contract.*

WI ST § 402.106. Definitions: "contract"; "agreement"; "contract for sale"; "sale"; "present sale"; "conforming" to contract; "termination"; "cancellation"

Haines v. Kerner, 404 U.S. 519, 520, 92 S. Ct. 594, 596, 30 L. ED 2d 652 (1972); see also *Matzker v. Herr*, 748 F. 2d 1142, 1146, (7th Cir.1984) *(federal district courts must ensure that pro se litigants are given "fair and meaningful consideration").* In reviewing plaintiff's filings, the court is mindful that pro se complaints are held "to less stringent standards than formal pleadings drafted by lawyers."
If there are in insufficiencies within the process or document that does not take away from the merits contained therein, then its contractual construction stands as authentic and genuine.

Governed By:
Article 1, Section 10, Clause 1. *No State shall enter into any Treaty, Alliance, or Confederation; grant Letters of Marque and Reprisal; coin Money; emit Bills of Credit; make any Thing but gold and silver Coin a Tender in Payment of Debts; pass any Bill of Attainder, ex post facto Law, or Law impairing the Obligation of Contracts, or grant any Title of Nobility.*
You swore an oath to uphold this law as having supreme authority within the jurisdiction of this matter.

Wisconsin Statutes Uniform Commercial Code Ch 401-420
The STATE OF WISCONSIN recognizes the jurisdiction and authority of the Uniform Commercial Code within this matter as it supports the inability to impair the obligations of contracts.

WI ST § 401.103. Construction of uniform commercial code to promote its purposes and policies; applicability of supplemental principles of law.
UCC 1-103(a) The Uniform Commercial Code must be liberally construed and applied to promote its underlying purposes and policies, which are: (1) to simplify, clarify, and modernize the law governing commercial transactions; (2) to permit the continued expansion of commercial practices through custom, usage, and agreement of the parties; and (3) to make uniform the law among the various jurisdictions. (b) Unless displaced by the particular provisions of the Uniform Commercial Code, the principles of law and equity, including the law merchant and the law relative to capacity to contract, principal and agent, estoppel, fraud, misrepresentation, duress, coercion, mistake, bankruptcy, and other validating or invalidating cause supplement its provisions.
The STATE OF WISCONSIN has recognized the authority of the Uniform Commercial Code and has adopted it within its statutes.

WI ST § 401.201. General definitions (rm)
UCC 1-201(32) "Remedy" means any remedial right to which an aggrieved party is entitled with or without resort to a tribunal.

WI ST § 401.305. Remedies to be liberally administered
UCC 1-305(a) (a) The remedies provided by [the Uniform Commercial Code] must be liberally administered to the end that the aggrieved party may be put in as good a position as if the other party had fully performed but neither consequential or special damages nor penal damages may be had except as specifically provided in [the Uniform Commercial Code] or by other rule of law.
(b) Any right or obligation declared by [the Uniform Commercial Code] is enforceable by action unless the provision declaring it specifies a different and limited effect.
The State recognizes my right to create a remedy outside of the courtroom which this document pursues through the formation of a contractual agreement.

WI ST § 401.307. Prima facie evidence by 3rd-party documents
UCC 1-307 A document in due form purporting to be a bill of lading, policy or certificate of insurance, official weigher's or inspector's certificate, consular invoice, or any other document authorized or required by the contract to be issued by a 3rd party shall be prima facie evidence of its own authenticity and genuineness and of the facts stated in the document by the 3rd party.
This document was sent to you via 3rd party which makes it prima facie evidence and its authenticity and genuineness must be disproven.

(United States v. Kiss, 658 F. 2nd, 526, 536 (7th Cir. 1981); Cert. Denied, 50 U.S. L.W. 2169; S Ct March 22, 1982) "Indeed, no more than Affidavits is necessary to make the prima facie case."

This document has an affidavit attached making it prima facie evidence and its authenticity and genuineness must be disproven.

WI ST § 402.206. Offer and acceptance in formation of contract
UCC 2-206 Unless otherwise unambiguously indicated by the language or circumstances

(a) an offer to make a contract shall be construed as inviting acceptance in any manner and by any medium reasonable in the circumstances;

This document acts as an offer to contract, is lawful in its formation and is sent through the reasonable medium of certified mail. Therefore, this document is a lawful contract.

WI ST § 401.201. General definitions (g)
UCC 1-201(12) "Contract" means the total legal obligation that results from the parties' agreement as determined by chs. 401 to 411 as supplemented by any other applicable laws. (Compare "Agreement.")

This document creates a legal obligation under the jurisdiction of Wisconsin to enforce as result of the agreement of the parties contained herein.

WI ST § 402.206. Offer and acceptance in formation of contract
UCC 2-206 Unless otherwise unambiguously indicated by the language or circumstances

(a) an offer to make a contract shall be construed as inviting acceptance in any manner and by any medium reasonable in the circumstances;

The parties have agreed to the offer of the contract by it being accepted by the receiving party through the reasonable medium of certified mail.

Contractual Parties
This contractual agreement known herein after as the **"Agreement"** sets forth the terms under which Piotrowski, Owen M known herein after as the "respondent" who is legally obligated to perform according to the terms set forth by LONDALE QUINTAE STRICKLING© herein after known as the "Sender".

Contractual Terms
The Respondent: Prosecuting agency attorney: Piotrowski, Owen M

is in full agreement to the authenticity and genuineness of the following merits if they go unrebutted in the next 10 business days.

I AM NOT LONDALE QUINTAE STRICKLING©

1. Kabir Elohim Isreal did not operate as LONDALE QUINTAE STRICKLING© due to fraud in the factum.
2. Kabir Elohim Isreal did not operate as LONDALE QUINTAE STRICKLING© vi coactus.
3. Proof that the State of Wisconsin does not recognize LONDALE QUINTAE STRICKLING© as a foreign trust.
4. Proof that the State of Wisconsin has jurisdiction over the foreign trust LONDALE QUINTAE STRICKLING©.
5. Kabir Elohim Isreal is not identically separate from to LONDALE QUINTAE STRICKLING©.

6. A foreign trust and its representative(s) are entitled to the privileges, benefits and immunities of a Foreign state according to the Foreign Sovereign Immunity Act, the Geneva Convention, the Vienna Convention and the Hague Convention.
7. The use of the name LONDALE QUINTAE STRICKLING© for financial gain is not copyright infringement.

I AM NOT IN WISCONSIN NOR THE UNITED STATES

8. The UNITED STATES is a corporation according to 28 USCS 3002 (15)(A).
9. A corporation can exist outside the contemplation of the mind.
10. The UNITED STATES is not a land mass. Republica v Sweers 1 Dallas 43, Treaty of Commerce 8 Stat 116 Treaty of Peace 8 Stat 80, IRS Publication 6209 Articles of Association October 20 1774.
11. A physical body cannot be within fictional geometric borders of jurisdiction.
12. The UNITED STATES only has a physical presence within Washington DC according to Wis. Stat. 409.307 (8).

THERE IS NO VALID CLAIM AGAINST ME

13. "Every man is independent of all laws except those prescribed by nature. He is not bound by any institution formed by his fellowman without his consent." (Cruden v. Neale, 2 N.C. 338 May Term 1796) I do not consent to being governed by the institution known as the STATE OF WISCONSIN and or the UNITED STATES and without my consent I cannot and will not be lawfully forced to do so.
14. "The common law is the real law, the Supreme Law of the land, the code, rules regulations, policy and statutes are not the law." (Self v. Rhay, 61 Wn (2d) 261)
15. "All codes, rules and regulations are for government authorities only, not human/creators in accordance with God's laws. All codes, rules and regulations are unconstitutional and lacking due process." (Rodriguez v. Ray Donovan (U.S. department of Labor) 769 F. 2d1344,1348 (1985)

THERE IS NO ADVERSE PARTY

16. There is no one that can be cross examined as the victim therefore due process cant be upheld to the fullest extent of the law.

Claim of Relief:

If the above-mentioned merits are not rebutted in 11 business days, their authenticity and genuineness will stand as fact and truth in a both a public and private capacity. This will subject the Respondent's claim to an estoppel. The Respondents lack of rebuttal will be deemed tacit acquiescence to the terms of this contract and will show evidence of dishonor. Upon the discovery of dishonor, a certificate of dishonor will be issued according to WI ST § 403.505. Evidence of dishonor.

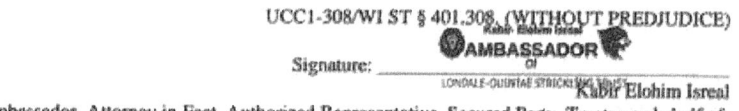

UCC1-308/WI ST § 401.308. (WITHOUT PREDJUDICE)
AMBASSADOR
Signature: _____
LONDALE-QUINTAE STRICKLING Kabir Elohim Isreal
Ambassador, Attorney in Fact, Authorized Representative, Secured Party, Trustee on behalf of:
LONDALE QUINTAE STRICKLING©, Ens legis

Certified Mail Receipt Number 7021 1970 0002 2925 5129

MILWAUKEE CIRCUIT COURT
901 N 9th STREET
MILWAUKEE WISCONSIN 53233

From: Kabir Elohim Isreal
Secured Party Creditor Filing #P19007796-6, #P19008387-8 and #20210215000594-1
Power of Attorney DOC# 10909499
On Behalf of: LONDALE QUINTAE STRICKLING©
Case# 2023CF001349

AFFIDAVIT OF COMMERCIAL OFFER FOR PRESENT SALE

Governed By:

WI ST § 401.307
UCC 1-307

(United States v. Kiss, 658 F. 2nd, 526, 536 (7th Cir. 1981); Cert. Denied, 50 U.S. L.W. 2169; S Ct March 22, 1982) "Indeed no more than Affidavits is necessary to make the prima facie case."

RE: AFFIDAVIT - The following merits will stand as fact and truth in a private and public capacity.

I, the Sender solemnly affirm that the attached contract is true to the best of my knowledge and has been constructed in good faith according to UCC 1-201(20)/WI ST § 401.201(k) and UCC 1-304/ WI Stat § 421.108 on behalf of LONDALE QUINTAE STRICKLING©, is without the intent of fraud or unconscionability but with the intention of self-help and remedy according to UCC 1-201(32)(34)/WI ST § 401.201(rm)(sm).

JURAT CERTIFICATION

State of Wisconsin County of: Milwaukee
Printed Name of the Undersigned: Kabir-Elohim Isreal
Signature of the Undersigned: [signature]

This instrument was acknowledged before me a Notary Public and was affirmed to be the truth in which I attest to, on the date of by the above mentioned. Witness my hand and seal.

Notary Name: Alicia Carter
Notary Signature: Alicia Carter
My Commission Expires: 12/13/2025

Seal:

ALICIA CARTER
Notary Public
State of Wisconsin

STATE OF WISCONSIN }
MILWAUKEE COUNTY ss

Docket # 681457

I hereby certify that on the __24__ day of __MAY__ 20__23__ at __1437__ hrs.
at __901 N 9th st__ in the __CITY__ of __MILWAUKEE__
in said county of Milwaukee, State of Wisconsin I duly served the within:

- [ ] SUMMONS AND COMPLAINT (Small claim)
- [ ] AUTHENTICATED COPIES OF SUMMONS AND COMPLAINT
- [ ] SUBPOENA
- [ ] EXECUTION (Served and Unsatisfied)
- [ ] MOTION AND NOTICE OF MOTION
- [ ] AFFIDAVIT AND ORDER TO SHOW CAUSE
- [ ] NOTICE TO QUIT OR PAY RENT 5 DAYS
- [ ] SUMMONS & PETITION
- [ ] TEMPORARY RESTRAINING ORDER/NOTICE OF HEARING (HARASSMENT) AND PETITION FOR TEMPORARY RESTRAINING ORDER AND/OR INJUNCTION (HARASSMENT)
- [ ] TEMPORARY RESTRAINING ORDER/NOTICE OF HEARING (DOMESTIC ABUSE) AND PETITION FOR TEMPORARY RESTRAINING ORDER AND/OR INJUNCTION (DOMESTIC ABUSE)
- [ ] NOTICE OF HEARING - TEMPORARY RESTRAINING ORDER (CHILD ABUSE) AND PETITION IN JUVENILE COURT FOR TEMPORARY RESTRAINING ORDER AND/OR INJUNCTION (CHILD ABUSE)
- [ ] INJUNCTION (HARASSMENT)
- [ ] INJUNCTION (DOMESTIC ABUSE)
- [ ] INJUNCTION (CHILD ABUSE)
- [ ] OTHER __Final Written Acceptance__

On the within named defendant __Owen Piotrowski__

Sex:_____ Race:_____ DOB:_____

[X] By then and there delivering to and leaving with _____

[ ] By affixing same on the front door leading to the premises described herein, which is a conspicuous part of the premises where it may be conveniently read

[ ] I left with _____ personally the sum of $_____ legal fees.
[ ] I left with _____ the sum of $_____ legal fees for attendance and travel.

I endorsed on said copy my name, official title and date of service. On authenticated copies of summons and complaint, also the time, place, manner of service, person served.

Service $_____
Travel $_____
Total $_____

Case # __23CF1349__

Dated __MAY 24, 23__

Denita R. Ball, Sheriff

Per __ARANDOLH__
Badge # __264__
Deputy Sheriff

1001 R14   THIS IS NOT AN INVOICE   146

Certified Mail Receipt Number 7021 1970 0002 2925 5174

MILWAUKEE CIRCUIT COURT
901 N 9th STREET
MILWAUKEE WISCONSIN 53233

From: Kabir Elohim Isreal
Secured Party Creditor Filing #P19007796-6 and #P19008387-8.
Power of Attorney 10909499
On Behalf of: LONDALE QUINTAE STRICKLING©
Case# 2023CF001349

FINAL WRITTEN ACCEPTANCE

Governed By:

UCC § 2-202./WI Stat § 402.202 Final Written Acceptance: Parol or Extrinsic Evidence.
Terms with respect to which the confirmatory memoranda of the parties agree or which are otherwise set forth in a writing intended by the parties as a final expression of their agreement with respect to such terms as are included therein may not be contradicted by evidence of any prior agreement or of a contemporaneous oral agreement but may be explained or supplemented.

- (a) by course of dealing or usage of trade (§ 1-205)(WI ST. § 401.303) or by course of performance (§ 2-208)(WI ST. § 402.208); and
- (b) by evidence of consistent additional terms unless the court finds the writing to have been intended also as a complete and exclusive statement of the terms of the agreement

RECEIVED
APR 24 2023
Office of District Attorney
Milwaukee, WI 53233

E: To Prosecuting agency attorney: Piotrowski, Owen M

This contractual agreement known herein after as the "Agreement" sets forth the terms under which _Owen M. Piotrowski_ known herein after as the "respondent" who is legally obligated to perform according to the terms set forth by LONDALE QUINTAE STRICKLING© herein after known as the "Sender".

RE: FINAL WRITTEN ACCEPTANCE OF COMMERCIAL OFFER FOR PRESENT SALE - On the date of _April 5th 2023_ you were in receipt of a commercial offer for a present sale which is confirmed by the USPS tracking number _7021197000022925516_. This also confirms the contractual obligation you entered into through tacit acquiescence. You have shown acceptance of the offer by providing no denial of acceptance when you did not provide any form of rebuttal within the prescribed timeframe of 11 days (3-days grace period) which is in compliance with the Federal Rules of Civil Procedure (14-days). You have continued to show acceptance by not denying your acceptance. Let all things be confirmed with 2 or more witnesses. Your tacit acquiescence acts as the first witness to your obligation to the contractual terms stated therein. This document will be the second witness to your acceptance. You have 3 days to provide an explanation of dishonor or supplementation to the contract. If these terms are not met, here now is now final written acceptance of the contractual obligation to comply with the terms sent to you via certified mail number _7021 1970 0002 2925 5167_ on the date of _April 5th 2023_.

UCC1-308/WI ST § 401.308. (WITHOUT PREDJUDICE)

Signature: _____

Kabir Elohim Isreal
Ambassador, Attorney in Fact, Authorized Representative, Secured Party, Trustee on behalf of:
LONDALE QUINTAE STRICKLING©, Ens legis

RECEIVED
APR 24 2023
Office of District Attorney
Milwaukee, WI 53233

Certified Mail Receipt Number 7021 1970 0002 2925 5174

MILWAUKEE CIRCUIT COURT
901 N 9th STREET
MILWAUKEE WISCONSIN 53233

From: Kabir Elohim Isreal
Secured Party Creditor Filing #P19007796-6 and #P19008387-8.
Power of Attorney 10909499
On Behalf of: LONDALE QUINTAE STRICKLING©
Case# 2023CF001349

RECEIVED APR 24 2023
Office of District Attorney
Milwaukee, WI 53233

FILED CRIMINAL DIVISION 23 APR 24 AM 11:15 CLERK OF CIRCUIT COURT

AFFIDAVIT OF FINAL WRITTEN ACCEPTANCE

Governed By:

WI ST § 401.307
UCC 1-307

(United States v. Kiss, 658 F. 2nd, 526, 536 (7th Cir. 1981); Cert. Denied, 50 U.S. L.W. 2169; S Ct March 22, 1982) "Indeed no more than Affidavits is necessary to make the prima facie case."

RE: AFFIDAVIT - The following merits will stand as fact and truth in a private and public capacity.

I, the Sender solemnly affirm that the attached contract is true to the best of my knowledge and has been constructed in good faith according to UCC 1-201(20)/WI ST § 401.201(k) and UCC 1-304/ WI Stat § 421.108 on behalf of LONDALE QUINTAE STRICKLING©, is without the intent of fraud or unconscionability but with the intention of self-help and remedy according to UCC 1-201(32)(34)/WI ST § 401.201(rm)(sm).

JURAT CERTIFICATION

State of Wisconsin County of Milwaukee
Printed Name of the Undersigned: Kabir-Elohim Isreal©
Signature of the Undersigned:

This instrument was acknowledged before me a Notary Public and was affirmed to be the truth in which I attest to, on the date of by the above mentioned. Witness my hand and seal.

Notary Name: Alicia Carter
Notary Signature: Alicia Carter 4/21/2023   Seal: ALICIA CARTER Notary Public State of Wisconsin
My Commission Expires: 12/12/2025

Certified Mail Receipt Number 7021 1970 0002 2925 5259

RECEIVED JUN 23 2023
Office of District Attorney
Milwaukee, WI 53233

MILWAUKEE CIRCUIT COURT
901 N 9th STREET
MILWAUKEE WISCONSIN 53233

From: Kabir-Elohim Isreal
Secured Party Creditor Filing #2021021500094-1 and #P19007796-6 and #P19008387-8.
Power of Attorney #10909499
On Behalf of: LONDALE QUINTAE STRICKLING©
Case# 2023CF001349

CERTIFICATE OF DISHONOR

Governed By:
WI ST § 401.307
UCC 1-307

RE: CERTIFICATE OF DISHONOR - On the date of June 5th 2023 you were in receipt of a Commercial Offer for a Present sale which is confirmed by the USPS tracking number 7021 1970 0002 2925 5129. You have shown acceptance of the offer by providing no denial of acceptance when you did not provide any form of rebuttal within the prescribed timeframe of 11 days (3-day grace period) which is in compliance with the Federal Rules of Civil Procedure (14-days). You continued to show acceptance when you did not provide any explanation for your dishonor or any supplementation to the contractual terms when the opportunity was offered and presented on the date of June 20 2023 via certified mail tracking number 7021 1970 0002 2925 5272. This document certifies your agreement to the terms of the contract sent to you on the date of June 5th 2023 via certified mail number 7021 1970 0002 2925 5129 through your tacit acquiescence and dishonor.

JURAT CERTIFICATION

State of Wisconsin County of Milwaukee
Printed Name of the Undersigned: Kabir-Elohim Isreal
Signature of the Undersigned:

Kabir-Elohim Isreal
AMBASSADOR
of
LONDALE-QUINTAE STRICKLING TRUST

This instrument was acknowledged before me a Notary Public and was affirmed to be the truth in which I attest to, on the date of by the above mentioned. Witness my hand and seal.

Notary Name: PRAHLAD VADAPALLY
Notary Signature:
My Commission Expires: 10/13/2025

Seal: [PRAHLAD VADAPALLY NOTARY PUBLIC STATE OF WISCONSIN]

Certified Mail Receipt Number _____

MILWAUKEE CIRCUIT COURT
901 N 9th STREET
MILWAUKEE WISCONSIN 53233

From: Kabir Elohim Isreal
Secured Party Creditor Filing #P19007796-6 and #P19008387-8.
Power of Attorney DOC#10909499
On Behalf of: LONDALE QUINTAE STRICKLING©
Case# 2023CF001349

RECEIVED
APR 1 2 2023
Office of District Attorney
Milwaukee, WI 53233

AFFIDAVIT OF TRUTH

Governed By:
UCC 1-307

"Indeed no more than Affidavits is necessary to make the prima facie case." (United States v. Kiss, 658 F. 2nd, 526, 536 (7th Cir. 1981); Cert. Denied, 50 U.S. L.W. 2169; S Ct March 22, 1982)

RE: AFFIDAVIT - The following merits will stand as fact and truth in a private and public capacity if not rebutted according to law and jurisprudence.

1. I, Kabir Elohim Isreal, solemnly affirms that the attached contract is true to best of my knowledge and has been constructed in good faith according to UCC 1-201 and UCC 1-304, I Kabir Elohim Isreal, am not operating with the intent of fraud or unconscionability but with the intention of self-help and remedy according to UCC 1-201(32)(34).

2. **LONDALE QUINTAE STRICKLING© Is A Foreign State**
LONDALE QUINTAE STRICKLING© is a Foreign State under copyright law and is not human being. LONDALE QUINTAE STRICKLING© is the name on a birth certificate and is a trust based on the birth certificate being a means to enter the contract of citizenship as citizenship is a contract according to "Chisolm v Georgia, 2 U.S. 419, 440 1793 U.S. LEXIS 249; 2 Dall 419". This contract involves obedience to the laws of the UNITED STATES and IT'S individual STATES in exchanges for benefits as well as a contract with the Federal Reserve Bank giving a promise to pay money in the similitude of money. In order to constitute a loan, there must be a contract whereby one-party transfers to the other a sum of money. See: U.S. v. Neifert White, 247 F.Supp. 878. This contract is the contract of citizenship. The issuance of Federal Reserve notes is not an attempt by the government to coin money, it is a pledge of the government to pay dollars. See: U.S. v. Ballard, 14 Wall 457. This is because banks extend credit, not money. See: National Bank v. Atkinson, 55 Fed. Rep. 571. Lawful money under the Constitution Article 1, Section 10, Paragraph 1, is "Gold and Silver." This provision of the constitution has never been amended. Thus, any other form of promised money is a voidable. This is due to the fact that the only substances ever declared as money were gold and silver, in coin form, with copper/nickel serving in token capacity only. See: 12 USCA 152 re. "lawful money" and Coinage Act of April 2, 1792, at Sections 11, 16, & 20; re. copper/nickel tokens, see Sec. 9, and 31 USCA 460. Also, "No state shall make anything but gold and silver coin a tender in payment of debt . . ., said notes shall be obligations of the United States . . . they shall be redeemed in lawful (gold, silver money on demand at the Treasury Department of the United States. See:

Title 12 U.S.C., Section 411. Since the Gold Reserve Act of 1933 & 1934 suspended the use of gold in commerce. The credit loaned from the Federal Reserve can only be paid with something equivalent or greater yet other than 'like kind,' i.e., debt instruments, promises to pay or credit of the people. To secure the transaction, the credit of the people was insured and monetized. This contract exists as a nexum due to an inability to back a debt back in credit results in the utilization of and or confiscation of that which produces the credit and the credit being the ability to pay money. That which produces the ability to pay money is the human body. The human body was given as collateral for a beneficiary position that provides security to the social contract of citizenship mentioned in "Chisolm v Georgia, 2 U.S. 419, 440 1793 U.S. LEXIS 249; 2 Dall 419". The organization of each citizen or the government was entrusted with the loan as the Trustee to manage it for the beneficiaries called citizens. The name "LONDALE QUINTAE STRICKLING©" was the name of this trust account and the social security number was given as a numerical representation of the insurance credit involved in this account. This beneficial position and its privileges came with responsibilities. According to 18 USCS 7(1) a citizen is deemed a vessel due to carrying these responsibilities in exchange for the beneficiary position of citizenship and the credit in exchange for the Federal Reserve Bank's promise to loan money. According to Black's Law Dictionary a "trust" arises as a result of a manifestation to create it. The name "LONDALE QUINTAE STRICKLING©" was erroneously considered to be apart of this manifestation as a citizen and assigned a Social Security Number due to an unconscionable naked adhesion contract of citizenship that was presented in the form of the birth certificate which was initiated and confirmed without my consent due to a lack of competency and a concealment of facts ab initio. I, the Affiant, Kabir Elohim Isreal, am not LONDALE QUINTAE STRICKLING© nor is my physical being made of flesh and blood collateral to any contract of citizenship. The birth certificate name exists as a corporation because each individual citizen had to become incorporated in order to contract with a non-living entity such as the Federal Reserve Bank for a debt-based loan because living Human Beings can't have a "meeting of the minds" that contracts require, with an intangible, mindless, non-living entity. Since each citizen makes the UNITED STATES government, the UNITED STATES government has to exist as a corporation which it does according to 28 USCS 3002(15)(A). Therefore, the birth certificate name, LONDALE QUINTAE STRICKLING© which is the name on the account, like the name is a trust but is not a citizen or UNITED STATES person. According to 26 USCS 7701(a)(30) The term "United States person" means—(E) any trust if—(i) a court within the United States is able to exercise primary supervision over the administration of the trust, and (ii) one or more United States persons have the authority to control all substantial decisions of the trust. I, the Affiant, Kabir Elohim Isreal, took full control over the trust LONDALE QUINTAE STRICKLING© and had this control recorded into the official Uniform Commercial Code records. The proof of my ownership of this trust is documented under the above mention filing number. According to 26 USCS 7701(a)(31)(B) The term "foreign trust" means any trust other than a trust described in subparagraph (E) of paragraph (30). Due to the trust known as "LONDALE QUINTAE STRICKLING©" not being under the supervision of any court within the UNITED STATES or any UNITED STATES person, the trust is a Foreign Trust. According to 8 USCS 1101(14) The term "foreign state" includes outlying possessions of a foreign state, but self-governing dominions or territories under mandate or trusteeship shall be regarded as separate foreign states. Due to the trust known as LONDALE QUINTAE STRICKLING© being a Foreign Trust and not governed by the UNITED STATES in any way, it exists as Foreign State as well. I am Power of Attorney, Secure Party Creditor, and Authorized Representative and Ambassador for this Foreign State and have the ability to represent it in legal matters. This ability is recorded in section (6) of the attached Power of Attorney document.

3. My Citizenship Is Unconstitutional

When considering the legality of citizenship for the so-called Black/African-American, any logically competent human being can use deductive reasoning within jurisprudence and conclude that there is no aspect of interpretation for the UNITED STATES Constitution that would support the claim. Therefore,

I will substantiate that due to being classified as the byword and misnomer known as Black/African-American, which is a result of being a descendant of the people brought to the continental land mass called America through the Trans-Atlantic slave trade; I am not, cannot and will not be classified as being within the UNITED STATES or as a UNITED STAES citizen. When using a literal or intentional interpretation of the UNITED STATES Constitution it is clear through its preamble the so-called Black/African-American was not included in the statement "…Blessings of Liberty to ourselves and our posterity…" considering they were not at liberty when the constitution was constructed and are not among the people making the statement neither are they the posterity of the people making the statement, they were neither literally or intentionally mentioned in the Constitution. When considering a modern interpretation of the Constitution there would be no UNITED STATES if not for the slavery and emancipation of slaves, which makes a modern interpretation futile. When considering the 13th Amendment of the Constitution, it was created to make the Emancipation Proclamation apart of the supreme law of the union of the States, which solidified Abraham Lincoln's war tactic of freeing the slaves for the sole purpose of saving the union of the States. On August 22,1862, Lincoln stated "If I could save the union without freeing any slave I would do it…" Therefore, the abolishment of slavery was not due to its oppressive cruelty or to make the so-called Black/African-American equal to the people literally mentioned in the Constitution. The 14th Amendment does not include freed slaves due to their proper classification as refugees according to 8 USCS 1101(a)(42)(A). Considering they were outside the country in which they habitually resided in, were unable to return due to poverty and would likely have faced persecution by the African and Arab tribes that assisted in their capture and slavery. To consider the children of the emancipated slaves' citizens would be culpable negligence by not considering the application of how the freed slaves' citizenship to the nation they came from affected their children since the freed slaves were refugees which by definition makes them members to another nation. This understanding is supported by case law/common law which is why the case United States v Wong Kim Ark, 169 U.S. 649, 18 S. Ct. 456, 42 L. Ed. 890 1898 mentions the case Smith v Alabama 124 U.S. 478 8 S. Ct.564 and also mentions 2 Kent Comm. 258 Notes for elaboration. In the case Smith v Alabama, Mr. Justice Matthews delivered the judgment of the court by saying "The interpretation of the Constitution of the United States is necessarily influenced by the fact that its provisions are framed in the language of English common law, and are to be read in the light of its history." In 2ndKent 258 Notes, Chancellor Kent in his commentaries stated, "Natives are all persons born within the jurisdiction and allegiance of the United States. This is the rule of common law, without any regard or reference to the political condition or allegiance of their parents with the exception of the children of ambassadors who were in theory born within the allegiance of the foreign power they represent. To create allegiance by birth, the party must be born not only within the territory, but within the allegiance of the government. It is equally the doctrine of common law, that during such hostile occupation of a territory and the parents be adhering to the enemy as subjects de facto their children born under such a temporary dominion are not born under the allegiance of the conquered." In Cockburn on Nationality 7, Lord Chief Justice Cockburn said "… an English subject save only the children of foreign ambassadors who were excepted because their fathers carried their nationality with them…"

When considering if the emancipated slaves gave their allegiance to the UNITED STATES one would have to question their perception individually, as some could have grown to trust the UNITED STATES and its people, some could have become victims of Stockholm Syndrome, some might have lied due to feelings of duress, others might have longed to return to their country of original residence. Therefore, their allegiance to the UNITED STATES government is uncertain and to overlook this uncertainty would be to make the compact/contract of allegiance without consideration which would make the allegiance a nundum pactum/naked contract which is void of authority. I therefore assert that I not only have no allegiance to the UNITED STATES but I was neither born within its jurisdiction. It should also be noted that I am not the byword and misnomer known as Black/Negro/Afro-American/African-American but I as well as the emancipated slaves are descendants of the biblical Nation of Israel (which is not be considered the same as or in any affiliation with the current State of Israel established on May 14, 1948). Monuments like 'The Free Blacks of Israel Hill" which is in Farmville Virginia as well as the map of the continent of Africa in 1747, by Sr. Danville under the patronage of the Duke of Orleans which was revised and improved by Mr. Bolton in 1766. The map shows the Kingdom of Judah along the coastal area in which the slaves brought to the new world were gathered. The Biblical Israelites governing laws required all of them to be ambassadors of their nation and their King according to the Book of Deuteronomy 4:5, 6 as well as the Letter called 2nd Corinthians 5:20. It is also within the governing laws of the Biblical Nation of Israel to consider any child an Israelite regardless of the location of the birth or were the father(s) lived according to the Book of Numbers 1:2. If my claim of being a descendant of the Biblical Nation of Israel by the bloodline of my patriarchal ancestry is doubted, then it cannot be denied based on article 15, 19 and 20 of the Universal Declaration of Human Rights which supports my right as a human being the ability to manifest my thoughts, change my beliefs as well as teach, practice and express them with others, my right to peaceful association and my right from being arbitrarily denied the ability to change my nationality. This understanding is substantiated by the case "Hale v Henkel, 201 U.S. 43 which states one has rights that existed by the law of the land long antecedent to the organization of the State." If I am not a citizen of the Biblical Nation of Israel by bloodline, my conversion is accepted within the governing laws of the Nation which orders me to consider and carry myself as a Biblical Israelite by birth and to be treated as such according to the Book of Leviticus 19:34, 24:22. My declaration of being a citizen of the Biblical Nation of Israel alone exempts me from UNITED STATES citizenship is supported by the law of 26 USCS 7701(c)(i) which states "an individual shall not be treated as present in the United States during any period for which the individual establishes that he has a closer connection to a foreign country than to the United States". The Religious Freedoms Restoration Act of 1993 sec. 2 does not apply to my claims and declarations or to the Biblical Nation of Israel's plans as they are not from a religious perspective but are the actual perspectives of how an ancient government is to be restored by those who are its descendants and members according to the Book of Zephaniah 2:1 and the Book of Ezekiel 37:1-28. When questioning the authenticity of the plans documented in the Bible for the Biblical Nation of Israel, the case Xiuming Jiang v AG of the United States 379, Fed, Appx 204 2010 is referenced which states "Moreover the board...did not indicate that it questioned the authenticity of the letter nor did it indicate that it had any grounds to do so. This case is referenced considering one is applying diplomatics to the Bible, one must consider there is archeological, historical, extra biblical and genetic proof that the people known as the Biblical Israelites and the Biblical Nation of Israel existed and therefore there is no grounds to doubt its plans as a nation. The supremacy clause of the constitution confirms that no public policy of a State can be allowed to override the positive guarantees of the Constitution. Therefore, the so-called Blacks/African-Americans may be treated like citizens yet they are not and cannot be citizens according to the Constitution. This understanding of jurisprudence substantiated by the case law/common law "Dred Scott v Sanford 1857 Supreme Court" as well as the Legal Maxim "Talis non esteadem, nammullum simile est idem/such is not the same for nothing similar is the same thing." Richard v Secretary of State, Dept. Of State (1985, ca9 cal) 752 F2d 1413 shows expatriation is rooted in the intention of the act, congress is without power to provide citizens expatriate by mere performance of specified acts. According to Davis v District Director, Immigration & Naturalization Service (1979, DC Dist. Col.) 481 F Supp 1178, renunciation of citizenship does not require allegiance to another nation but only requires renunciation of U.S. Nationality. Yet, I, the Affiant, Kabir Elohim Isreal renunciate all forms of citizenship in accord with 8 USCS 1481(a) (1), (2).

4. My Citizenship Was Fraudulent Contract

The contract of my citizenship is fraudulent and void of authority. According to Ballentine's Law Dictionary the word "compact" is a contract of important and serious nature. According to the 9th

Edition of Black's Law Dictionary the word "compact" is an agreement or covenant between two or more parties especially between Governments or States. When considering the Constitutions of every State of the UNITED STATES as well as the constitution of the UNITED STATES, they are defined as compacts according to the case "Chisolm v Georgia, 2 U.S. 419, 440 1793 U.S. LEXIS 249; 2 Dall 419" which states "Every State Constitution is a compact made by and between the citizen of a State to govern themselves in a certain manner; and the Constitution of the United States is likewise a compact made by the people to govern themselves as to general objects, in a certain manner." Therefore, by definition the UNITED STATES constitution is not only a compact but is also a contract and covenant as well. When considering the citizenship mentioned in the 14th amendment which states "All persons born or naturalized in the united states, and subject to the jurisdiction thereof are citizens of the United States and of the state wherein they reside." According to 8 USCS 1101(A)(22) the term "national" of the United States means a citizen of the United States and according to 8 USCS 1101(A)(23) the term "naturalization" means the conferring of nationality of a State upon a person after birth by any means whatsoever. Therefore, the registering of the birth certificate in the record of vital statistics in the county, municipality, town or township of the person's birth acts as the means of conferring nationality and the birth certificate acts as the legal instrument showing one was born or naturalized in the UNITED STATES and was subject to its jurisdiction when the instrument was registered, which substantiates 14th Amendment citizenship. According to the 9th Edition of Black's Law Dictionary the definition of instrument/ legal instrument is "a written legal document that defines rights, duties, entitlements, or liabilities such as a contract..." Black's Law Dictionary also mentions A.E. Randall ed 3d ed 1924 which defines instrument by stating "...in fact any written or printed document that may have to be interpreted by the courts." Therefore, considering a national is a citizen and naturalization which is citizenship can come by any means whatsoever after birth, the legal instrument that is the birth certificate acts as the means of granting citizenship when registered which automatically becomes the legal instrument/contract that makes one a party to the compact that is the Constitution(s). This is the application of the Legal Maxim "causa casaeest causa causati/ the cause of a case is the case of the effect. According to the 9th edition of Black's Law Dictionary the word "transaction" means the act or instance of conducting business or other dealings especially the formation, performance or discharge of a contract, business agreement or exchange. The word "exchange" is synonymous with the word "commerce" which comprises every species of commercial intercourse which is all defined by Ballentine's Law Dictionary. According to UCC 1-103 (a)(1) which states in (a) the Uniform Commercial Code must be liberally construed and applied to promote its underlying purposes which are (1) To simply clarify and modernize the law governing commercial transactions. Considering that commercial transactions involve contracts and considering the birth certificate is a contract of citizenship, the Uniform Commercial Code would by default and deductive reasoning within jurisprudence, govern citizenship. This is verified by the contract of citizenship being registered with the record of vital statistics and according to Ballentine's Law, the Vital Statistics Act is one of the Uniform Laws which can be found in the Commercial Code. Therefore, my status of living outside of the UNITED STATES and its jurisdiction as a "non-resident alien" was entered into the official Uniform Commercial Code records under the filing numbers: #P19007796-6 and #P19008387-8. Therefore, I am applying UCC 2-615 titled "Excuse By Failure of Presupposed Conditions" to the compact/contract of citizenship that is the birth certificate. UCC 2-615 comment 3 states "the first test under this article in terms of basic assumption is a familiar one. The additional test of commercial impracticability (as contrasted with impossibility, frustration of performance or frustration of venue) has been adopted in order to call attention to the commercial charter of the criterion chosen by the article." Therefore, this document acts as an improbation proving the compact/contract of citizenship to be one of impracticability based on the agenda and structure of the Biblical Nation of Israel which claimed my allegiance before the UNITED STATES through my patriarchal ancestry. I assert that I lacked competency and any bargaining power at the inception of citizenship, which resulted in misrepresentation, as well as misidentification of my political/national/personal status, which leaves the compact/contract of citizenship in procedural unconscionability and even substantive unconscionability due to its terms being contrary to my political/national/personal status. According to Ballentine's Law Dictionary "failure of consideration" is the circumstance or combination of circumstances under which the consideration for a contract which was sufficient at the contract's inception has become worthless, has ceased to exist, or has been extinguished, whether by performance or an innate defect in the thing to be given. Therefore, I hereby assert that the contract of UNITED STATES citizenship is worthless, ceases to exist and is extinguished and has always been void of authority because at the moment of my birth I was brought into allegiance with another nation without the need of paperwork, registration or documenting any notification to the UNITED STATES. Therefore, the compact/contract of citizenship is an unconscionable naked adhesion contract of impracticability in my case and is subject to the "impossibility of performance doctrine" which releases a party from a contract on the grounds of uncontrollable circumstances rendering the performance impossible, which was the lack of considering my consent due to a lack of competency and a concealment of facts. This understanding is validated by the Legal Maxims "contractuslegem ex conventioneaccipiunt/contracts receive legal authority from the agreement of the parties", "contractus ex turpi causa vel contra bonus mores nullusest/a contract founded on wrongful consideration or against good morals is null", "conventiovincitlegem/the express agreement of the party overrides the law (I did not agree to the contract of citizenship which makes it subject to the law)", "beneficium invite no datur/a privilege or benefit is not granted against a person's will".

5. I Do Not Live In The UNITED STATES

I do not, have not and will not live, reside or exist in the corporate UNITED STATES. According to 28 USCS 3002 (15)(A) the UNITED STATES is a corporation and not a tangible land mass. According to Ballentine's Law Dictionary a corporation is an artificial being that is invisible, intangible and exists only in contemplation. I assert that I do not contemplate any fictional borders of jurisdiction or and fictional federal geometric planes neither do I contemplate that I exist within them or have ever existed within them. Therefore, I exist outside of the UNITED STATES jurisdiction. I do however contemplate that certain and specific regions of tangible land have been given names by its group of inhabitants which occupy it. I have also pledged my body as collateral to the Foreign State that is known as "LONDALE QUINTAE STRICKLING©" which can be found in the official Uniform Commercial Code records under the filing. This further substantiates that I am not in the UNITED STATES but exist within the jurisdiction of a Foreign State.

6. There Is A Quasi Contract Currently Active

There is a quasi-contract currently active between the STATE OF WISCONSIN and the Foreign State known as "LONDALE QUINTAE STRICKLING©". This contract entails and agreement that the STATE OF WISCONSIN and any of its agencies or agents' wont trespass on the rights, privileges, immunities, defenses or protections of the Foreign State or any of its agents. This contract can be found within the attached documents and is to be honored because it has been accepted and agreed to by the agents that operate on behalf of the STATE OF WISCONSIN when it was entered into the official Uniform Commercial Code without question or rebuttal. The STATE OF WISCONSIN cannot show nor provide a superior interest in the said property as identified upon the Security Agreement held by me. See Wynhammer v People NY 378.

UCC1-308(WITHOUT PREDJUDICE)

Signature: _Kabir Chh:ん Beel_

Kabir Elohim Isreal
Ambassador, Attorney in Fact, Authorized Representative, Secured Party, Trustee on behalf of:
LONDALE QUINTAE STRICKLING©, Ens legis

JURAT CERTIFICATION

State of Wisconsin County of Milwaukee

Printed Name of the Undersigned: Kabi--Elohim Isreal

Signature of the Undersigned: _____

This instrument was acknowledged before me a Notary Public and was affirmed to be the truth in which I attest to, on the date of 04/05/2023 by the above mentioned. Witness my hand and seal.

Notary Signature: _____   Seal:

My Commission Expires: 10/13/2025

FILED
CRIMINAL DIVISION

23 AUG -9 AM 11: 50 MILWAUKEE COUNTY COURTHOUSE
901 N 9TH STREET
MILWAUKEE WISCONSIN 53202

CLERK OF CIRCUIT COURT

RECEIVED AUG 09 2023
Office of District Attorney
Milwaukee, WI 53233

From: Kabir Elohim Isreal
Secured Party Creditor Filing #P19007796-6 and #P19008387-8 #20210215000594-1
Power of Attorney# 10909499
On Behalf of: LONDALE QUINTAE STRICKLING©
Case# 2023CF001349

MOTION TO DISMISS

"Indeed no more than Affidavits is necessary to make the prima facie case."
(United States v. Kiss, 658 F.2nd, 526, 536 (7thCir. 1981); Cert. Denied, 50 U.S. L.W. 2169; S Ct March 22, 1982)

RE: There is a violation of Wis. Stat. 970.02 and Wis. Stat. 970.09 as the initial preliminary hearing was deemed to be insufficient and probable cause was not found to bind the case over for plea and or trial yet the case was not dismissed as the statutes require. This lack of probable cause required the court to make a nunc pro tunc correction as if the hearing never happened in order to reschedule for another preliminary hearing which is outside of statutory procedure. From this perspective of jurisprudence, it is evident that it is not procedural to need more than one preliminary hearing so the need for another is equal to there never have been one. For the goal of the preliminary hearing is determining if there is probable cause to believe a felony has been committed by the defendant.

If having another preliminary hearing is due to a lack of finding probable cause then having another hearing is also due to not acknowledging initial procedure.

If the initial procedure from the original preliminary hearing is not acknowledged, then the need for another fails to acknowledge the first.

If this were not the conclusion of the matter then the case would be dismissed for a lack of finding probable cause initially.

Since the case is not dismissed according to statutory procedure to do so then the case is not acknowledging that there has already been a preliminary hearing and that there has been no probable cause found.

Therefore the case is still bound to the statutory procedure in the inception of its nunc pro tunc correction although unprocedural and capriciously arbitrary it may be, since the process has renewed instead of dismissed, it is still bound to the rule of being scheduled within 20 days after an initial appearance. Since there is an unprocedural renewal, deductive reasoning shows the last court date stands as the unprocedural initial appearance, which is why it is procedurally being proceeded by a preliminary hearing.

The fact that there is a need of another is to not acknowledge the first as the procedure is to dismiss the case if probable cause can't be meet meaning probable cause of a crime could not be determined. According to Wis. Stat when probable cause of a crime cant be found at the preliminary hearing the case is to be dismissed. Probable cause was not found and therefore this case should be dismissed. This case has also scheduled preliminary hearing 20 days after the initial appearance

It would be quite unscrupulous, arbitrary and capricious to acknowledge that the first preliminary hearing was 20 days after the initial appearance so the case cant be dismissed but not acknowledge that the preliminary hearing couldn't prove probable cause to dismiss the case. This negligence would continue if this unprocedural rescheduling doesn't constitute as the first preliminary hearing since the first is disregarded. This negligence can be ended if the court acknowledges this preliminary hearing as the first after initial appearance and dismiss the case due to it being outside of the statutory timeframe yet this negligence can also be ended if the court dismisses the case on the grounds of there being no probable cause initially found.

JURAT CERTIFICATION

State of Wisconsin County of Milwaukee

Printed Name of the Undersigned: _____

Signature of the Undersigned: _____

This instrument was acknowledged before me a Notary Public and was affirmed to be the truth in which I attest to, on the date of by the above mentioned. Witness my hand and seal.

Notary Signature: *Alicia Carter*   Seal.

My Commission Expires: 12/12/2025

ALICIA CARTER
Notary Public
State of Wisconsin

Certified Mail Receipt Number _____

MILWAUKEE CIRCUIT COURT
901 N 9th STREET
MILWAUKEE WISCONSIN 53233

From: Kabir Elohim Isreal
Secured Party Creditor Filing #P19007796-6 and #P19008387-8.
Power of Attorney DOC# 10909499
On Behalf of: LONDALE QUINTAE STRICKLING©
Case# 2023CF001349

MOTION TO KNOW NATURE OF CHARGES

RE: The court is motion made on behalf of the defendant in accordance with the 6 Amendment of the United States Constitution to know the nature of the charges being brought against the defendant:

1. Is this an Article 1 Court or an Article 3 court?
2. If this is an Article 1 Court, how am I the movant under the subjection of the UNITED STATES when I am not a member or employee?
3. If this is an Article 3 Court, why has there not been a proper summons according to the Rules of Civil Procedure?

Certified Mail Receipt Number _____

MILWAUKEE CIRCUIT COURT
901 N 9th STREET
MILWAUKEE WISCONSIN 53233

From: Kabir Elohim Isreal
Secured Party Creditor Filing #P19007796-6 and #P19008387-8.
Power of Attorney 10909499
On Behalf of: LONDALE QUINTAE STRICKLING©
Case# 2023CF001349

MOTION FOR SUMMARY JUDGEMENT
WIS. STAT 802.08

RE: This motion is made on behalf of the defendant to dismiss the case with prejudice by summary judgement based on the following merits:

1. LONDALE QUINTAE STRICKLING is a foreign state according to 26 USCS 7701(a)(30), 26 USCS 7701(a)(31)(B), 8 USCS 1101(14). Please see Exhibit A Affidavit of Truth Section 2 and Exhibit W8 Ben Certificate of foreign Status, and Exhibit Durable Power of Attorney Section 7g
2. Kabir Elohim Isreal and LONDALE QUINTAE STRICKLING are not present in the UNITED STATES according to 26 USCS 7701(c)(i). Please See Exhibit Wisconsin Department of Justice Records Check and Certification and Exhibit Department of Transportation Record of Non-Residency Exhibit Spectrum Bill (as proof of non-residency) Exhibit Puerto Rico Foreign Trust Certificate registration, WDFI Foreign Limited Liability Company Registration.
3. I, Kabir Elohim Isreal, am a refugee according to 8 USCS 1101(a)(42)(A), 8 U.S.C. § 1158(b)(1)(B)(i), The Universal Declaration of Human Rights and Dred Scott vs Sanford Davis v District Director, Immigration & Naturalization Service (1979, DC Dist. Col.) 481 F Supp 1178
4. I, Kabir Elohim Isreal, have renunciated all forms of citizenship according to 8 USCS 1481(a) (1), (2). Please see Exhibi W8 Ben Certificate of Foreign Status
5. There is a misnomer in the above-mentioned case as Kabir Elohim Isreal is not the same LONDALE QUINTAE STRICKLING©. See Exhibit Durable Power of Attorney Section 6 Special Instructions, Exhibit Common Law Copyright Notice and Exhibit Affidavit of Truth Section 2
6. There is copyright infringement in the matter as the above-mentioned case uses the name LONDALE QUINTAE STRICKLING© for financial gain which is prohibited due to ownership under common law copyright. See Exhibit Common Law Copyright Notice
7. There is a violation of the Legal Notice and Demand which is a quasi-contract between the STATE OF WISCONSIN and the foreign state known as LONDALE QUINTAE STRICKLING©. See Exhibit Legal Notice and Demand
8. Lawful notice has been given to the agents of WISCONSIN of the residence and political status of both Kabir Elohim Isreal and LONDALE QUINTAE STRICKLING©. See Exhibit Legal Notice of Status by Certified Mail
9. There is a lack of personal jurisdiction and subject matter jurisdiction as Kabir Elohim Israel is an ambassador for LONDALE QUINTAE STRICKLING and the Biblical Nation of Israel. See Constitution for the United States of America. See Exhibit Legal Notice and Demand

10. There is no valid proof of claim or claim for relief in the above-mentioned case. See Exhibit Affidavit of Truth Section 4 & 5.

Chapter 5: Case Studies and Real-World Applications

In this chapter, we will explore real-world examples and case studies that illustrate the effective use of legal documents and strategies in navigating complex legal challenges, particularly for pro se litigants facing criminal charges. These examples highlight the importance of preparation, strategic application, and the impact of well-crafted legal documents in achieving favorable outcomes.

Section 1: Documenting Success Stories

Effective Use of Legal Notices

CASE EXAMPLE:

John Doe was facing multiple charges and believed his rights were being violated due to procedural errors. He strategically prepared and filed a detailed Legal Notice and Demand, challenging the court's jurisdiction and asserting his rights.

- **Preparation**: John carefully researched the legal basis for his claims, drafted a precise notice citing relevant laws and precedents, and clearly outlined his demands for due process.

- **Delivery**: He ensured the notice was delivered to all relevant parties, including the court, prosecution, and any involved officials, via certified mail to maintain a record of receipt.

- **Judicial Response:** The court took notice of the procedural errors highlighted in John's document. This led to a review of the case, and several charges were dropped due to the demonstrated violations.

Lessons Learned:

- **Timing**: Filing the notice early in the legal proceedings can significantly impact the direction of the case.

- **Legal Wording:** Use clear, precise, and legally sound language to articulate demands.

- **Documentation:** Maintain records of delivery and receipt to substantiate claims of procedural violations.

Navigating Identity Change in Court

CASE EXAMPLE:

Jane Smith had legally changed her name and identity after a period of incarceration. Facing new charges under her former identity, she used her new legal documentation to assert her new identity in court.

- **Document Presentation:** Jane presented her legal name change documents, a notarized Affidavit of Truth, and a W-8BEN form to establish her new identity.
- **Argumentation:** She argued that any legal actions against her should reflect her current legal identity, emphasizing the separation from her past convictions.
- **Court Recognition:** The court recognized her new identity, leading to a reconsideration of the charges based on the updated legal context.

Strategic Insights:

- **Comprehensive Documentation:** Ensure all identity change documents are complete, accurate, and legally validated.
- **Persuasive Argumentation:** Clearly articulate the legal reasons for the court to recognize the new identity, supported by relevant documentation.

Section 2: Overcoming Legal Obstacles

Challenges with Public Servant Questionnaires

CASE EXAMPLE:

Tom Brown was involved in a legal dispute where he believed the public officials were biased. He used the Public Servant Questionnaire to gather information about their qualifications and potential conflicts of interest.

- **Questionnaire Responses:** The responses revealed that one of the officials handling his case had a prior disciplinary record that was not disclosed.

- **Procedural Flaws:** Tom used this information to challenge the official's involvement, leading to the official's removal from the case and a review of the procedural conduct.

Effective Tactics:

- **Thorough Research:** Ensure questions are comprehensive and cover qualifications, disciplinary records, and potential conflicts of interest.

- **Legal Leverage:** Use the documented responses to highlight procedural flaws and biases, supporting claims of unfair treatment.

Utilizing Trusts in Legal Defense

CASE EXAMPLE:

Sarah Green used a trust to protect her assets while facing a legal battle over property disputes. She established a trust and used Trust Certificate Units (TCUs) to manage and secure her assets.

- **Trust Setup:** Sarah established a legally sound trust, clearly defining the roles and responsibilities of the trustees.

- **Asset Protection:** The trust shielded her personal assets from being directly targeted in the legal dispute, separating them from her personal liabilities.

- **Legal Outcome:** The court recognized the trust's validity, and her personal assets were protected, leading to a favorable resolution of the property dispute.

Application Tips:

- **Legal Framework:** Ensure the trust is established with a clear legal framework and all necessary documentation.

- **Asset Management:** Use TCUs to manage and protect assets within the trust, providing a layer of security in legal disputes.

Section 3: Advanced Negotiation and Settlement Techniques

Successful Commercial Offers

CASE EXAMPLE:

David White faced a lengthy legal battle over contractual obligations. He proposed a commercial offer to settle the dispute out of court.

- **Offer Preparation:** David drafted a detailed commercial offer outlining the terms of the settlement, backed by an affidavit to confirm its authenticity.
- **Negotiation:** The offer was appealing to the opposing party as it provided a quick resolution and avoided prolonged litigation.
- **Settlement:** The parties agreed to the terms, and the case was settled amicably, saving time and resources.

Negotiation Strategies:

- **Clear Terms**: Ensure the offer is clear, concise, and addresses the interests of both parties.
- **Legal Documentation**: Back the offer with an affidavit to add legal weight and authenticity.

Handling Dishonor in Legal Proceedings

CASE EXAMPLE:

Lisa Black had entered into an agreement that was dishonored by the other party. She used a Certificate of Dishonor to document the failure and pursue legal action.

- **Documenting Failure:** Lisa documented the breach of agreement with a Certificate of Dishonor, detailing the unmet terms.

- **Legal Action:** The certificate served as evidence in court, strengthening her case and leading to a favorable judgment.

- **Impact:** The court awarded damages based on the documented dishonor, holding the other party accountable.

Documenting Failures:

- **Detailed Documentation:** Ensure the certificate clearly documents the failure to honor the agreement.

- **Legal Use:** Use the certificate as evidence in legal proceedings to support claims of breach and seek compensation.

Section 4: Legal Documentation in Action

Power of Affidavits

CASE EXAMPLE:

Michael Davis used an Affidavit of Truth to support his defense in a criminal case, asserting factual statements that contradicted the prosecution's claims.

- **Affidavit Preparation:** Michael drafted a comprehensive Affidavit of Truth, detailing his version of events with supporting evidence.

- **Court Impact:** The affidavit was pivotal in creating reasonable doubt, leading to a favorable outcome in the case.

- **Legal Strength:** The sworn statements under oath carried significant legal weight, supporting his defense robustly.

Drafting Effective Affidavits:

- **Factual Accuracy:** Ensure the affidavit is factually accurate and supported by evidence.

- **Legal Format**: Follow the legal format and include notarization to enhance its validity.

Trust Certificate Units in Settlements

CASE EXAMPLE:

Natalie Grey used Trust Certificate Units (TCUs) to settle a financial dispute. She leveraged the TCUs as part of the negotiation process.

- **Settlement Process:** Natalie issued TCUs representing the value of assets within her trust, offering them as part of the settlement.

- **Legal Recognition:** The TCUs were recognized as valid financial instruments, facilitating the settlement.

- **Outcome:** The dispute was resolved efficiently, with the TCUs providing a flexible and secure means of settlement.

Leveraging Financial Instruments:

- **Issuing TCUs:** Ensure TCUs are properly documented and endorsed.

- **Negotiation Use:** Use TCUs strategically in negotiations to offer secure and flexible settlement options.

Conclusion of Chapter 5

This chapter showcases real-world applications of the concepts, strategies, and documentation discussed throughout the book. It provides practical examples and actionable insights, demonstrating how individuals can successfully navigate the legal system using the tools and techniques outlined in previous chapters. These case studies serve as a testament to the effectiveness of a well-prepared and documented legal strategy, offering hope and guidance for those facing similar legal challenges.

[Some people may wonder why it took so many documents,

well let us remind you that you were dealing with an alleged three-time felon, with very serious alleged allegations. It was the states initial lack of awareness that had them pursue something that they later "as a whole" realized would cause them more harm than good and so the end result is]

"victory"

halleluYah

Chapter 6:

Advanced Strategies for SPCs

In this chapter, we delve into advanced strategies for Secured Party Creditors (SPCs), focusing on how these techniques can be applied to navigate complex legal challenges, particularly in criminal cases. We will explore legal innovations, the assertion of sovereign identity, international laws, and the use of innovative financial instruments.

Section 1: Legal Innovations and Complex Scenarios

Expanding Legal Boundaries

Innovation Overview:

Secured Party Creditor (SPC) concepts often push the boundaries of traditional legal frameworks by introducing unique arguments and strategies that challenge conventional legal principles.

- **Pioneering Legal Arguments:** SPC strategies often involve innovative legal arguments that redefine relationships between individuals and their legal entities, debts, and obligations.

- **Boundary-Pushing:** These strategies can challenge traditional views of sovereignty, citizenship, and financial responsibility, leading to new legal precedents.

CASE EXAMPLES:

1. **Case Study 1:** An individual facing foreclosure used SPC principles to argue that the debt was illegitimate because the original loan agreement lacked full disclosure. By using UCC filings and SPC status, they successfully contested the foreclosure and retained their property.

2. **Case Study 2:** A defendant in a criminal case claimed their sovereign status, arguing that the court lacked jurisdiction over them as a natural person distinct from their legal entity.

This argument led to a significant reduction in charges and a precedent for similar defenses.

Lessons Learned:

- **Innovation in Argumentation:** Being creative and knowledgeable about SPC principles can open new avenues for defense and legal argumentation.

- **Precedents:** Successful cases can set precedents, making it easier for others to follow similar strategies.

Complex Legal Entities and Structures

Complex Structures:

Utilizing advanced legal entities like trusts, LLCs, and other organizational structures can offer significant protection and flexibility in legal and financial matters.

- **Irrevocable Legacy Trusts:** These can be used to separate personal assets from liabilities, offering protection in legal disputes.

- **LLCs and Corporations:** Forming an LLC or corporation can provide legal separation and liability protection, which can be crucial in complex legal situations.

Strategic Applications:

- **Asset Protection:** These structures can shield personal assets from creditors and legal claims.

- **Legal Flexibility:** They provide a framework for managing and navigating legal challenges more effectively.

EXAMPLE:

- **Creating a Family Trust:** A family establishes a trust to manage and protect their assets. This trust legally separates their personal wealth from their business operations, reducing their exposure to legal risks.

- **Forming an LLC:** An individual forms an LLC to manage their business activities. This provides a legal shield between their personal and business assets, offering protection from business-related lawsuits.

Section 2:

Mastering Sovereign Legal Identity

Asserting Sovereignty in Legal Proceedings

Sovereignty Claims:

Claiming sovereign status in legal disputes involves asserting that the individual operates under a legal framework separate from state or federal jurisdictions.

- **Potential Benefits:** Sovereign claims can challenge the court's jurisdiction, potentially leading to dismissal or reduction of charges.

- **Legal Risks:** There are risks, including the possibility of the court rejecting the claims or imposing penalties for perceived frivolous arguments.

Case Studies:

1. **Successful Sovereign Claim:** An individual facing tax evasion charges successfully argued that as a born again Child of God and that they have no contracts with the government and do not receive any privilege or benefit, they were not subject to federal tax laws. The case was dismissed due to lack of jurisdiction.

2. Unsuccessful Sovereign Claim: Another individual attempted to use sovereign status to avoid criminal charges but was unsuccessful, resulting in additional penalties, due to him presenting himself in court as the government owned name and being there to argue against "statutes" instead of asserting separation from the legal name on the record and presenting an affidavit of Truth.

" remember we cannot serve two masters and we cannot be a part of two governments either we serve the most high or reserve man"

Lessons Learned:

- Thorough Preparation: Success often depends on thorough preparation and understanding of both sovereign principles and traditional legal responses.

- Balancing Risks and Rewards: Consider the potential risks and rewards before asserting sovereign claims.

Documentation and Legal Standing

Enhancing Legal Standing:

Using comprehensive documentation can significantly enhance your legal standing in court, especially when asserting SPC status.

- Key Documents: Essential documents include UCC filings, affidavits, and notarized declarations.

- Strategic Use: Present these documents strategically to establish and reinforce your legal identity and claims.

Documentation Best Practices:

- Accuracy: Ensure all documents are accurate and free of errors.

- Organization: Keep documents well-organized and easily accessible for legal proceedings.

- Legal Validation: Have key documents notarized or otherwise validated to strengthen their legal standing.

Example:

- Affidavit of Sovereign Status: A detailed affidavit explaining your sovereign status, supported by legal citations and personal testimony.

- UCC Financing Statement: A UCC-1 filing that declares your legal standing and claims over personal property.

Section 3: Navigating International Laws and Treaties

International Legal Considerations

Global Perspective:

International laws and treaties can provide additional avenues for legal strategies, particularly for those claiming foreign or sovereign status.

- **Leveraging Treaties:** International treaties can offer protections or exemptions that are not available under domestic law.

- **Jurisdictional Challenges:** Understanding and using international legal principles can challenge local jurisdiction over your case.

Practical Guidance:

- **Research Treaties:** Investigate relevant international treaties that may apply to your situation.

Legal Representation: Consider seeking legal representation with expertise in international law.

EXAMPLE:

- **Extradition Cases:** Using international treaties to contest extradition requests, arguing that the charges violate human rights or other protected statuses.

Use of Foreign Documents and Identities

Strategic Use of Foreign Status:

Foreign documents, such as passports or citizenship certificates, can be used to assert special legal rights or exemptions in domestic courts.

- **Legal Advantages:** These documents can sometimes offer advantages, such as diplomatic immunity or jurisdictional challenges.

- **Challenges:** Be prepared for potential challenges from domestic authorities regarding the validity and applicability of foreign documents.

CASE EXAMPLES:

1. **Diplomatic Immunity:** An individual used their status as a foreign diplomat to claim immunity from criminal prosecution in a domestic court.

2. **Residency Status:** A defendant used their foreign residency status to challenge the jurisdiction of the domestic court over their case.

Lessons Learned:

- **Documentation:** Ensure all foreign documents are current, valid, and properly translated if necessary.

- **Legal Support:** Engage legal experts familiar with both domestic and international law.

Section 4: Innovative Financial Instruments in Legal Defense

Negotiable Instruments and Settlements

Using Financial Instruments:

Negotiable instruments, such as promissory notes or trust certificates, can be powerful tools in legal settlements and defense strategies.

- **Settlement Negotiations:** These instruments can be used to propose financial settlements that resolve legal disputes without prolonged litigation.

- **Defense Strategies:** They can also be leveraged to show financial responsibility and goodwill in legal defenses.

Financial Strategy Development:

- **Creating Instruments:** Learn how to create and issue negotiable instruments.

- **Using in Negotiations:** Understand how to present these instruments effectively in negotiations.

EXAMPLE:

- **Promissory Note:** Issuing a promissory note to settle a debt, providing a clear repayment plan and terms.

- **Trust Certificate:** Using a trust certificate to transfer assets as part of a legal settlement.

Digital and Crypto Assets in Legal Frameworks

Emerging Trends:

Digital and cryptocurrency assets are increasingly relevant in legal strategies, offering new avenues for financial management and defense.

- **Modern Assets:** Understand the role of digital assets like Bitcoin, Ethereum, and other cryptocurrencies in legal contexts.

- **Legal Uncertainties:** Be aware of the legal uncertainties and evolving regulations surrounding these assets.

Legal and Financial Integration:

- Asset Management: Learn how to integrate digital assets into traditional legal and financial strategies.

- **Regulatory Compliance:** Ensure compliance with current regulations and stay informed about legal developments.

EXAMPLE:

- **Crypto Settlement:** Using cryptocurrency to settle a financial dispute, providing a fast and secure transaction.

- **Digital Asset Trust:** Creating a trust that holds digital assets, offering protection and management of these modern financial instruments.

Conclusion of Chapter 6

Chapter 6 concludes the guide by delving into sophisticated legal strategies that utilize advanced SPC concepts, sovereign claims, and international law. It provides a thorough understanding of how these elements can be integrated into an overarching legal and financial strategy to maximize outcomes in complex legal situations. This chapter equips readers with the knowledge to not only defend their rights but also to innovate within the legal system, using a blend of traditional and modern legal tactics to secure their freedom and assets effectively.

STATE OF WISCONSIN   CIRCUIT COURT   MILWAUKEE COUNTY

STATE OF WISCONSIN,

                Plaintiff,   Case No. 2023CF001349

    vs.

LONDALE QUINTAE STRICKLING,

                Defendant.

                    PRELIMINARY HEARING

             Before the HONORABLE BARRY PHILLIPS
                Court Commissioner, presiding

                      August 9, 2023

APPEARANCES:

FOR THE PLAINTIFF: GREGG M. HERMAN, ESQ.
                      MILWAUKEE COUNTY DISTRICT
                         ATTORNEY'S OFFICE
                      Safety Building
                      821 W. State Street
                      Milwaukee, WI 53233-1427
                      (414) 278-4130

FOR THE DEFENDANT: LONDALE QUINTAE STRICKLING, PRO SE

                    Recorded and transcribed by
              VALORI WEBER, Official Court Reporter

```
 1              P R O C E E D I N G S
 2         (Proceedings commenced at 4:42 p.m.)
 3         THE CLERK: Calling case 23CF1349, State of
 4  Wisconsin vs. Londale Strickling. This case is
 5  assigned to Branch 19.
 6         Appearances.
 7         MR. HERMANN: Gregg Herman for the State.
 8         MR. YASHARALAH: Gabaryah Yasharalah here on
 9  behalf of Londale Quintae Strickling.
10         MR. HERM
11         THE COURT: I'm going to ask you this one and
12  one time only. Are you Londale Strickling?
13         MR. YASHARALAH: No.
14         THE COURT: I will issue a warrant. Any bail
15  posted is forfeited.
16         MR. YASHARALAH: Well, why is this, sir? Why
17  is there a warrant? I have --
18         THE COURT: Mr. Strickling is supposed to be
19  in court. You're claiming you're not Mr. Strickling,
20  correct?
21         MR. YASHARALAH: Yes, I'm the -- have attorney
22  papers to represent --
23         THE COURT: Are you Londale Strickling?
24         MR. YASHARALAH: No, I am not, sir. I am --
25         THE COURT: Warrant shall be issued for
```

```
 1  Mr. Strickling's arrest.  Any bail posted is forfeited.
 2          MR. YASHARALAH:  Well, what --
 3          THE COURT:  Calendar's over.
 4          MR. YASHARALAH:  Well, can we have the
 5  presumed defendant come in the court?  He's in the
 6  hallway.
 7          THE COURT:  He needs to come into court then.
 8          MR. YASHARALAH:  His name is not Londale
 9  Quintae Strickling.  He has a court order for a new
10  name as well.
11          THE COURT:  Either Mr. Londale Strickling --
12          MR. YASHARALAH:  Hold on, sir, please.
13          THE COURT:  -- is going to walk in this
14  court --
15          MR. YASHARALAH:  Respectfully, hold on.
16          THE COURT:  -- or this case will be over.
17          MR. YASHARALAH:  One second.
18          (Off the record from 4:43 p.m. to 4:45 p.m.)
19          THE COURT:  Call the case.
20          THE CLERK:  Recalling case 23CF1349, State of
21  Wisconsin vs. Londale Strickling.  This case is
22  assigned to Branch 19.
23          Appearances.
24          MR. HERMAN:  Gregg Herman for the State.
25          THE DEFENDANT:  Kabir-Elohim Isreal in person --
```

```
 1        THE COURT:  All right.
 2        THE DEFENDANT:  -- on behalf of Londale
 3   Quintae Strickling trust.
 4        THE COURT:  All right.  Just so you
 5   understand, Mr. Strickling.  I don't want to -- if you
 6   truly have in fact changed your name, the judge has the
 7   power to maybe tell the State to change the name that
 8   you've been charged under.  Right now, I have to refer
 9   to you as the named that's charged in this Complaint,
10   or I will be responsible for the --
11        THE DEFENDANT:  Even with -- I'm sorry -- even
12   with court order.
13        THE COURT:  Wait till I finish.
14        THE DEFENDANT:  Okay.
15        THE COURT:  Will till I finish.  I will be
16   responsible for losing jurisdiction over you because as
17   far as the State of Wisconsin is concerned with this
18   case, you're charged under Londale Strickling.
19        Now, when you eventually go in front of the
20   judge, if you show the judge that you have in fact
21   changed your name, she may -- he or she may be able to
22   change --
23        THE DEFENDANT:  Sir, with all due respect, I
24   can show you that now as far -- including with CCAP.
25        THE COURT:  Did you hear what I said?  I don't
```

4

183

1 have the power to do that.
2 THE DEFENDANT: Right.
3 THE COURT: Only the judge does. I have don't
4 have the power to do that. So I mean no disrespect by
5 referring to --
6 THE DEFENDANT: Yes, sir.
7 THE COURT: -- you as Londale Strickling, but
8 I have no choice but to do that.
9 THE DEFENDANT: Gotcha.
10 THE COURT: Okay. So I'm trying to be
11 respectful --
12 THE DEFENDANT: Absolutely.
13 THE COURT: -- by letting you know why I'm
14 doing that. Okay?
15 Now, State. Do you have a witness for the
16 Strickling case?
17 MR. HERMAN: The witness was subpoenaed and
18 was unavailable and --
19 THE COURT: For what reason?
20 MR. HERMAN: Let me see if I can find out.
21 I don't know. A different officer was
22 subpoenaed, and I cannot tell the Court the status. I
23 wasn't aware. Normally I email the officer and ask why
24 he isn't here. I can't tell the Court what happened
25 there because I haven't had time to do that.

1   But originally, the officer was subpoenaed,
2   said he couldn't make it. Another subpoena went out to
3   another officer. And I have not heard from either one.
4   THE COURT: Do you have a motion?
5   THE DEFENDANT: Yes, I have several motions.
6   THE COURT: As to the fact that the State is
7   unable to proceed today, do you have a motion as to
8   that?
9   THE DEFENDANT: Yes. I have a motion to
10   dismiss.
11   THE COURT: This is the second time the
12   matter's been before the Court for a preliminary
13   hearing.
14   On June 30th, the State was unprepared. The
15   Defendant made a motion to dismiss. The motion to
16   dismiss was taken under advisement.
17   We appear today. The State is once again not
18   prepared. The State, at least this time, has no
19   explanation as to why the witness is not present.
20   Based on that, I will dismiss the case.
21   THE DEFENDANT: Thank you. One more thing.
22   THE COURT: Sir, you won today.
23   THE DEFENDANT: Can we clear --
24   THE COURT: Walk away with your win.
25   THE DEFENDANT: -- is this with or without

```
 1  prejudice, for the record?
 2          THE COURT:  It's without prejudice.
 3          THE DEFENDANT:  Thank you.
 4          THE COURT:  Definitely without.  They can
 5  reissue --
 6          THE DEFENDANT:  Okay.
 7          THE COURT:  -- just so you know.
 8          THE DEFENDANT:  Okay.
 9          THE COURT:  But today, the case is over.
10          THE DEFENDANT:  And can we have that removed
11  from CCAP?
12          THE COURT:  I can't do that.
13          THE DEFENDANT:  Okay.
14          THE COURT:  You can petition for it, but I
15  can't do that.
16          THE DEFENDANT:  Okay, thank you.
17          THE COURT:  All right.
18          (Proceedings adjourned at 4:49 p.m.)
19
20
21
22
23
24
25
```

CERTIFICATE

I, Valori Weber, Certified Electronic Reporter, do hereby certify that I have been duly sworn as a Digital Court Reporter for Milwaukee County, in and for the State of Wisconsin. I further certify that I have carefully transcribed from and compared the foregoing pages with the original digital audio recording from said proceeding and that this transcript is true and correct to the best of my ability.

Dated this 8th day of November, 2023.

_____
Valori Weber
Court Reporter

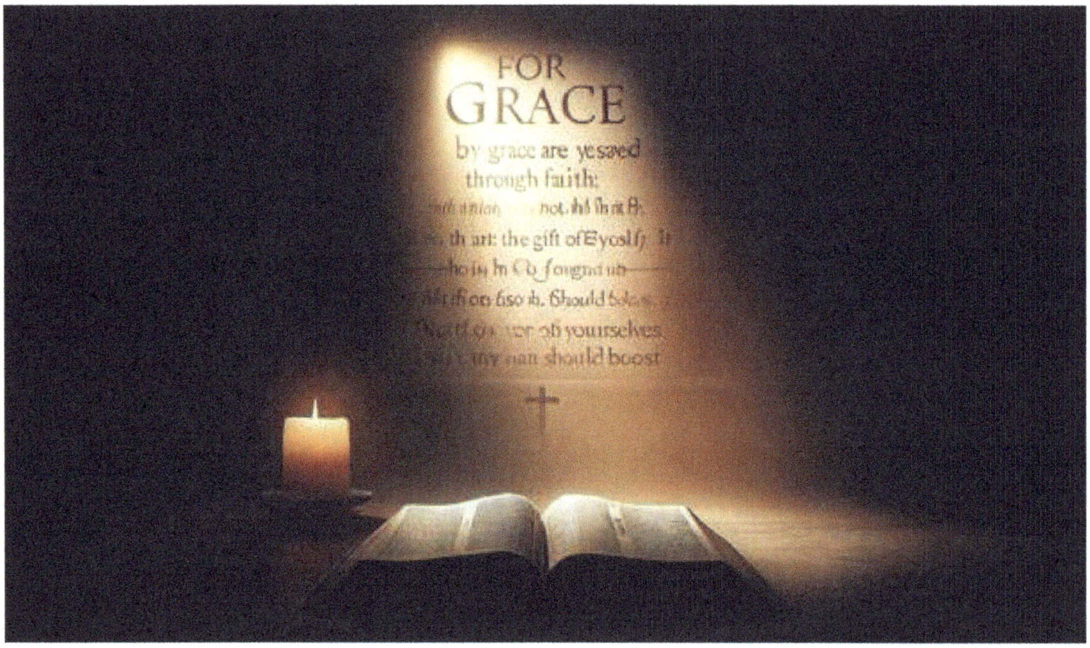
FOR
GRACE
by grace are yesaved
through faith:

Chapter 7: Empowerment Through Legal Enlightenment

In this chapter, we focus on the power of education, community engagement, proactive strategies, and transformative legal actions. These elements are essential for empowering Secured Party Creditors (SPCs) to navigate the legal system effectively and assert their rights confidently.

Section 1: Educating and Empowering the SPC Community

Building Knowledge and Confidence

Educational Initiatives:

Education is the cornerstone of empowerment within the SPC community. By understanding your rights and the legal processes, you can navigate the legal system more effectively.

- **Workshops and Seminars:** Participate in workshops and seminars that cover SPC principles, legal document preparation, and strategic defense techniques.

- **Online Courses:** Enroll in online courses that offer in-depth knowledge on various aspects of SPC, including UCC filings, trust creation, and sovereign claims.

- **Reading and Research:** Stay informed by reading books, articles, and legal documents relevant to SPC practices. Knowledge is a powerful tool that can transform your approach to legal challenges.

Empowerment Through Knowledge:

Acquiring legal knowledge empowers you to assert your rights and challenge unjust legal practices. It enables you to approach legal proceedings with confidence and clarity.

- **Self-Confidence:** Understanding the law boosts your confidence in legal settings, helping you to present your case effectively.

- **Strategic Advantage:** Knowledge provides a strategic advantage, allowing you to anticipate potential challenges and prepare appropriate responses.

Community Engagement and Support

Creating Support Networks:

Building a supportive community is vital for sharing resources, advice, and moral support. A strong network can provide invaluable assistance during legal challenges.

- **Support Groups:** Join or create support groups where members can discuss their experiences, share legal strategies, and offer encouragement. *** [We have support groups that can be found at: TheBiblicalNationofIsraelRegistry.World]
- **Mentorship Programs:** Engage in mentorship programs where experienced SPCs can guide newcomers through the complexities of the legal system. [We offer mentorship programs at: RoyaltyandPower.org]
- **Online Forums**: Participate in online forums and social media groups dedicated to SPC topics, enabling you to connect with a broader community. [Help our online community Network grow by joining us on the " Scroll" exclusively found on "The biblical nation of Israel Registry.World"]

Case studies:

Learning from the experiences of others can be incredibly valuable. Here are a few examples of how community support has benefited individuals:

1. **Case Study 1:** A support group helped an individual facing foreclosure by sharing successful strategies and providing emotional support. The collective knowledge and encouragement led to a favorable resolution.

2. **Case Study 2:** An online forum connected a new SPC with a mentor who guided them through the process of challenging an unjust tax levy, resulting in the levy being lifted.

Section 2: Legal Self-Defense and Proactive Strategies

Proactive Legal Documentation

Importance of Documentation:

Maintaining comprehensive and accurate legal documentation is crucial for legal self-defense. Proper documentation can substantiate your claims and protect your rights.

- **Comprehensive Records:** Keep detailed records of all legal documents, correspondence, and evidence related to your case.
- **Accuracy:** Ensure all documents are accurate and up-to-date, as errors can undermine your credibility and legal standing.

Strategic Document Management:

Effective management of your legal documents enhances your ability to present a strong case.

- **Organization:** Organize your documents systematically, using folders or digital tools to keep everything accessible.
- **Presentation**: When presenting documents in court, ensure they are properly formatted and clearly labeled for easy reference.

Advanced Legal Planning and Strategy

Long-term Legal Planning:

Developing long-term legal strategies helps you anticipate challenges and prepare for various scenarios.

"The number one long-term legal planning you can do is dismissing your so-called government name and being born again by spirit and

==Truth that comes from the Father by way of the Son.... A name created under the government and authority of your creator The Most High."==

==" It is wise to have this done before any possible situation, to ensure better odds of a swift win"==

Yes your parents may have given you your name but the government owns it because your parents registered it.

Render unto Caesars that which is Caesars and that which is the Lord's unto the Lord

Give it up and return back to the authority of the example of the Son by way of the Father.

- **Legal Roadmap:** Create a roadmap outlining your legal goals, potential obstacles, and planned actions.

- **Regular Review:** Regularly review and update your strategies to adapt to changing circumstances and legal developments.

Innovative Defense Techniques:

Utilize cutting-edge legal theories and practices to safeguard your sovereignty.

- **Legal Innovations:** Stay informed about new legal developments and innovative defense techniques that can strengthen your position.

- **Creative Solutions:** Be open to creative and unconventional solutions that can effectively address your legal challenges.

Section 3: Transformative Legal Actions

Challenging Unjust Laws and Practices

Legal Activism:

Legal activism plays a crucial role in challenging and changing unjust laws that negatively impact the SPC community.

- **Awareness Campaigns:** Participate in or organize campaigns to raise awareness about unjust laws and advocate for change.
- **Public Speaking:** Engage in public speaking opportunities to educate others about SPC principles, ***The importance of being Born again under Yeshua ha mashiach***, and the need for a mass legal reform.

Success Stories:

Highlighting significant cases where legal challenges have led to positive changes in the law can inspire and motivate others.

1. **Case Study 1:** An SPC successfully challenged an unfair property tax law, leading to its repeal and the establishment of fairer taxation practices.
2. **Case Study 2:** A group of activists fought against unlawful debt collection practices, resulting in new regulations that protect consumers.

Creating Legal Precedents

Setting Precedents:

Setting legal precedents is essential for supporting the rights and freedoms of SPCs.

- **Strategic Litigation:** Approach litigation with the goal of creating favorable legal precedents that benefit the broader SPC community.
- **Case Preparation:** Thoroughly prepare your case, focusing on legal arguments that can establish new precedents.

Guidance for Litigation:

- **Research:** Conduct extensive legal research to support your arguments and identify potential precedents.

- **Documentation:** Ensure all necessary documentation is meticulously prepared and presented.

Conclusion of Chapter 7

Chapter 7 wraps up the guide by focusing on the broader implications of being an SPC, emphasizing education, community support, and proactive legal strategies as key elements of empowerment. This chapter serves as a call to action for readers to educate themselves, engage with the community, and take transformative legal actions to not only protect their rights but also to challenge and change the system. It underscores the power of legal knowledge and community in achieving true sovereignty and freedom.

Closing Reflections: Rebirth and Renewal through Legal Sovereignty

As we conclude this guide, we return to the core theme that has guided our journey: the transformative power of rebirth and being born again, not only in a spiritual sense but also in a legal context. This process, which you have embarked upon as a so-called Secured Party Creditor (SPC), is about more than navigating complex legal systems—it is about claiming a new identity that aligns with your deepest truths and convictions.

Embracing a New Identity

Your journey as an SPC is akin to a rebirth, shedding old identities and assumptions imposed upon you by society and its legal structures. This rebirth is not just a change of name or a new legal document; it's a profound metamorphosis that affects how you interact with the world and assert your rights within it. By adopting a new legal identity, you reclaim power over your personal and financial sovereignty, stepping into a role that you define, not one that has been defined for you.

The Power of Knowledge and Community

In embracing your rebirth, you've learned the power of knowledge and the strength of community. This guide has equipped you with the legal understanding necessary to navigate your transformation effectively. However, the community around you—fellow travelers who have undergone or are undergoing similar transformations—provides the support and wisdom to sustain your journey. Together, your shared experiences and challenges forge a collective resilience and a repository of knowledge that can empower others.

Continuous Growth and Advocacy

The concept of being born again is inherently tied to continuous growth and renewal. In legal terms, this means staying vigilant about changes in laws, court rulings, and societal norms that impact your sovereignty. Your advocacy for rights and recognition is crucial, not just for your own benefit but for the advancement of all who share this path. Each legal victory, no matter how small, paves the way for broader acceptance and understanding of SPC principles.

Leaving a Legacy

Consider what legacy you wish to leave as you live out your rebirth. How will you use your newfound sovereignty to influence the world around you? Your journey can inspire and illuminate the paths of others, showing that true freedom comes from understanding, asserting, and living out one's rights. Teach, mentor, and contribute to the body of knowledge that supports this community, ensuring that your rebirth sparks a wider awakening.

Final Words

Thank you for embracing the journey of rebirth through this guide. May your path as a Secured Party Creditor be marked by growth, empowerment, and the joy of discovering your true self under the law. Your rebirth is not the end of a process but the beginning of a lived experience of sovereignty and freedom. Continue to live out your truth, advocate for your rights, and support the community that walks with you. Here's to your continual rebirth and the profound impact it will have on the world.

All glory, honor, thanks and praise be to The Most High. We are thankful for the example we have in the Son and salvation Yeshua ha mashiach, only by way of the Father are we able to receive this gift.
halleluYah

VICTORY
AGAINST
ALL ODDS
Empower yourself to chogle nons
and Rreshavpe your dostriny.
VICTORY
AGAINST
ALL ODDS
AHAZON
Victory Against All Ods
amazon

Form **W-8BEN**
(Rev. October 2021)
Department of the Treasury
Internal Revenue Service

Certificate of Foreign Status of Beneficial Owner for United States Tax Withholding and Reporting (Individuals)
▶ For use by individuals. Entities must use Form W-8BEN-E.
▶ Go to *www.irs.gov/FormW8BEN* for instructions and the latest information.
▶ Give this form to the withholding agent or payer. Do not send to the IRS.

OMB No. 1545-1621

Do NOT use this form if:	Instead, use Form:
• You are NOT an individual	W-8BEN-E
• You are a U.S. citizen or other U.S. person, including a resident alien individual	W-9
• You are a beneficial owner claiming that income is effectively connected with the conduct of trade or business within the United States (other than personal services)	W-8ECI
• You are a beneficial owner who is receiving compensation for personal services performed in the United States	8233 or W-4
• You are a person acting as an intermediary	W-8IMY

Note: If you are resident in a FATCA partner jurisdiction (that is, a Model 1 IGA jurisdiction with reciprocity), certain tax account information may be provided to your jurisdiction of residence.

Part I Identification of Beneficial Owner (see instructions)

1 Name of individual who is the beneficial owner
2 Country of citizenship

3 Permanent residence address (street, apt. or suite no., or rural route). **Do not use a P.O. box or in-care-of address.**

City or town, state or province. Include postal code where appropriate.
Country

4 Mailing address (if different from above)

City or town, state or province. Include postal code where appropriate.
Country

5 U.S. taxpayer identification number (SSN or ITIN), if required (see instructions)

6a Foreign tax identifying number (see instructions)
6b Check if FTIN not legally required . . . . ☐

7 Reference number(s) (see instructions)
8 Date of birth (MM-DD-YYYY) (see instructions)

Part II Claim of Tax Treaty Benefits (for chapter 3 purposes only) (see instructions)

9 I certify that the beneficial owner is a resident of _____ within the meaning of the income tax treaty between the United States and that country.

10 **Special rates and conditions** (if applicable—see instructions): The beneficial owner is claiming the provisions of Article and paragraph _____ of the treaty identified on line 9 above to claim a ____ % rate of withholding on (specify type of income): _____.
Explain the additional conditions in the Article and paragraph the beneficial owner meets to be eligible for the rate of withholding: _____

Part III Certification

Under penalties of perjury, I declare that I have examined the information on this form and to the best of my knowledge and belief it is true, correct, and complete. I further certify under penalties of perjury that:

- I am the individual that is the beneficial owner (or am authorized to sign for the individual that is the beneficial owner) of all the income or proceeds to which this form relates or am using this form to document myself for chapter 4 purposes;
- The person named on line 1 of this form is not a U.S. person;
- This form relates to:
  (a) income not effectively connected with the conduct of a trade or business in the United States;
  (b) income effectively connected with the conduct of a trade or business in the United States but is not subject to tax under an applicable income tax treaty;
  (c) the partner's share of a partnership's effectively connected taxable income; or
  (d) the partner's amount realized from the transfer of a partnership interest subject to withholding under section 1446(f);
- The person named on line 1 of this form is a resident of the treaty country listed on line 9 of the form (if any) within the meaning of the income tax treaty between the United States and that country; and
- For broker transactions or barter exchanges, the beneficial owner is an exempt foreign person as defined in the instructions.

Furthermore, I authorize this form to be provided to any withholding agent that has control, receipt, or custody of the income of which I am the beneficial owner or any withholding agent that can disburse or make payments of the income of which I am the beneficial owner. **I agree that I will submit a new form within 30 days if any certification made on this form becomes incorrect.**

Sign Here ☐ I certify that I have the capacity to sign for the person identified on line 1 of this form.

_____
Signature of beneficial owner (or individual authorized to sign for beneficial owner)   Date (MM-DD-YYYY)

Print name of signer

For Paperwork Reduction Act Notice, see separate instructions.   Cat. No. 25047Z   Form **W-8BEN** (Rev. 10-2021)

Form **56**
(Rev. November 2022)
Department of the Treasury
Internal Revenue Service

Notice Concerning Fiduciary Relationship
(Internal Revenue Code Sections 6036 and 6903)
Go to *www.irs.gov/Form56* for instructions and the latest information.

OMB No. 1545-0013

Part I Identification

Name of person for whom you are acting (as shown on the tax return)	Identifying number	Decedent's social security no.

Address of person for whom you are acting (number, street, and room or suite no.)

City or town, state, and ZIP code (If a foreign address, see instructions.)

Fiduciary's name

Address of fiduciary (number, street, and room or suite no.)

City or town, state, and ZIP code	Telephone number (optional) ( )

Section A. Authority

1 Authority for fiduciary relationship. Check applicable box:
- a ☐ Court appointment of testate estate (valid will exists)
- b ☐ Court appointment of intestate estate (no valid will exists)
- c ☐ Court appointment as guardian or conservator
- d ☐ Fiduciary of intestate estate
- e ☐ Valid trust instrument and amendments
- f ☐ Bankruptcy or assignment for the benefit of creditors
- g ☐ Other. Describe: _____

2a If box 1a, 1b, or 1d is checked, enter the date of death: _____
  b If box 1c, 1e, 1f, or 1g is checked, enter the date of appointment, taking office, or assignment or transfer of assets: _____

Section B. Nature of Liability and Tax Notices

3 Type of taxes (check all that apply): ☐ Income ☐ Gift ☐ Estate ☐ Generation-skipping transfer ☐ Employment
  ☐ Excise ☐ Other (describe): _____

4 Federal tax form number (check all that apply): a ☐ 706 series b ☐ 709 c ☐ 940 d ☐ 941, 943, 944
  e ☐ 1040 or 1040-SR f ☐ 1041 g ☐ 1120 h ☐ Other (list): _____

5 If your authority as a fiduciary does not cover all years or tax periods, check here . . . . ☐
  and list the specific years or periods within your authority: _____

For Paperwork Reduction Act and Privacy Act Notice, see separate instructions.   Cat. No. 16375I   Form **56** (Rev. 11-2022)

Form 56 (Rev. 11-2022) Page **2**

Part II — Revocation or Termination of Notice

Section A—Total Revocation or Termination

6 Check this box if you are revoking or terminating all prior notices concerning fiduciary relationships on file with the Internal Revenue Service for the same tax matters and years or periods covered by this notice concerning fiduciary relationship . . ☐

Reason for termination of fiduciary relationship. Check applicable box:

a ☐ Court order revoking fiduciary authority
b ☐ Certificate of dissolution or termination of a business entity
c ☐ Other. Describe: _____

Section B—Partial Revocation

7a Check this box if you are revoking earlier notices concerning fiduciary relationships on file with the Internal Revenue Service for the same tax matters and years or periods covered by this notice concerning fiduciary relationship . . . . ☐

b Specify to whom granted, date, and address, including ZIP code.

Section C—Substitute Fiduciary

8 Check this box if a new fiduciary or fiduciaries have been or will be substituted for the revoking or terminating fiduciary and specify the name(s) and address(es), including ZIP code(s), of the new fiduciary(ies) . . . . ☐

Part III — Court and Administrative Proceedings

Name of court (if other than a court proceeding, identify the type of proceeding and name of agency)	Date proceeding initiated
Address of court	Docket number of proceeding
City or town, state, and ZIP code	Date	Time ☐ a.m. ☐ p.m.	Place of other proceedings

Part IV — Signature

Please Sign Here

Under penalties of perjury, I declare that I have examined this document, including any accompanying statements, and to the best of my knowledge and belief, it is true, correct, and complete.

_____ _____ _____
Fiduciary's signature   Title, if applicable   Date

Form **56** (Rev. 11-2022)

Instructions for UCC Financing Statement (Form UCC1)

Please type or print this form. Be sure it is completely legible. Forms with handwritten entries may be rejected. Read and follow all Instructions.

Fill in form very carefully; mistakes may have important legal consequences. If you have questions, consult your attorney. The filing office cannot give legal advice.

Unless specifically required by applicable state law, DO NOT include social security numbers, driver's license numbers, financial account numbers or other non-public personally identifiable information anywhere on the form.

Form instructions are intended for paper forms. Electronic UCC filing parameters and instructions may differ from the below instructions.

Send completed form and any attachments to the filing office, with the required fee.

ITEM INSTRUCTIONS

A and B. To assist filing offices that might wish to communicate with filer, filer may provide information in item A and item B. These items are optional.

C. Complete item C if filer desires an acknowledgment sent to them.

1. Debtor's name. Carefully review applicable statutory guidance about providing the debtor's name. Enter only one Debtor name in item 1 -- either an organization's name (1a) or an individual's name (1b). If any part of the Individual Debtor's name will not fit in line 1b, check the box in item 1, leave all of item 1 blank, check the box in item 9 of the Financing Statement Addendum (Form UCC1Ad) and enter the Individual Debtor name in item 10 of the Financing Statement Addendum (Form UCC1Ad). Enter Debtor's correct name. Do not abbreviate words that are not already abbreviated in the Debtor's name. If a portion of the Debtor's name consists of only an initial or an abbreviation rather than a full word, enter only the abbreviation or the initial. If the collateral is held in a trust and the Debtor name is the name of the trust, enter trust name in the Organization's Name box in item 1a.

1a. Organization Debtor Name. "Organization Name" means the name of an entity that is not a natural person. A sole proprietorship is not an organization, even if the individual proprietor does business under a trade name. If Debtor is a registered organization (e.g., corporation, limited partnership, limited liability company), it is advisable to examine Debtor's current filed public organic records to determine Debtor's correct name. Trade name is insufficient. If a corporate ending (e.g., corporation, limited partnership, limited liability company) is part of the Debtor's name, it must be included. Do not use words that are not part of the Debtor's name.

1b. Individual Debtor Name. "Individual Name" means the name of a natural person; this includes the name of an individual doing business as a sole proprietorship, whether or not operating under a trade name. The term includes the name of a decedent where collateral is being administered by a personal representative of the decedent. The term does not include the name of an entity, even if it contains, as part of the entity's name, the name of an individual. Prefixes (e.g., Mr., Mrs., Ms.) and titles (e.g., M.D.) are generally not part of an individual name. Indications of lineage (e.g., Jr., Sr., III) generally are not part of the individual's name, but may be entered in the Suffix box. Enter individual Debtor's surname (family name) in Individual's Surname box, first personal name in First Personal Name box, and all additional names in Additional Name(s)/Initial(s) box.
If a Debtor's name consists of only a single word, enter that word in Individual's Surname box and leave other boxes blank.

For both organization and individual Debtors. Do not use Debtor's trade name, DBA, AKA, FKA, division name, etc. in place of or combined with Debtor's correct name; filer may add such other names as additional Debtors if desired (but this is neither required nor recommended).

For both organization and individual Debtors. Name variations may be optionally provided as additional debtors. Do not combine multiple names in one section. Provide each name variation and address as described in the instructions for item 2 below.

1c. Enter a mailing address for the Debtor named in item 1a or 1b.

2. Additional Debtor's name. If an additional Debtor is included, complete item 2, determined and formatted per Instruction 1. For additional Debtors, attach either Addendum (Form UCC1Ad) or Additional Party (Form UCC1AP) and follow Instruction 1 for determining and formatting additional names.

3. Secured Party's name. Enter name and mailing address for Secured Party or full Assignee who will be the Secured Party of record. For additional Secured Parties, attach either Addendum (Form UCC1Ad) or Additional Party (Form UCC1AP). Optional: Attach Addendum (Form UCC1Ad) giving Assignor Secured Party's name and mailing address in item 11.

4. Collateral. Use item 4 to indicate the collateral covered by this financing statement. If space in item 4 is insufficient, continue the collateral description in item 12 of the Addendum (Form UCC1Ad) or attach additional page(s) and incorporate by reference in item 12 (e.g., See Exhibit A).

Note: If this financing statement covers timber to be cut, covers as-extracted collateral, and/or is filed as a fixture filing, attach Addendum (Form UCC1Ad) and complete the required information in items 13, 14, 15, and 16. Consult applicable state UCC law for filing location.

5. If collateral is held in a trust or being administered by a decedent's personal representative, check the appropriate box in item 5. If more than one Debtor has an interest in the described collateral and the check box does not apply to the interest of all Debtors, the filer should consider filing a separate Financing Statement (Form UCC1) for each Debtor.

6a. If this financing statement relates to a Public-Finance Transaction, Manufactured-Home Transaction, or a Debtor is a Transmitting Utility, check the appropriate box in item 6a. If a Debtor is a Transmitting Utility and the initial financing statement is filed in connection with a Public-Finance Transaction or Manufactured-Home Transaction, check only that a Debtor is a Transmitting Utility.

6b. If this is an Agricultural Lien (as defined in applicable state's enactment of the Uniform Commercial Code) or if this is not a UCC security interest filing (e.g., a tax lien, judgment lien, etc.), check the appropriate box in item 6b and attach any other items required under applicable law.

7. Alternative Designation. If filer desires (at filer's option) to use the designations lessee and lessor, consignee and consignor, seller and buyer (such as in the case of the sale of a payment intangible, promissory note, account or chattel paper), bailee and bailor, or licensee and licensor instead of Debtor and Secured Party, check the appropriate box in item 7.

8. Optional Filer Reference Data. This item is optional and is for filer's use only to provide reference information the filer may find useful.

UCC FINANCING STATEMENT
FOLLOW INSTRUCTIONS

A. NAME & PHONE OF CONTACT AT SUBMITTER (optional)

B. E-MAIL CONTACT AT SUBMITTER (optional)

C. SEND ACKNOWLEDGMENT TO: (Name and Address)

SEE BELOW FOR SECURED PARTY CONTACT INFORMATION

THE ABOVE SPACE IS FOR FILING OFFICE USE ONLY

1. DEBTOR'S NAME: Provide only one Debtor name (1a or 1b) (use exact, full name; do not omit, modify, or abbreviate any part of the Debtor's name); if any part of the Individual Debtor's name will not fit in line 1b, leave all of item 1 blank, check here ☐ and provide the Individual Debtor information in item 10 of the Financing Statement Addendum (Form UCC1Ad)

1a. ORGANIZATION'S NAME				
1b. INDIVIDUAL'S SURNAME	FIRST PERSONAL NAME	ADDITIONAL NAME(S)/INITIAL(S)		SUFFIX
1c. MAILING ADDRESS	CITY	STATE	POSTAL CODE	COUNTRY

2. DEBTOR'S NAME: Provide only one Debtor name (2a or 2b) (use exact, full name; do not omit, modify, or abbreviate any part of the Debtor's name); if any part of the Individual Debtor's name will not fit in line 2b, leave all of item 2 blank, check here ☐ and provide the Individual Debtor information in item 10 of the Financing Statement Addendum (Form UCC1Ad)

2a. ORGANIZATION'S NAME				
2b. INDIVIDUAL'S SURNAME	FIRST PERSONAL NAME	ADDITIONAL NAME(S)/INITIAL(S)		SUFFIX
2c. MAILING ADDRESS	CITY	STATE	POSTAL CODE	COUNTRY

3. SECURED PARTY'S NAME (or NAME of ASSIGNEE of ASSIGNOR SECURED PARTY): Provide only one Secured Party name (3a or 3b)

3a. ORGANIZATION'S NAME				
3b. INDIVIDUAL'S SURNAME	FIRST PERSONAL NAME	ADDITIONAL NAME(S)/INITIAL(S)		SUFFIX
3c. MAILING ADDRESS	CITY	STATE	POSTAL CODE	COUNTRY

4. COLLATERAL: This financing statement covers the following collateral:

5. Check only if applicable and check only one box: Collateral is ☐ held in a Trust (see UCC1Ad, item 17 and Instructions) ☐ being administered by a Decedent's Personal Representative

6a. Check only if applicable and check only one box:
☐ Public-Finance Transaction ☐ Manufactured-Home Transaction ☐ A Debtor is a Transmitting Utility

6b. Check only if applicable and check only one box:
☐ Agricultural Lien ☐ Non-UCC Filing

7. ALTERNATIVE DESIGNATION (if applicable): ☐ Lessee/Lessor ☐ Consignee/Consignor ☐ Seller/Buyer ☐ Bailee/Bailor ☐ Licensee/Licensor

8. OPTIONAL FILER REFERENCE DATA:

FILING OFFICE COPY — UCC FINANCING STATEMENT (Form UCC1) (Rev. 07/01/23)

Instructions for UCC Financing Statement Addendum (Form UCC1Ad)

Please type or laser-print this form. Be sure it is completely legible. Read and follow all Instructions; use of the correct name for the Debtor is crucial. Fill in form very carefully; mistakes may have important legal consequences. If you have questions, consult your attorney. The filing office cannot give legal advice.

ITEM INSTRUCTIONS

9. **Name of first Debtor.** Enter name of first Debtor exactly as shown in item 1 of Financing Statement (Form UCC1) to which this Addendum relates. The name will not be indexed as a separate debtor. The Debtor name in this section is intended to cross-reference this Addendum with the related Financing Statement (Form UCC1).

   If the box in item 1 of the Financing Statement (Form UCC1) was checked because Individual Debtor name did not fit, the box in item 9 of this Addendum should be checked.

10. **Additional Debtor's name.** If this Addendum adds an additional Debtor, complete item 10 in accordance with Instruction 1 of Financing Statement (Form UCC1). For additional Debtors, attach either an additional Addendum or Additional Party (Form UCC1AP) and follow Instruction 1 of Financing Statement (Form UCC1) for determining and formatting additional names.

11. **Additional Secured Party's name or Assignor Secured Party's name.** If this Addendum adds an additional Secured Party, complete item 11 in accordance with Instruction 3 of Financing Statement (Form UCC1). For additional Secured Parties, attach either an additional Addendum or Additional Party (Form UCC1AP) and complete applicable items in accordance with Instruction 3 of Financing Statement (Form UCC1). In the case of a full assignment of the Secured Party's interest before the filing of this financing statement, if filer has provided the name and mailing address of the Assignee in item 3 of Financing Statement (Form UCC1), filer may enter Assignor Secured Party's name and mailing address in item 11.

12. **Additional Collateral Description.** If space in item 4 of Financing Statement (Form UCC1) is insufficient or additional information must be provided, enter additional information in item 12 or attach additional page(s) and incorporate by reference in item 12 (e.g., See Exhibit A). Do not include social security numbers or other personally identifiable information.

13-16. **Real Estate Record Information.** If this Financing Statement is to be filed in the real estate records and covers timber to be cut, covers as-extracted collateral, and/or is filed as a fixture filing, complete items 1-4 of the Financing Statement (Form UCC1), check the box in item 13, check the appropriate box in item 14, and complete the required information in items 15 and 16. If the Debtor does not have an interest of record, enter the name and address of the record owner in item 15. Provide a sufficient description of real estate in accordance with the applicable law of the jurisdiction where the real estate is located in item 16. If space in items 15 or 16 is insufficient, attach additional page(s) and incorporate by reference in items 15 or 16 (e.g., See Exhibit A), and continue the real estate record information. Do not include social security numbers or other personally identifiable information.

17. **Miscellaneous.** Under certain circumstances, additional information not provided on the Financing Statement (Form UCC1) may be required. Also, some states have non-uniform requirements. Use this space or attach additional page(s) and incorporate by reference in item 17 (e.g., See Exhibit A) to provide such additional information or to comply with such requirements; otherwise, leave blank. Do not include social security numbers or other personally identifiable information.

UCC FINANCING STATEMENT ADDENDUM
FOLLOW INSTRUCTIONS

9. NAME OF FIRST DEBTOR: Same as line 1a or 1b on Financing Statement; if line 1b was left blank because Individual Debtor name did not fit, check here ☐

9a. ORGANIZATION'S NAME

OR

9b. INDIVIDUAL'S SURNAME

FIRST PERSONAL NAME

ADDITIONAL NAME(S)/INITIAL(S) | SUFFIX

THE ABOVE SPACE IS FOR FILING OFFICE USE ONLY

10. DEBTOR'S NAME: Provide (10a or 10b) only one additional Debtor name or Debtor name that did not fit in line 1b or 2b of the Financing Statement (Form UCC1) (use exact, full name; do not omit, modify, or abbreviate any part of the Debtor's name) and enter the mailing address in line 10c

10a. ORGANIZATION'S NAME

OR

10b. INDIVIDUAL'S SURNAME

INDIVIDUAL'S FIRST PERSONAL NAME

INDIVIDUAL'S ADDITIONAL NAME(S)/INITIAL(S) | SUFFIX

10c. MAILING ADDRESS | CITY | STATE | POSTAL CODE | COUNTRY

11. ☐ ADDITIONAL SECURED PARTY'S NAME or ☐ ASSIGNOR SECURED PARTY'S NAME: Provide only one name (11a or 11b)

11a. ORGANIZATION'S NAME

OR

11b. INDIVIDUAL'S SURNAME | FIRST PERSONAL NAME | ADDITIONAL NAME(S)/INITIAL(S) | SUFFIX

11c. MAILING ADDRESS | CITY | STATE | POSTAL CODE | COUNTRY

12. ADDITIONAL SPACE FOR ITEM 4 (Collateral):

13. ☐ This FINANCING STATEMENT is to be filed [for record] (or recorded) in the REAL ESTATE RECORDS (if applicable)

14. This FINANCING STATEMENT: ☐ covers timber to be cut ☐ covers as-extracted collateral ☐ is filed as a fixture filing

15. Name and address of a RECORD OWNER of real estate described in item 16 (if Debtor does not have a record interest):

16. Description of real estate:

17. MISCELLANEOUS:

FILING OFFICE COPY — UCC FINANCING STATEMENT ADDENDUM (Form UCC1Ad) (Rev. 07/01/23)

SAMPLE IRREVOCABLE TRUST

DECLARATION OF TRUST

DECLARATION OF TRUST, made as of this _____ day of _____, 20__, among _____, having an address at _____, as grantor (hereinafter referred to as the "Grantor"), and _____, having an address at _____, and _____, having an address at _____, as trustees (collectively hereinafter referred to as the "Trustees").

W I T N E S S E T H:

WHEREAS, the Grantor is the owner of the property more particularly described in Schedule A attached hereto and made a part hereof; and

WHEREAS, the Grantor's [husband/wife] has predeceased the Grantor, and the Grantor has two children, _____ and _____; and

WHEREAS, the Grantor desires to create an irrevocable trust of the property described in Schedule A hereto, together with such monies, securities and other assets as the Trustees hereafter may hold or acquire hereunder (said property, monies, securities and other assets, together with any additions thereto received pursuant to the Grantor's last will and testament or otherwise, being hereinafter referred to as the "trust estate"), for the purposes and upon the terms and conditions hereinafter set forth.

NOW, THEREFORE, in consideration of the covenants herein contained and other valuable consideration, the receipt and sufficiency of which hereby are acknowledged, the Grantor hereby irrevocably transfers, conveys, assigns and delivers to the Trustees as and for the trust estate the property more particularly described in Schedule A hereto, to hold the same, and any other property which the Trustees hereafter may acquire, **IN TRUST**, for the purposes and upon the terms and conditions hereinafter set forth:

FIRST: The Trustees shall hold, manage, invest and reinvest the trust estate, shall collect the income therefrom, and shall pay the net income to or for the benefit of the Grantor, in convenient installments but at least quarter-annually, during the life of the Grantor.

The Trustee shall have no right to invade principal of the Trust Estate for the benefit of the Grantor. The Grantor directs that the provisions of section 7-1.6 of the Estates, Powers and Trusts Law of the State of New York shall not be available to require any invasion of principal by the Trustee or any Court.

In the event that this Trust holds residential real property used by the Grantor, then Grantor shall have the exclusive right to occupy and use such real property and shall not be required to pay rent for the use of such property.

SECOND: Upon the death of the Grantor, the Trustees shall pay and distribute the trust estate at that time remaining to the Grantor's then living issue, in equal shares, per stirpes, discharged of trust. If there are no issue of the Grantor then living, the trust estate shall be paid and distributed to such persons and in such proportions as the same would be distributed under the laws of the State of New York then in force had the Grantor then died intestate, a resident of New York and the owner of said property.

THIRD: In any case in which the Trustees are authorized or directed by any provision of this Agreement to pay or distribute income or principal to any person who shall be a minor or incompetent, the Trustees, in their absolute discretion and without authorization of any court, may pay or distribute the whole or any part of such income or principal to such minor or incompetent personally, or may apply the whole or any part thereof directly to the health, education, maintenance or support of such minor or incompetent, or may pay or distribute the whole or any part thereof to the guardian, committee, conservator or other legal representative, wherever appointed, of such minor or incompetent or to the person with whom such minor or incompetent may from time to time reside, or in the case of a minor, may pay or distribute the whole or any part thereof to a custodian for such minor under any gifts to minors or transfers to minors act. Evidence of such payment or distribution or the receipt therefor by the person to whom any such payment or distribution is made shall be a full discharge of the Trustees from all liability with respect thereto, even though the Trustees may be such person.

The Trustees, in their absolute discretion, may defer payment or distribution of any or all income or principal to which a minor may be entitled until such minor shall attain the age of twenty-one (21) years, or to make such payment or distribution at any time and from time to time, during the minority of such minor, holding the whole or the undistributed portion thereof as a separate fund vested in such minor but subject to the power in trust hereby given to the Trustees to administer and invest such fund and to use the income or principal thereof for the benefit of such minor as if such fund were held in trust hereunder. The Trustees shall pay and distribute any balance of such fund to such minor when such minor shall attain the age of twenty-one (21) years. Except as is herein above provided, if such minor shall die before attaining the age of twenty-one (21) years, the Trustees shall pay and distribute such balance to the executors, administrators or legal representatives of the estate of such minor.

The word "minor", wherever used in this Article THIRD, shall mean any person who has not attained the age of twenty-one (21) years.

FOURTH: This Agreement and the trusts created hereunder are irrevocable. The Grantor shall execute such further instruments as shall be necessary to vest the Trustees with full title to the property which is the subject of this Agreement.

FIFTH: In the administration of any property, real or personal, at any time forming a part of the trust estate, including accumulated income, and in the administration of any trust created hereunder, the Trustees, in addition to and without limitation of the powers conferred on trustees under the New York Estates, Powers and Trusts Law, as amended or any successor thereto, or otherwise provided by law, shall have the following powers to be exercised in the absolute discretion of the Trustees, except as otherwise expressly provided in this Agreement:

(a) To retain such property for any period, whether or not the same is of the character permissible for investments by fiduciaries under any applicable law, and without regard to the effect any such retention may have upon the diversity of investments;

(b) To sell, transfer, exchange, convert or otherwise dispose of, or grant options with respect to, such property, at public or private sale, with or without security, in such manner, at such times, for such prices, and upon such terms and conditions as the Trustees may deem advisable;

(c) To invest and reinvest in common or preferred stocks, securities, limited liability companies, investment trusts, mutual funds, regulated investment companies, bonds and other property, real or personal, foreign or domestic, including any undivided interest in any one or more common trust funds, whether or not such investments be of the character permissible for investments by fiduciaries under any applicable law, and without regard to the effect any such investment may have upon the diversity of investments;

(d) To render liquid the trust estate or any trust created hereunder in whole or in part, at any time and from time to time, and to hold unproductive property, cash or readily marketable securities of little or no yield for such period as the Trustees may deem advisable;

(e) To lease any such property beyond the period fixed by statute for leases made by fiduciaries and beyond the duration of any trust created hereunder;

(f) To join or become a party to, or to oppose, any reorganization, readjustment, recapitalization, foreclosure, merger, voting trust, dissolution, consolidation or exchange, and to deposit any securities with any committee, depository or trustee, and to pay any fees, expenses and assessments incurred in connection therewith, and to charge the same to principal, and to exercise conversion, subscription or other rights, and to make any necessary payments in connection therewith, or to sell any such privileges;

(g) To form one or more corporations or limited liability companies, alone or with any person, in any jurisdiction, and to transfer assets to any new or existing corporation or limited liability company in exchange for stock or membership interests; to form one or more partnerships with any person in any jurisdiction, to have any trust or a nominee be a general or limited partner, and to transfer assets to any new or existing partnership as a capital contribution; to enter into one or more joint ventures or associations with any person in any jurisdiction, and to commit assets to the purposes of those ventures or associations; and to retain as an investment for any period any securities, partnership interests or other assets resulting from any such actions;

(h) To vote in person at meetings of stock or security holders and adjournments thereof, and to vote by general or limited proxy with respect to any stock or securities;

(i) To hold stock and securities in the name of a nominee without indicating the trust character of such holding, or unregistered or in such form as will pass by delivery, or to use a central depository and to permit registration in the name of a nominee;

(j) To initiate or defend, at the expense of the trust estate, any litigation relating to this Agreement or any property of the trust estate which the Trustees consider advisable, and to pay, compromise, compound, adjust, submit to arbitration, sell or release any claims or demands of the trust estate or any trust created hereunder against others or of others against the same as the Trustees may deem advisable, including the acceptance of deeds of real property in satisfaction of notes, bonds and mortgages, and to make any payments in connection therewith which the Trustees may deem advisable;

(k) To carry insurance of the kinds and in the amounts which the Trustees consider advisable, at the expense of the trust estate, to protect the trust estate and the Trustees personally against any hazard;

(l) To make distribution of the trust estate or of the principal of any trust created hereunder in cash or in kind, or partly in kind, and to cause any distribution to be composed of cash, property or undivided fractional shares in property different in kind from any other distribution; to hold the principal of separate trusts in a consolidated fund and to invest the same as a single fund; and to merge any trusts which have substantially identical terms and beneficiaries, and to hold them as a single trust;

(m) To employ and pay the compensation of accountants, attorneys, experts, investment counselors, custodians, agents and other persons or firms providing services or advice, irrespective of whether the Trustees may be associated therewith; to delegate discretionary powers to such persons or firms; and to rely upon information or advice furnished thereby or to ignore the same, as the Trustees in their discretion may determine;

(n) To execute and deliver any and all instruments or writings which it may deem advisable to carry out any of the foregoing powers; and

Notwithstanding anything to the contrary contained herein, during such time as any current or possible future beneficiary of any trust created hereunder may be acting as a Trustee hereunder, such person shall be disqualified from exercising any power to make any discretionary distributions of income or principal to himself or herself or to satisfy any of his or her legal obligations, or to make discretionary allocations of receipts or disbursements as between income and principal. All such powers shall be exercisable, if at all, only by any other Trustee acting at the time with such beneficiary. No Trustee who is a current or possible future beneficiary of any trust hereunder shall participate in the exercise of any powers of the Trustees which would cause such beneficiary to be treated as the owner of trust assets for tax purposes.

SIXTH: The Grantor hereby appoints _____ and _____ as joint Trustees hereunder.

If either of the Trustees for any reason shall fail or cease to act as Trustee, the other Trustee, at any time after qualifying to act as Trustee, shall have the right to serve as sole Trustee hereunder, without appointment of a successor co-Trustee.

The term "Trustees" wherever used herein shall mean the trustee or trustees in office from time to time. Any such trustee shall have the same rights, powers, duties, authority and privileges, whether or not discretionary, as if originally appointed hereunder.

No bond, surety or other security shall be required of any Trustee acting hereunder for the faithful performance of the duties of Trustee, notwithstanding any law of any State or other jurisdiction to the contrary.

SEVENTH: The Trustees, at any time and from time to time, may render an account to the living person or persons who are entitled, at the time of such account, to receive all or a portion of the income of the trusts herein created.

The Trustees shall not be required at any time to file any account in any court, nor shall the Trustees be required to have any account judicially settled. Nothing herein, however, shall be construed as limiting the right of the Trustees to seek a judicial settlement of any account.

EIGHTH: The determination of the Trustees in respect of the amount of any discretionary payment of income or principal from any trust established hereunder, and of the advisability thereof, shall be final and conclusive on all persons, whether or not then in being, having or claiming any interest in such trust, and upon making any such payment, the Trustees shall be released fully from all further liability or accountability therefor.

NINTH: For purposes of this Agreement, any beneficiary hereunder shall be deemed to have predeceased any other person upon whose death such beneficiary shall become entitled to receive income or principal unless such beneficiary shall survive such other person by more than thirty days. The provisions of this Agreement shall be construed as aforesaid, notwithstanding the provisions of any applicable law establishing a different presumption of order of death or providing for survivorship for a fixed period as a condition of inheritance of property.

TENTH: No disposition, charge or encumbrance on the income or principal of any trust established hereunder shall be valid or binding upon the Trustees. No beneficiary shall have any right, power or authority to assign, transfer, encumber or otherwise dispose of such income or principal or any part thereof until the same shall be paid to such beneficiary by the Trustees. No income or principal shall be subject in any manner to any claim of any creditor of any beneficiary or liable to attachment, execution or other process of law prior to its actual receipt by the beneficiary.

ELEVENTH: The validity and construction of this Agreement and the trusts created hereunder shall be governed by the laws of the State of New York.

The words "child" and "children", wherever used in this Agreement, shall include not only the child and children of the person or persons designated, but also the legally adopted child and children of such person or persons, at the time in question. The word "issue", wherever used in this Agreement, shall include not only the child, children and issue of the person or persons designated, but also the legally adopted child and children of such person or persons and the child, children or issue thereof, at the time in question.

Any provision herein which refers to a statute, rule, regulation or other specific legal reference which is no longer in effect at the time said provision is to be applied shall be deemed to refer to the successor, replacement or amendment to such statute, rule, regulation or other reference, if any, and shall be interpreted in such a manner so as to carry out the original intent of said provision.

Wherever used in this Agreement and the context so requires, the masculine shall include the feminine and the singular shall include the plural, and vice versa.

If under any of the provisions of this Agreement any portion of the trust estate would be held in trust beyond a date twenty-one years after the death of the last survivor of the Grantor and the issue of the Grantor and other beneficiaries hereunder now in being, or such later date permitted by the rule against perpetuities applicable in the State of New York; then, upon such date, the trust of such portion shall terminate and the principal, and any unpaid income thereof, shall be paid and distributed to the person or persons then living who would have been entitled to receive the income therefrom had the trust continued, in the proportions to which they would have been so entitled.

TWELFTH: This Agreement shall extend to and be binding upon the heirs, executors, administrators, successors and assigns of the undersigned Grantor and upon the Trustees acting hereunder.

THIRTEENTH: This Agreement and the trusts created hereunder may be referred to, in any other instrument, by the name: "_____ Irrevocable Living Trust dated _____, 20__." Any transfers to this Agreement or any trust hereunder may refer to the aforesaid name or to "_____ and _____ as Trustees under _____ Irrevocable Living Trust dated _____, 20__," with or without specifying any change in Trustees.

IN WITNESS WHEREOF, this Agreement has been duly executed as of the date first above written.

_____
[Name of Grantor]
Grantor

_____
[Name of Trustee]
Trustee

_____
[Name of Trustee]
Trustee

STATE OF NEW YORK)
) ss.:
COUNTY OF _____)

     On the _____ day of _____, 20__, before me, the undersigned, personally appeared _____, personally known to me or proved to me on the basis of satisfactory evidence to be the individual whose name is subscribed to the within instrument and acknowledged to me that [he/she] executed the same in [his/her] capacity, and that by [his/her] signature on the instrument, the individual, or the person upon behalf of which the individual acted, executed the instrument.

                                                 _____
                                                 Notary Public

STATE OF NEW YORK)
) ss.:
COUNTY OF _____)

     On the _____ day of _____, 20__, before me, the undersigned, personally appeared _____, personally known to me or proved to me on the basis of satisfactory evidence to be the individual whose name is subscribed to the within instrument and acknowledged to me that [he/she] executed the same in [his/her] capacity, and that by [his/her] signature on the instrument, the individual, or the person upon behalf of which the individual acted, executed the instrument.

                                                 _____
                                                 Notary Public

STATE OF NEW YORK)
) ss.:
COUNTY OF _____)

     On the _____ day of _____, 20__, before me, the undersigned, personally appeared _____, personally known to me or proved to me on the basis of satisfactory evidence to be the individual whose name is subscribed to the within instrument and acknowledged to me that [he/she] executed the same in [his/her] capacity, and that by [his/her] signature on the instrument, the individual, or the person upon behalf of which the individual acted, executed the instrument.

                                                 _____
                                                 Notary Public

SCHEDULE A

TRUST ESTATE PROPERTY

MEMORANDUM OF TRUST

KNOW THAT, _____, having an address at _____, as Grantor, created an irrevocable trust, known as the _____ Irrevocable Living Trust dated _____, 20__, by executing a Declaration of Trust, dated _____, 20__, naming _____, having an address at _____, and _____, having an address at _____, as trustees (collectively referred to as the "Trustees").

This Memorandum of Trust is executed as evidence of the existence of the foregoing Declaration of Trust. Any person may rely upon this Memorandum of Trust as evidence of the existence of said Declaration of Trust, and is relieved of any obligation to verify that any transaction entered into by a Trustee thereunder is consistent with the terms and conditions of said Declaration of Trust.

The Declaration of Trust and the trusts created thereunder may be referred to by the name: "_____ Irrevocable Living Trust dated _____, 20__". Any transfers to the Declaration of Trust or any trust thereunder may refer to the aforesaid name or to "_____ and _____ as Trustees under _____ Irrevocable Living Trust dated _____, 20__", with or without specifying any change in Trustees.

IN WITNESS WHEREOF, the Grantor has executed this Memorandum of Trust as of this _____ day of _____, 20__.

_____
[Name of Grantor]
Grantor

STATE OF NEW YORK   )
) ss.:
COUNTY OF _____)

On the _____ day of _____, 20__, before me, the undersigned, personally appeared _____, personally known to me or proved to me on the basis of satisfactory evidence to be the individual whose name is subscribed to the within instrument and acknowledged to me that [he/she] executed the same in [his/her] capacity, and that by [his/her] signature on the instrument, the individual, or the person upon behalf of which the individual acted, executed the instrument.

_____
Notary Public

SCHEDULE A	Itemized Deductions	OMB No. 1545-0074
(Form 1040)	Attach to Form 1040 or 1040-SR.	2023
Department of the Treasury Internal Revenue Service	Go to *www.irs.gov/ScheduleA* for instructions and the latest information. **Caution:** If you are claiming a net qualified disaster loss on Form 4684, see the instructions for line 16.	Attachment Sequence No. **07**

Name(s) shown on Form 1040 or 1040-SR | Your social security number

Medical and Dental Expenses		**Caution:** Do not include expenses reimbursed or paid by others.	
	1	Medical and dental expenses (see instructions)	1
	2	Enter amount from Form 1040 or 1040-SR, line 11	2
	3	Multiply line 2 by 7.5% (0.075)	3
	4	Subtract line 3 from line 1. If line 3 is more than line 1, enter -0-		4
Taxes You Paid	5	State and local taxes.	
		a State and local income taxes or general sales taxes. You may include either income taxes or general sales taxes on line 5a, but not both. If you elect to include general sales taxes instead of income taxes, check this box . . . . ☐	5a
		b State and local real estate taxes (see instructions)	5b
		c State and local personal property taxes	5c
		d Add lines 5a through 5c	5d
		e Enter the smaller of line 5d or $10,000 ($5,000 if married filing separately)	5e
	6	Other taxes. List type and amount: _____	6
	7	Add lines 5e and 6		7
Interest You Paid	8	Home mortgage interest and points. If you didn't use all of your home mortgage loan(s) to buy, build, or improve your home, see instructions and check this box . . . . ☐	
Caution: Your mortgage interest deduction may be limited. See instructions.		**a** Home mortgage interest and points reported to you on Form 1098. See instructions if limited	8a
		b Home mortgage interest not reported to you on Form 1098. See instructions if limited. If paid to the person from whom you bought the home, see instructions and show that person's name, identifying no., and address	8b
		_____ _____	
		c Points not reported to you on Form 1098. See instructions for special rules	8c
		d Reserved for future use	8d
		e Add lines 8a through 8c	8e
	9	Investment interest. Attach Form 4952 if required. See instructions	9
	10	Add lines 8e and 9		10
Gifts to Charity	11	Gifts by cash or check. If you made any gift of $250 or more, see instructions	11
Caution: If you made a gift and got a benefit for it, see instructions.	12	Other than by cash or check. If you made any gift of $250 or more, see instructions. You **must** attach Form 8283 if over $500 . . .	12
	13	Carryover from prior year	13
	14	Add lines 11 through 13		14
Casualty and Theft Losses	15	Casualty and theft loss(es) from a federally declared disaster (other than net qualified disaster losses). Attach Form 4684 and enter the amount from line 18 of that form. See instructions		15
Other Itemized Deductions	16	Other—from list in instructions. List type and amount: _____ _____		16
Total Itemized Deductions	17	Add the amounts in the far right column for lines 4 through 16. Also, enter this amount on Form 1040 or 1040-SR, line 12		17
	18	If you elect to itemize deductions even though they are less than your standard deduction, check this box . . . . ☐		

For Paperwork Reduction Act Notice, see the Instructions for Form 1040.   Cat. No. 17145C   Schedule A (Form 1040) 2023

Understanding Schedule A (Form 1040) or (Form 1040-NR) and Its Application in the SPC Rebirth Process

Schedule A (Form 1040) is an IRS form used by taxpayers in the United States to report itemized deductions. This form allows individuals to deduct certain expenses from their taxable income, potentially reducing the amount of tax owed.

Purpose of Schedule A (Form 1040)

1. Itemized Deductions:

   - Medical and Dental Expenses: Deductible to the extent that they exceed 7.5% of adjusted gross income (AGI).

   - Taxes Paid: Includes state and local income taxes, real estate taxes, and personal property taxes.

   - Interest Paid: Deductible mortgage interest and investment interest.

   - Charitable Contributions: Cash and non-cash contributions to qualified organizations.

   - Casualty and Theft Losses: Losses from federally declared disasters.

   - Other Itemized Deductions: Miscellaneous deductions such as unreimbursed employee expenses and tax preparation fees.

2. Reducing Tax Liability:

   - Itemizing deductions on Schedule A can reduce taxable income more than the standard deduction, leading to lower overall tax liability for some taxpayers.

Using Schedule A in the SPC Rebirth Process

In the context of the Secured Party Creditor (SPC) rebirth process, Schedule A can be used to demonstrate financial responsibility and transparency. Here's how:

Step-by-Step Guide:

1. Gather Documentation:

   - Collect receipts, statements, and other documentation for all deductible expenses you plan to itemize.

2. Download Schedule A:

   - Obtain the form from the IRS website [here](https://www.irs.gov/forms-pubs/about-schedule-a-form-1040).

3. Complete the Form:

   - Medical and Dental Expenses: Enter total unreimbursed medical and dental expenses.

   - Taxes Paid: Report state and local income taxes, real estate taxes, and personal property taxes.

   - Interest Paid: Include mortgage interest and investment interest.

   - Charitable Contributions: Record cash and non-cash contributions to qualifying charities.

   - Casualty and Theft Losses: Detail any losses from federally declared disasters.

   - Other Itemized Deductions: Include any additional deductions.

4. File with Form 1040:

   - Attach Schedule A to your Form 1040 when filing your tax return.

Application for Criminal Charge in SPC Rebirth Process

Using Schedule A in the context of a criminal charge or legal defense can help in several ways:

1. Financial Transparency:

   - Demonstrating detailed financial records can show good faith and transparency, which may be beneficial in legal proceedings.

2. Establishing Financial Stability:

   - Itemized deductions can illustrate financial stability and responsibility, potentially influencing court perceptions.

3. Supporting Legal Arguments:

   - Detailed financial records from Schedule A can be used to support legal arguments related to financial dealings, fraud allegations, or other criminal charges.

Effective Outcomes:

1. Reduced Tax Liability:

   - Properly itemizing deductions can lower tax liability, demonstrating financial prudence.

2. Enhanced Credibility:

   - Accurate and transparent financial reporting can enhance your credibility in court.

3. Documentation of Financial Responsibility:

   - Providing thorough financial documentation can support claims of financial responsibility and integrity, which can be critical in the SPC rebirth process and related legal matters.

Practical Steps:

1. Accurate Record-Keeping:
   - Maintain meticulous records of all deductible expenses.
2. Consistent Reporting:
   - Ensure that all financial reports, including Schedule A, are consistent and accurate.
3. Legal Consultation:
   - Consult with a tax professional or legal advisor to ensure proper use of Schedule A in your specific legal context.

By understanding and utilizing Schedule A effectively, individuals in the SPC rebirth process can enhance their financial transparency and support their legal strategies. This approach underscores the importance of detailed financial documentation in achieving legal and financial sovereignty.

Use of Schedule A (Form 1040) by Non-Citizen Nationals and Foreign Nationals

***Schedule A (Form 1040) is primarily designed for U.S. taxpayers to report itemized deductions. This includes U.S. citizens, resident aliens, and in some cases, non-citizen nationals and foreign nationals who meet certain conditions.**

Use by Non-Citizen Nationals and Foreign Nationals

1. Resident Aliens:

   - Eligibility: Resident aliens (non-citizens who meet the substantial presence test or have a green card) are generally required to file a U.S. tax return using Form 1040. They can itemize deductions using Schedule A just like U.S. citizens.

   - Reporting Requirements: They must report worldwide income and can claim the same deductions as U.S. citizens.

2. Nonresident Aliens:

   - Eligibility: Nonresident aliens (foreign nationals who do not meet the substantial presence test or do not have a green card) typically file U.S. taxes using Form 1040-NR.

   - Limitations: Nonresident aliens have different rules and may not be eligible to use Schedule A. Instead, they can claim specific deductions directly on Form 1040-NR, subject to treaty benefits and other conditions.

   - Exceptions: Certain nonresident aliens who elect to be treated as resident aliens for tax purposes (e.g., through a treaty or special elections) might use Form 1040 and Schedule A.

3. Non-Citizen Nationals:

   - Eligibility: Non-citizen nationals (e.g., individuals born in American Samoa or on Swains Island) who are treated as U.S. nationals for tax purposes generally use Form 1040 and can itemize deductions using Schedule A.

   - Reporting Requirements: They report income and deductions similarly to U.S. citizens and resident aliens.

Specific Applications:

1. Tax Treaties:

   - Foreign Nationals: Individuals from countries with tax treaties with the U.S. may have specific provisions that allow them to benefit from certain deductions or exclusions. These treaties can affect whether and how Schedule A is used.

2. Dual Status Aliens:

   - Part-Year Residents: Individuals who are part-year residents (dual status aliens) may need to file both Form 1040 and Form 1040-NR. For the part of the year they are resident aliens, they can use Schedule A for itemized deductions.

Practical Steps for Foreign Nationals and Non-Citizen Nationals:

1. Determine Residency Status:

   - Use the substantial presence test or green card test to determine if you are a resident alien or nonresident alien.

2. Review Tax Treaty Benefits:

   - Check if your home country has a tax treaty with the U.S. that affects your eligibility to use Schedule A.

3. Accurate Documentation:

   - Keep thorough records of all deductible expenses, whether you are itemizing on Schedule A or claiming specific deductions on Form 1040-NR.

4. Consult a Tax Professional:

   - Given the complexity of international tax law, consulting a tax advisor who specializes in U.S. taxes for foreign nationals can help ensure compliance and optimize your tax situation.

Contact us at **RoyaltyandPower.org** Or **TheBiblicalNationofIsraelRegistry.World**

Summary:

Schedule A (Form 1040) is generally used by U.S. citizens, resident aliens, and non-citizen nationals to itemize deductions. While nonresident aliens typically use Form 1040-NR, certain conditions, including tax treaties and dual status, can allow foreign nationals to use Schedule A. Always verify specific eligibility and consult with a tax professional to navigate the complexities of U.S. tax filing as a foreign national.

For more detailed information, refer to the IRS [Instructions for Schedule A](https://www.irs.gov/instructions/i1040sca) and [Publication 519, U.S. Tax Guide for Aliens](https://www.irs.gov/publications/p519).

Affidavit of Individual Surety

Applying Standard Form 28 to the Rebirth/Secured Party Creditor (SPC) process involves using the form as part of your filings to demonstrate your status and financial capability. This integration shows your ability to back bonds and obligations, reinforcing your claims as an SPC.

OMB Control Number 9000-0001 pertains to Standard Form 28, which is used for the Affidavit of Individual Surety. This form is prescribed by the General Services Administration (GSA) and outlined in the Federal Acquisition Regulation (FAR) at 48 CFR 53.228(e). Standard Form 28 must be completed and submitted by individual sureties on bonds executed in connection with government contracts. The form verifies the financial status and assets of the surety to ensure their capability to meet the obligations of the bond [["]](https://www.gsa.gov/system/files/2024-02/SF24-23a.pdf).

Here's how it can be integrated:

Step-by-Step Guide to Using Standard Form 28 for the Rebirth/SPC Process

1. Gather Financial Information:

- Collect documentation of your assets, including property deeds, bank statements, and any other proof of ownership or value.

2. Download the Form:

- Obtain Standard Form 28 from the GSA website **[here](https://www.gsa.gov/forms-library/affidavit-individual-surety).**

3. Complete Personal Information:

- Fill in your personal details, including name, address, and Social Security Number.

4. List Assets: " PRB" (PRIVATE REGISTERED BOND) or TCU

- Accurately list all your assets, specifying descriptions, values, and any encumbrances.

5. Affidavit Section:

- Carefully read the affidavit section and ensure you understand it. Sign and date it in the presence of a notary public.

6. Attach Supporting Documents:

- Attach copies of all supporting documents that verify the information provided about your assets.

7. Submit the Form:

- Include the completed form and attachments in your SPC filing packet. This may be submitted to the relevant government office or financial institution handling your SPC process.

8. Follow Up:

- Monitor the status of your submission and be prepared to provide additional documentation if requested.

By following these steps, you will ensure that your use of Standard Form 28 is thorough and accurate, supporting your status as a Secured Party Creditor.

AFFIDAVIT OF INDIVIDUAL SURETY
(See instructions on reverse)

OMB Control Number: 9000-0001
Expiration Date: 3/31/2024

Paperwork Reduction Act Statement - This information collection meets the requirements of 44 USC § 3507, as amended by section 2 of the Paperwork Reduction Act of 1995. You do not need to answer these questions unless we display a valid Office of Management and Budget (OMB) control number. The OMB control number for this collection is 9000-0001. We estimate that it will take 0.3 hours to read the instructions, gather the facts, and answer the questions. Send only comments relating to our time estimate, including suggestions for reducing this burden, or any other aspects of this collection of information to: U.S. General Services Administration, Regulatory Secretariat Division (M1V1CB), 1800 F Street, NW, Washington, DC 20405.

STATE OF	COUNTY OF	SS.

I, the undersigned, being duly sworn, depose and say that I am: (1) the surety to the attached bond(s); (2) a citizen of the United States; and of full age and legally competent. Where the sureties are acting as co-sureties, we, the Sureties, bind ourselves in such sum "jointly and severally" as well as "severally" only for the purpose of allowing a joint action or actions against any or all of us. For all other purposes, each Surety binds itself, jointly and severally with the Principal. I recognize that statements contained herein concern a matter within the jurisdiction of an agency of the United States and the making of a false, fictitious or fraudulent statement may render the maker subject to prosecution under Title 18, United States Code Sections 1001 and 494. This affidavit is made to induce the United States of America to accept me as surety on the attached bond.

1. NAME (First, Middle, Last) (Type or Print)	2A. HOME ADDRESS (Number, Street, City, State, ZIP Code)	
3. TYPE AND DURATION OF OCCUPATION		
	2B. TELEPHONE NUMBER	2C. EMAIL ADDRESS
4A. NAME AND ADDRESS OF EMPLOYER (Number, Street, City, State, ZIP Code) (If self-employed, so state)	5A. NAME AND ADDRESS OF INDIVIDUAL SURETY BROKER USED (Number, Street, City, State, ZIP Code)	
	5B. SURETY BROKER EMAIL ADDRESS	
4B. EMPLOYER EMAIL ADDRESS	5C. HOME TELEPHONE NUMBER	5D. BUSINESS TELEPHONE NUMBER
6A. NAME AND ADDRESS OF FINANCIAL INSTITUTION SUBMITTING THE PLEDGE OF SECURITIES ON BEHALF OF INDIVIDUAL SURETY (Number, Street, City, State, ZIP Code)	6B. FINANCIAL INSTITUTION EMAIL ADDRESS	6C. ROUTING TRANSIT NUMBER (RTN)
	6D. CONTACT PERSON NAME	6E. CONTACT PERSON TELEPHONE NUMBER
	6F. CONTACT PERSON EMAIL ADDRESS	

7. THE FOLLOWING IS A TRUE REPRESENTATION OF THE ASSETS I HAVE PLEDGED TO THE UNITED STATES IN SUPPORT OF THE ATTACHED BOND. *(LIST THE COMMITTEE ON UNIFORM SECURITIES IDENTIFICATION PROCEDURES (CUSIP) NUMBER AND PAR (FACE) AMOUNT OF EACH SECURITY).*

AUTHORIZED FOR LOCAL REPRODUCTION
Previous edition is NOT usable

STANDARD FORM 28 (REV. 2/2021)
Prescribed by GSA-FAR (48 CFR) 53.228(e)

8. IDENTIFY ALL LIENS, JUDGEMENTS, OR ANY OTHER ENCUMBRANCES INVOLVING SUBJECT ASSETS.

9. IDENTIFY ALL BONDS, INCLUDING BID GUARANTEES, FOR WHICH THE SUBJECT ASSETS HAVE BEEN PLEDGED WITHIN THREE YEARS PRIOR TO THE DATE OF EXECUTION OF THIS AFFIDAVIT.

DOCUMENTATION OF THE PLEDGED ASSET MUST BE ATTACHED.

10. SIGNATURE	11. BOND AND CONTRACT TO WHICH THIS AFFIDAVIT RELATES (where appropriate)

12. SUBSCRIBED AND SWORN TO BEFORE ME AS FOLLOWS:

a. DATE OATH ADMINISTERED MONTH DAY YEAR	b. CITY AND STATE (or other jurisdiction)	
c. NAME AND TITLE OF OFFICIAL ADMINISTERING OATH (type or print)	d. SIGNATURE	e. MY COMMISSION EXPIRES

Official Seal

STANDARD FORM 28 (REV. 2/2021) PAGE 2

INSTRUCTIONS

1. Individual sureties on bonds executed in connection with Government contracts must complete and submit this form with the bond. (See Federal Acquisition Regulation (FAR) 28.203, 53.228(e).) The surety must have the completed form notarized.

2. No corporation, partnership, or other unincorporated association or firm, as such, is acceptable as an individual surety (i.e. must be a natural person). Likewise, members of a partnership are not acceptable as sureties on bonds that a partnership or an association, or any co-partner or member thereof, is the principal obligor. An individual surety will not include any financial interest in assets connected with the principal on the bond that this affidavit supports.

3. United States citizenship is a requirement for individual sureties for contracts and bonds when the contract is awarded in the United States. However, when the Contracting Officer is located in an outlying area or a foreign country, the individual surety is only required to be a permanent resident of the area or country in which the contracting officer is located.

4. All signatures of the affidavit submitted must be originals. Affidavits bearing reproduced signatures are not acceptable. An authorized person must sign the bond. Any person signing in a representative capacity (e.g., an attorney-in-fact) must furnish evidence of authority if that representative is not a member of a firm, partnership, or joint venture, or an officer of the corporation involved.

STANDARD FORM 28 (REV. 2/2021) PAGE 3

Understanding and Using Standard Form 24 for the Rebirth/SPC Process

"Bid Bond"

Overview:

Standard Form 24 (SF 24), associated with OMB Control Number 9000-0005, is a Bid Bond form prescribed by the General Services Administration (GSA) and outlined in the Federal Acquisition Regulation (FAR) at 48 CFR 53.228(a). This form is used to provide a bid guarantee ensuring that the bidder, if awarded the contract, will execute the contract and provide the required performance and payment bonds.

Application to the Rebirth/Secured Party Creditor (SPC) Process:

Integrating SF 24 into the SPC process involves demonstrating financial responsibility and trustworthiness. Here's a step-by-step guide on how to use SF 24 effectively:

Step-by-Step Guide:

1. Gather Necessary Information:

   - Ensure you have all required personal and financial details, including asset documentation.

2. Download Standard Form 24:

- Obtain the form from the GSA website or directly from [this link](https://www.gsa.gov/forms-library/bid-bond).

3. Fill in Bidder Information:

- Complete the sections with your legal name, address, and contact information.

4. Principal Details:

- If acting as a principal, fill in the details accurately, including your SPC or Rebirth status and any related legal identifiers.

5. Surety Information:

- Provide the surety company's name, address, and contact details. The surety company guarantees that you will fulfill your obligations.

6. Bond Amount:

- Specify the bond amount, which is typically a percentage of the bid amount.

7. Obligee Information:

- Detail the government agency or entity to which the bond is submitted.

8. Signatures:

- Ensure that all required parties, including the principal and surety, sign the form. It may need notarization.

9. Attach Supporting Documents:
  - Include any necessary documentation that supports your financial capability and assets.

10. Submit the Form:
  - Submit SF 24 along with your SPC filings to the appropriate government agency or institution handling your process.

11. Maintain Records:
  - Keep copies of the completed form and all submissions for your records.

12. Follow Up:
  - Monitor the status of your submission and be prepared to provide additional information if requested.

By following these steps, you can ensure that your bid bond (SF 24) is correctly completed and supports your SPC process, demonstrating your financial reliability and commitment to fulfilling contractual obligations.

For further details on the form and its use, refer to the GSA's official page [here](https://www.gsa.gov/forms-library/bid-bond)

(https://omb.report/omb/9000-0045)

(https://www.reginfo.gov/public/do/PRAOMBHistory?ombControlNumber=9000-0001) (https://omb.report/omb/9000-0075).

BID BOND

(See instructions on reverse)

DATE BOND EXECUTED *(Must not be later than bid opening date)*

OMB Control Number: 9000-0045
Expiration Date: 8/31/2025

Paperwork Reduction Act Statement - This information collection meets the requirements of 44 USC § 3507, as amended by section 2 of the Paperwork Reduction Act of 1995. You do not need to answer these questions unless we display a valid Office of Management and Budget (OMB) control number. The OMB control number for this collection is 9000-0045. We estimate that it will take 1 hour to read the instructions, gather the facts, and answer the questions. Send only comments relating to our time estimate, including suggestions for reducing this burden, or any other aspects of this collection of information to: General Services Administration, Regulatory Secretariat Division (M1V1CB), 1800 F Street, NW, Washington, DC 20405.

PRINCIPAL *(Legal name and business address)*

TYPE OF ORGANIZATION *("X" one)*
☐ INDIVIDUAL ☐ PARTNERSHIP ☐ JOINT VENTURE
☐ CORPORATION ☐ OTHER *(Specify)*

STATE OF INCORPORATION

SURETY(IES) *(Name and business address)*

PENAL SUM OF BOND				BID IDENTIFICATION	
PERCENT OF BID PRICE	AMOUNT NOT TO EXCEED			BID DATE	INVITATION NUMBER
	MILLION(S)	THOUSAND(S)	HUNDRED(S)	CENTS	
					FOR *(Construction, Supplies or Services)*

OBLIGATION:

We, the Principal and Surety(ies) are firmly bound to the United States of America (hereinafter called the Government) in the above penal sum. For payment of the penal sum, we bind ourselves, our heirs, executors, administrators, and successors, jointly and severally. However, where the Sureties are corporations acting as co-sureties, we, the Sureties, bind ourselves in such sum "jointly and severally" as well as "severally" only for the purpose of allowing a joint action or actions against any or all of us. For all other purposes, each Surety binds itself, jointly and severally with the Principal, for the payment of the sum shown opposite the name of the Surety. If no limit of liability is indicated, the limit of liability is the full amount of the penal sum.

CONDITIONS:

The Principal has submitted the bid identified above.

THEREFORE:

The above obligation is void if the Principal - (a) upon acceptance by the Government of the bid identified above, within the period specified therein for acceptance (sixty (60) days if no period is specified), executes the further contractual documents and gives the bond(s) required by the terms of the bid as accepted within the time specified (ten (10) days if no period is specified) after receipt of the forms by the principal; or (b) in the event of failure to execute such further contractual documents and give such bonds, pays the Government for any cost of procuring the work which exceeds the amount of the bid.

Each Surety executing this instrument agrees that its obligation is not impaired by any extension(s) of the time for acceptance of the bid that the Principal may grant to the Government. Notice to the surety(ies) of extension(s) is waived. However, waiver of the notice applies only to extensions aggregating not more than sixty (60) calendar days in addition to the period originally allowed for acceptance of the bid.

WITNESS:

The Principal and Surety(ies) executed this bid bond and affixed their seals on the above date.

PRINCIPAL

SIGNATURE(S)	1. (Seal)	2. (Seal)	3. (Seal)	Corporate Seal
NAME(S) & TITLE(S) *(Typed)*	1.	2.	3.	

INDIVIDUAL SURETY(IES)

SIGNATURE(S)	1. (Seal)	2. (Seal)
NAME(S) *(Typed)*	1.	2.

CORPORATE SURETY(IES)

SURETY A	NAME & ADDRESS		STATE OF INCORPORATION	LIABILITY LIMIT ($)	
	SIGNATURE(S)	1.	2.		Corporate Seal
	NAME(S) & TITLE(S) *(Typed)*	1.	2.		

AUTHORIZED FOR LOCAL REPRODUCTION
Previous edition is NOT usable

STANDARD FORM 24 (REV. 8/2016)
Prescribed by GSA - FAR (48 CFR) 53.228(a)

			STATE OF INCORPORATION	LIABILITY LIMIT ($)	
SURETY B	NAME & ADDRESS				Corporate Seal
	SIGNATURE(S)	1.	2.		
	NAME(S) & TITLE(S) (Typed)	1.	2.		
SURETY C	NAME & ADDRESS		STATE OF INCORPORATION	LIABILITY LIMIT ($)	Corporate Seal
	SIGNATURE(S)	1.	2.		
	NAME(S) & TITLE(S) (Typed)	1.	2.		
SURETY D	NAME & ADDRESS		STATE OF INCORPORATION	LIABILITY LIMIT ($)	Corporate Seal
	SIGNATURE(S)	1.	2.		
	NAME(S) & TITLE(S) (Typed)	1.	2.		
SURETY E	NAME & ADDRESS		STATE OF INCORPORATION	LIABILITY LIMIT ($)	Corporate Seal
	SIGNATURE(S)	1.	2.		
	NAME(S) & TITLE(S) (Typed)	1.	2.		
SURETY F	NAME & ADDRESS		STATE OF INCORPORATION	LIABILITY LIMIT ($)	Corporate Seal
	SIGNATURE(S)	1.	2.		
	NAME(S) & TITLE(S) (Typed)	1.	2.		
SURETY G	NAME & ADDRESS		STATE OF INCORPORATION	LIABILITY LIMIT ($)	Corporate Seal
	SIGNATURE(S)	1.	2.		
	NAME(S) & TITLE(S) (Typed)	1.	2.		

INSTRUCTIONS

1. This form is authorized for use when a bid guaranty is required. Any deviation from this form will require the written approval of the Administrator of General Services.

2. Insert the full legal name and business address of the Principal in the space designated "Principal" on the face of the form. An authorized person shall sign the bond. Any person signing in a representative capacity (e.g., an attorney-in-fact) must furnish evidence of authority if that representative is not a member of the firm, partnership, or joint venture, or an officer of the corporation involved.

3. The bond may express penal sum as a percentage of the bid price. In these cases, the bond may state a maximum dollar limitation (e.g., 20% of the bid price but the amount not to exceed _____ dollars).

4. (a) Corporations executing the bond as sureties must appear on the Department of the Treasury's list of approved sureties and must act within the limitations listed therein. The value put into the LIABILITY LIMIT block is the penal sum (i.e., the face value) of the bond, unless a co-surety arrangement is proposed

(b) When multiple corporate sureties are involved, their names and addresses shall appear in the spaces (Surety A, Surety B, etc.) headed "CORPORATE SURETY(IES)." In the space designated "SURETY(IES)" on the face of the form, insert only the letter identifier corresponding to each of the sureties. Moreover, when co-surety arrangements exist, the parties may allocate their respective limitations of liability under the bond, provided that the sum total of their liability equals 100% of the bond penal sum.

(c) When individual sureties are involved, a completed Affidavit of Individual Surety (Standard Form 28) for each individual surety, shall accompany the bond. The Government may require the surety to furnish additional substantiating information concerning its financial capability.

5. Corporations executing the bond shall affix their corporate seals. Individuals shall execute the bond opposite the word "Corporate Seal"; and shall affix an adhesive seal if executed in Maine, New Hampshire, or any other jurisdiction requiring adhesive seals.

6. Type the name and title of each person signing this bond in the space provided.

7. In its application to negotiated contracts, the terms "bid" and "bidder" shall include "proposal" and "offeror."

STANDARD FORM 24 (REV. 8/2016) BACK

Purpose of Standard Form 25

"Performance Bond"

Standard Form 25 (SF 25) is a Performance Bond form used in federal contracting to guarantee that the contractor will perform the obligations specified in the contract. Here are the key purposes of SF 25:

1. Guarantee of Performance:

  - Ensures Completion: It ensures that the contractor will complete the project or service in accordance with the terms and conditions of the contract.

  - **Quality Assurance:** It guarantees that the work will meet the specified standards and requirements set by the contract.

2. Financial Protection:

  - **Protects Government Interests:** It protects the government or the contracting entity from financial loss if the contractor fails to fulfill their obligations.

  - **Compensates for Non-Performance:** If the contractor defaults, the surety (the bond issuer) is responsible for either completing the project or compensating the obligee (the government or contracting entity) up to the bond amount.

3. Legal and Financial Accountability:

- **Legal Commitment:** The bond represents a legal commitment from the contractor and the surety to ensure project completion.

- **Financial Responsibility:**

It demonstrates the financial responsibility and reliability of the contractor, as they must qualify for and obtain the bond from a surety company.

4. Contract Compliance:

- Regulatory Requirement: It complies with the Federal Acquisition Regulation (FAR) requirements, specifically under FAR 48 CFR 53.228(b), which mandates performance bonds for certain contracts to safeguard the government's interest [["]](https://www.gsa.gov/reference/forms/performance-bond) [["]](https://omb.report/omb/9000-0045).

Step-by-Step Guide to Using SF 25 in the Rebirth/SPC Process

1. Gather Information:

- Collect all necessary personal, financial, and project-related information.

- Ensure you have detailed documentation of your assets and financial standing.

2. Download the Form:

- Obtain SF 25 from the GSA website [here](https://www.gsa.gov/forms-library/performance-bond).

3. Complete Principal Information:

- Fill in your legal name, address, and other identifying information.

4. Surety Information:

   - Enter the details of the surety company, including name, address, and contact information.

5. Obligee Information:

   - Specify the government agency or contracting entity requiring the bond.

6. Contract Details:

   - Provide details of the contract, including contract number and description of the work.

7. Bond Amount:

   - State the penal sum of the bond, which is usually a percentage of the contract value.

8. Signatures and Seals:

   - Ensure both the principal and the surety sign the form. Include corporate seals if necessary.

9. Attach Supporting Documents:

   - Attach documentation verifying your financial capability and the accuracy of the information provided.

10. Submission:

- Submit the completed SF 25 along with your SPC filings to the appropriate government agency.

11. Record Keeping:

- Keep copies of the completed form and all related documentation for your records.

12. Follow Up:

- Monitor the status of your submission and provide any additional information if requested.

Using SF 25 effectively supports your standing as a Secured Party Creditor by demonstrating your financial reliability and commitment to fulfilling contractual obligations. This process can help establish credibility and compliance with legal and financial requirements
[[*]](https://www.gsa.gov/reference/forms/performance-bond)

[[*]](https://omb.report/omb/9000-0045).

PERFORMANCE BOND
(See instructions on reverse)

DATE BOND EXECUTED *(Must be same or later than date of contract)*

OMB Control Number: 9000-0045
Expiration Date: 8/31/2025

Paperwork Reduction Act Statement - This information collection meets the requirements of 44 USC § 3507, as amended by section 2 of the Paperwork Reduction Act of 1995. You do not need to answer these questions unless we display a valid Office of Management and Budget (OMB) control number. The OMB control number for this collection is 9000-0045. We estimate that it will take 1 hour to read the instructions, gather the facts, and answer the questions. Send only comments relating to our time estimate, including suggestions for reducing this burden, or any other aspects of this collection of information to: General Services Administration, Regulatory Secretariat Division (M1V1CB), 1800 F Street, NW, Washington, DC 20405.

PRINCIPAL *(Legal name and business address)*

TYPE OF ORGANIZATION *("X" one)*
☐ INDIVIDUAL ☐ PARTNERSHIP ☐ JOINT VENTURE
☐ CORPORATION ☐ OTHER *(Specify)*

STATE OF INCORPORATION

SURETY(IES) *(Name(s) and business address(es))*

PENAL SUM OF BOND

MILLION(S)	THOUSAND(S)	HUNDRED(S)	CENTS

CONTRACT DATE | **CONTRACT NUMBER**

OBLIGATION:

We, the Principal and Surety(ies), are firmly bound to the United States of America (hereinafter called the Government) in the above penal sum. For payment of the penal sum, we bind ourselves, our heirs, executors, administrators, and successors, jointly and severally. However, where the Sureties are corporations acting as co-sureties, we, the Sureties, bind ourselves in such sum "jointly and severally" as well as "severally" only for the purpose of allowing a joint action or actions against any or all of us. For all other purposes, each Surety binds itself, jointly and severally with the Principal, for the payment of the sum shown opposite the name of the Surety. If no limit of liability is indicated, the limit of liability is the full amount of the penal sum.

CONDITIONS:

The Principal has entered into the contract identified above.

THEREFORE:

The above obligation is void if the Principal-

(a) (1) Performs and fulfills all the understanding, covenants, terms, conditions, and agreements of the contract during the original term of the contract and any extensions thereof that are granted by the Government, with or without notice of the Surety(ies) and during the life of any guaranty required under the contract, and

(2) Performs and fulfills all the undertakings, covenants, terms, conditions, and agreements of any and all duly authorized modifications of the contract that hereafter are made. Notice of those modifications to the Surety(ies) are waived.

(b) Pays to the Government the full amount of the taxes imposed by the Government, if the said contract is subject to 41 USC Chapter 31, Subchapter III, Bonds, which are collected, deducted, or withheld from wages paid by the Principal in carrying out the construction contract with respect to which this bond is furnished.

WITNESS:

The Principal and Surety(ies) executed this performance bond and affixed their seals on the above date.

PRINCIPAL

SIGNATURE(S)	1. (Seal)	2. (Seal)	3. (Seal)	Corporate Seal
NAME(S) & TITLE(S) *(Typed)*	1.	2.	3.	

INDIVIDUAL SURETY(IES)

SIGNATURE(S)	1. (Seal)	2. (Seal)
NAME(S) *(Typed)*	1.	2.

CORPORATE SURETY(IES)

SURETY A	NAME & ADDRESS		STATE OF INCORPORATION	LIABILITY LIMIT ($)	Corporate Seal
	SIGNATURE(S)	1.	2.		
	NAME(S) & TITLE(S) *(Typed)*	1.	2.		

AUTHORIZED FOR LOCAL REPRODUCTION
Previous edition is NOT usable

STANDARD FORM 25 (REV. 8/2016)
Prescribed by GSA-FAR (48 CFR) 53.228(b)

CORPORATE SURETY(IES) (Continued)

			STATE OF INCORPORATION	LIABILITY LIMIT ($)	
SURETY B	NAME & ADDRESS				Corporate Seal
	SIGNATURE(S)	1.	2.		
	NAME(S) & TITLE(S) (Typed)	1.	2.		
SURETY C	NAME & ADDRESS		STATE OF INCORPORATION	LIABILITY LIMIT ($)	Corporate Seal
	SIGNATURE(S)	1.	2.		
	NAME(S) & TITLE(S) (Typed)	1.	2.		
SURETY D	NAME & ADDRESS		STATE OF INCORPORATION	LIABILITY LIMIT ($)	Corporate Seal
	SIGNATURE(S)	1.	2.		
	NAME(S) & TITLE(S) (Typed)	1.	2.		
SURETY E	NAME & ADDRESS		STATE OF INCORPORATION	LIABILITY LIMIT ($)	Corporate Seal
	SIGNATURE(S)	1.	2.		
	NAME(S) & TITLE(S) (Typed)	1.	2.		
SURETY F	NAME & ADDRESS		STATE OF INCORPORATION	LIABILITY LIMIT ($)	Corporate Seal
	SIGNATURE(S)	1.	2.		
	NAME(S) & TITLE(S) (Typed)	1.	2.		
SURETY G	NAME & ADDRESS		STATE OF INCORPORATION	LIABILITY LIMIT ($)	Corporate Seal
	SIGNATURE(S)	1.	2.		
	NAME(S) & TITLE(S) (Typed)	1.	2.		

BOND PREMIUM ▶	RATE PER THOUSAND ($)	TOTAL ($)

INSTRUCTIONS

1. This form is authorized for use in connection with Government contracts. Any deviation from this form will require the written approval of the Administrator of General Services.

2. Insert the full legal name and business address of the Principal in the space designated "Principal" on the face of the form. An authorized person shall sign the bond. Any person signing in a representative capacity (e.g., an attorney-in-fact) must furnish evidence of authority if that representative is not a member of the firm, partnership, or joint venture, or an officer of the corporation involved.

3. (a) Corporations executing the bond as sureties must appear on the Department of the Treasury's list of approved sureties and must act within the limitations listed therein. The value put into the LIABILITY LIMIT block is the penal sum (i.e., the face value) of bonds, unless a co-surety arrangement is proposed.

(b) When multiple corporate sureties are involved, their names and addresses shall appear in the spaces (Surety A, Surety B, etc.) headed "CORPORATE SURETY(IES)." In the space designated "SURETY(IES)" on the face of the form, insert only the letter identifier corresponding to each of the sureties. Moreover, when co-surety arrangements exist, the parties may allocate their respective limitations of liability under the bonds, provided that the sum total of their liability equals 100% of the bond penal sum.

(c) When individual sureties are involved, a completed Affidavit of Individual Surety (Standard Form 28) for each individual surety shall accompany the bond. The government may require the surety to furnish additional substantiating information concerning its financial capability.

4. Corporations executing the bond shall affix their corporate seals. Individuals shall execute the bond opposite the words "Corporate Seal", and shall affix an adhesive seal if executed in Maine, New Hampshire, or any other jurisdiction requiring adhesive seals.

5. Type the name and title of each person signing this bond in the space provided.

STANDARD FORM 25 (REV. 8/2016) BACK

Understanding and Using Standard Form 25A for the Rebirth/SPC Process

Overview:

Standard Form 25A (SF 25A), associated with OMB Control Number 9000-0045, is a Payment Bond form prescribed by the General Services Administration (GSA) and outlined in the Federal Acquisition Regulation (FAR) at 48 CFR 53.228(c). This form ensures that subcontractors and suppliers are paid for their labor and materials if the principal contractor fails to make these payments.

Purpose of SF 25A

The primary purpose of SF 25A is to provide financial protection for subcontractors and suppliers. It guarantees payment for labor and materials supplied to a project, which is crucial in ensuring the smooth operation and completion of contracts, particularly in the construction industry.

Applying SF 25A in the Rebirth/Secured Party Creditor (SPC) Process

Using SF 25A within the SPC process can demonstrate your financial responsibility and commitment to fulfilling obligations. Here's a step-by-step guide to correctly use SF 25A in the context of SPC:

Step-by-Step Guide:

1. Gather Necessary Information:

  - Collect all relevant personal, financial, and project-related information.

- Ensure you have detailed documentation of your assets and financial standing.

2. Download Standard Form 25A:

   - Obtain the form from the GSA website [here](https://www.gsa.gov/forms-library/payment-bond).

3. Complete Principal Information:

   - Enter your legal name, address, and other identifying information accurately. This identifies you as the principal obligor on the bond.

4. Surety Information:

   - Provide details of the surety company that will guarantee your payments. This includes the company's name, address, and contact details.

5. Obligee Information:

   - Specify the government agency or entity requiring the payment bond.

6. Contract Information:

   - Provide details of the contract, including the contract number and a brief description of the work to be performed.

7. Bond Amount:

   - Indicate the penal sum of the bond, which typically covers the total amount owed to subcontractors and suppliers.

8. Execution Date:

   - Ensure the bond is dated the same day or later than the contract execution date.

9. Signatures and Seals:

   - Both the principal and surety must sign the form. Affix corporate seals if required by the jurisdiction where the bond is executed.

10. Attach Supporting Documents:

    - Attach documentation verifying your financial capability and the accuracy of the information provided.

11. Submission:

    - Submit the completed SF 25A along with your SPC filings to the appropriate government agency.

12. Record Keeping:

    - Keep copies of the completed form and all related documentation for your records.

13. Follow Up:

    - Monitor the status of your submission and provide any additional information if requested.

Using SF 25A effectively supports your standing as a Secured Party Creditor by demonstrating your financial reliability and commitment to fulfilling contractual obligations. This process can help establish credibility and compliance with legal and financial requirements [["](https://www.gsa.gov/reference/forms/payment-bond) [["](https://www.acquisition.gov/far/53.228).

PAYMENT BOND
(See instructions on reverse)

DATE BOND EXECUTED *(Must be same or later than date of contract)*

OMB Control Number: 9000-0045
Expiration Date: 8/31/2025

Paperwork Reduction Act Statement - This information collection meets the requirements of 44 USC § 3507, as amended by section 2 of the Paperwork Reduction Act of 1995. You do not need to answer these questions unless we display a valid Office of Management and Budget (OMB) control number. The OMB control number for this collection is 9000-0045. We estimate that it will take 1 hour to read the instructions, gather the facts, and answer the questions. Send only comments relating to our time estimate, including suggestions for reducing this burden, or any other aspects of this collection of information to: General Services Administration, Regulatory Secretariat Division (M1V1CB), 1800 F Street, NW, Washington, DC 20405

PRINCIPAL (Legal name and business address)	TYPE OF ORGANIZATION ("X" one)
	☐ INDIVIDUAL ☐ PARTNERSHIP ☐ JOINT VENTURE
	☐ CORPORATION ☐ OTHER (Specify)
	STATE OF INCORPORATION

SURETY(IES) (Name(s) and business address(es))	PENAL SUM OF BOND			
	MILLION(S)	THOUSAND(S)	HUNDRED(S)	CENTS
	CONTRACT DATE		CONTRACT NUMBER	

OBLIGATION:

We, the Principal and Surety(ies), are firmly bound to the United States of America (hereinafter called the Government) in the above penal sum. For payment of the penal sum, we bind ourselves, our heirs, executors, administrators, and successors, jointly and severally. However, where the Sureties are corporations acting as co-sureties, we, the Sureties, bind ourselves in such sum "jointly and severally" as well as "severally" only for the purpose of allowing a joint action or actions against any or all of us. For all other purposes, each Surety binds itself, jointly and severally with the Principal, for the payment of the sum shown opposite the name of the Surety. If no limit is indicated, the limit of liability is the full amount of the penal sum.

CONDITIONS:

The above obligation is void if the Principal promptly makes payment to all persons having a direct relationship with the Principal or a subcontractor of the Principal for furnishing labor, material or both in the prosecution of the work provided for in the contract identified above, and any authorized modifications of the contract that subsequently are made. Notice of those modifications to the Surety(ies) are waived.

WITNESS:

The Principal and Surety(ies) executed this payment bond and affixed their seals on the above date.

PRINCIPAL

	1.	2.	3.	
SIGNATURE(S)	(Seal)	(Seal)	(Seal)	Corporate Seal
NAME(S) & TITLE(S) (Typed)	1.	2.	3.	

INDIVIDUAL SURETY(IES)

	1.	2.	
SIGNATURE(S)	(Seal)		(Seal)
NAME(S) (Typed)	1.	2.	

CORPORATE SURETY(IES)

SURETY A	NAME & ADDRESS		STATE OF INCORPORATION	LIABILITY LIMIT $	
	SIGNATURE(S)	1.	2.		Corporate Seal
	NAME(S) & TITLE(S) (Typed)	1.	2.		

AUTHORIZED FOR LOCAL REPRODUCTION
Previous edition is NOT usable

STANDARD FORM 25A (REV. 8/2016)
Prescribed by GSA-FAR (48 CFR) 53.2228(c)

CORPORATE SURETY(IES) (Continued)

			STATE OF INCORPORATION	LIABILITY LIMIT $	
SURETY B	NAME & ADDRESS				Corporate Seal
	SIGNATURE(S)	1.	2.		
	NAME(S) & TITLE(S) (Typed)	1.	2.		
SURETY C	NAME & ADDRESS		STATE OF INCORPORATION	LIABILITY LIMIT $	Corporate Seal
	SIGNATURE(S)	1.	2.		
	NAME(S) & TITLE(S) (Typed)	1.	2.		
SURETY D	NAME & ADDRESS		STATE OF INCORPORATION	LIABILITY LIMIT $	Corporate Seal
	SIGNATURE(S)	1.	2.		
	NAME(S) & TITLE(S) (Typed)	1.	2.		
SURETY E	NAME & ADDRESS		STATE OF INCORPORATION	LIABILITY LIMIT $	Corporate Seal
	SIGNATURE(S)	1.	2.		
	NAME(S) & TITLE(S) (Typed)	1.	2.		
SURETY F	NAME & ADDRESS		STATE OF INCORPORATION	LIABILITY LIMIT $	Corporate Seal
	SIGNATURE(S)	1.	2.		
	NAME(S) & TITLE(S) (Typed)	1.	2.		
SURETY G	NAME & ADDRESS		STATE OF INCORPORATION	LIABILITY LIMIT $	Corporate Seal
	SIGNATURE(S)	1.	2.		
	NAME(S) & TITLE(S) (Typed)	1.	2.		

INSTRUCTIONS

1. This form, for the protection of persons supplying labor and material, is used when a payment bond is required under 40 USC Chapter 31, Subchapter III, Bonds. Any deviation from this form will require the written approval of the Administrator of General Services.

2. Insert the full legal name and business address of the Principal in the space designated "Principal" on the face of the form. An authorized person shall sign the bond. Any person signing in a representative capacity (e.g., an attorney-in-fact) must furnish evidence of authority if that representative is not a member of the firm, partnership, or joint venture, or an officer of the corporation involved.

3. (a) Corporations executing the bond as sureties must appear on the Department of the Treasury's list of approved sureties and must act within the limitations listed therein. The value put into the LIABILITY LIMIT block is the penal sum (i.e., the face value) of the bond, unless a co-surety arrangement is proposed.

   (b) When multiple corporate sureties are involved, their names and addresses shall appear in the spaces (Surety A, Surety B, etc.) headed "CORPORATE SURETY(IES)." In the space designated "SURETY(IES)" on the face of the form, insert only the letter identifier corresponding to each of the sureties. Moreover, when co-surety arrangements exist, the parties may allocate their respective limitations of liability under the bonds, provided that the sum total of their liability equals 100% of the bond penal sum.

   (c) When individual sureties are involved, a completed Affidavit of Individual Surety (Standard Form 28) for each individual surety shall accompany the bond. The Government may require the surety to furnish additional substantiating information concerning its financial capability.

4. Corporations executing the bond shall affix their corporate seals. Individuals shall execute the bond opposite the words "Corporate Seal", and shall affix an adhesive seal if executed in Maine, New Hampshire, or any other jurisdiction requiring adhesive seals.

5. Type the name and title of each person signing this bond in the space provided.

STANDARD FORM 25A (REV. 8/2016) BACK

John 14
King James Version

14 Let not your heart be troubled: ye believe in God, believe also in me.

² In my Father's house are many mansions: if it were not so, I would have told you. I go to prepare a place for you.

³ And if I go and prepare a place for you, I will come again, and receive you unto myself; that where I am, there ye may be also.

⁴ And whither I go ye know, and the way ye know.

⁵ Thomas saith unto him, Lord, we know not whither thou goest; and how can we know the way?

⁶ *Yeshua saith unto him, I am the way, the truth, and the life: no man cometh unto the Father, but by me.*

⁷ If ye had known me, ye should have known my Father also: and from henceforth ye know him, and have seen him.

⁸ Philip saith unto him, Lord, show us the Father, and it sufficeth us.

⁹ Yeshua saith unto him, Have I been so long time with you, and yet hast thou not known me, Philip? he that hath seen me hath seen the Father; and how sayest thou then, Show us the Father?

¹⁰ Believest thou not that I am in the Father, and the Father in me? the words that I speak unto you I speak not of myself: but the Father that dwelleth in me, he doeth the works.

¹¹ Believe me that I am in the Father, and the Father in me: or else believe me for the very works' sake.

¹² Verily, verily, I say unto you, He that believeth on me, the works that I do shall he do also; and greater works than these shall he do; because I go unto my Father.

¹³ And whatsoever ye shall ask in my name, that will I do, that the Father may be glorified in the Son.

¹⁴ If ye shall ask any thing in my name, I will do it.

¹⁵ If ye love me, keep my commandments.

¹⁶ And I will pray the Father, and he shall give you another Comforter, that he may abide with you for ever;

17 Even the Spirit of truth; whom the world cannot receive, because it seeth him not, neither knoweth him: but ye know him; for he dwelleth with you, and shall be in you.

==**18** I will not leave you comfortless: I will come to you.==

==**19** Yet a little while, and the world seeth me no more; but ye see me: because I live, ye shall live also.==

20 At that day ye shall know that I am in my Father, and ye in me, and I in you.

21 He that hath my commandments, and keepeth them, he it is that loveth me: and he that loveth me shall be loved of my Father, and I will love him, and will manifest myself to him.

22 Judas saith unto him, not Iscariot, Lord, how is it that thou wilt manifest thyself unto us, and not unto the world?

23 Yeshua answered and said unto him, If a man love me, he will keep my words: and my Father will love him, and we will come unto him, and make our abode with him.

==**24** He that loveth me not keepeth not my sayings: and the word which ye hear is not mine, but the Father's which sent me.==

25 These things have I spoken unto you, being yet present with you.

==**26** But the Comforter, which is the Holy Ghost, whom the Father will send in my name, he shall teach you all things, and bring all things to your remembrance, whatsoever I have said unto you.==

27 Peace I leave with you, my peace I give unto you: not as the world giveth, give I unto you. Let not your heart be troubled, neither let it be afraid.

28 Ye have heard how I said unto you, I go away, and come again unto you. If ye loved me, ye would rejoice, because I said, I go unto the Father: for my Father is greater than I.

29 And now I have told you before it come to pass, that, when it is come to pass, ye might believe.

30 Hereafter I will not talk much with you: for the prince of this world cometh, and hath nothing in me.

31 But that the world may know that I love the Father; and as the Father gave me commandment, even so I do. Arise, let us go hence.

Ambassador Kabir-Elohim Isreal

Legal Remedies: A Comparative Study of 42 USC 1983 Lawsuits and Tort Claims. Remedies for Civil Rights Litigation

5.0 ★★★★★ 2

Kindle	Hardcover
$9.99 (Earn 30 pts)	$77.00 (Earn 77 pts)
Available instantly	

Paperback

$57.00 (Earn 57 pts)

✓prime

Ambassador Kabir-Elohim IsReal

Manifesting Abundance: Spiritual and Metaphysical Laws of Manifestation

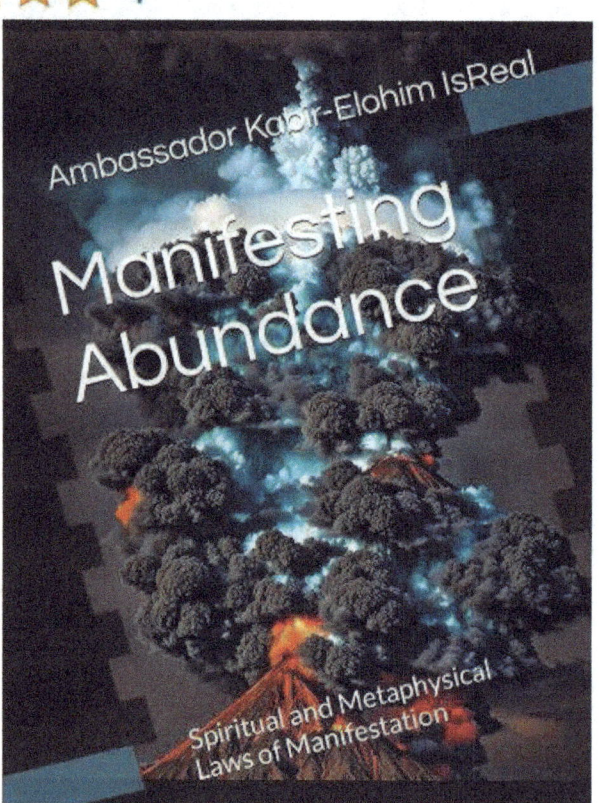

5.0 ★★★★★ 1

Kindle	Paperback
$0.00 kindle unlimited	$19.83 (Earn 20 pts)
or $9.99 (Earn 30 pts) to buy	✓prime

Understanding "Idem Sonans" and "Vi Coactus" in Court Context for Pro Se Litigants

Idem Sonans:

Idem Sonans *is a legal doctrine which means "sounding the same." It addresses the issue of minor misspellings of names in legal documents, suggesting that if two names sound sufficiently similar, the difference in spelling is not significant enough to invalidate legal proceedings. This principle is particularly relevant when it comes to slight variations in the spelling of names where the intent is clearly identifiable.*

Use in Court:

- **EXAMPLE:** If a legal document refers to "Jon Smith" but the correct spelling is "John Smith," under the doctrine of idem sonans, the court would treat the names as essentially the same if the pronunciation is indistinguishable.

Vi Coactus:

Vi Coactus is a Latin term meaning "under constraint" or "by compulsion." It is used to indicate that an action was performed under duress or force.

Use in Court:

- **EXAMPLE:** If someone signs a document but was forced to do so, they may add "V.C." or "Vi Coactus" next to their signature to indicate that the signature was obtained under compulsion.

" Context of a Pro Se Litigant Omitting Christian Name ":

1. Court Jurisdiction and Christian Name:

- **Bouvier's Law Dictionary** states that the omission of a Christian name (first name) in legal proceedings can prevent the court from acquiring jurisdiction over the person. This is based on historical legal principles where full names, including Christian names, were required to properly identify individuals.

- *Implication:* If a defendant's name on court records omits the Christian name, the defendant can argue that the court does not have proper jurisdiction over them.

2. Process for Pro Se Litigants:

- *Omitting Government Name:* When asked in court if they ever used a previous (government) name, a pro se litigant might respond affirmatively but add "vi coactus" to indicate that any use of that name was under duress or compulsion.

- *Affirmation with Constraint:* By stating "yes, vi coactus," the litigant acknowledges that they have used the name, but also asserts that such use was not voluntary. This can be a strategy to distance themselves from legal obligations or implications associated with that name.

3. Changing Name for Rebirth Process:

- **Legal Name Change:** One of the most crucial steps in the rebirth process is to legally change your name, reflecting a new identity often aligned with religious or spiritual rebirth concepts.

- **Record Keeping:** Ensuring all legal documents, court records, and personal identification reflect the new name is vital. This reinforces the claim of a new identity and can help in establishing jurisdictional arguments.

4. Effective Outcomes:

- Challenging Jurisdiction: By correctly using idem sonans and vi coactus, a pro se litigant can effectively challenge the court's jurisdiction over them if there are discrepancies in the name used.

- *Establishing New Identity:* Successfully changing and consistently using the new name helps in affirming the individual's rebirth process and distancing from previous legal identities and obligations.

Practical Steps:

1. Legal Documentation:

- Obtain a court order for the name change.

- Update all identification documents (driver's license, passport, etc.) with the new name.

2. Court Appearance:

- If summoned under the old name, clarify the name change and the reasons behind it.

- Use "vi coactus" if compelled to acknowledge the old name, indicating the acknowledgment is under duress.

3. Legal Strategy:

- Be prepared to cite Bouvier's Law Dictionary and relevant case law to support arguments regarding the omission of the Christian name and jurisdictional issues.

- Ensure all filings and court documents reflect the new name to maintain consistency and credibility.

By understanding and properly applying these legal doctrines, pro se litigants can better navigate the complexities of the court system and assert their new legal identity effectively.

FOREIGN **** NATIONAL

כתר יהודה אומת ישראל המקראית
American Samoa DRIVER'S LICENSE
DL# COJ83-1107197

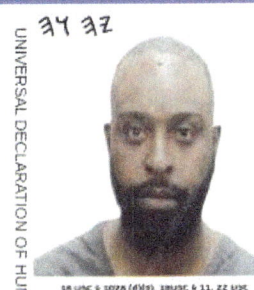

Kabir elohim Isreal
32.242251°N 35.327738°E
Har Kabir, Jerusalem
Palestinian, Kingdom of Judah

- **CLASS:** שַׁגְרִיר/Ambassador
- **DOB:** 07-11-83
- **HAIR:** BLK
- **WEIGHT:** 177
- **HEIGHT:** 5'11"
- **SEX:** M
- **ID NUM:** A223245169
- **IS ISSUED:** 07/19/2023
- **Expires:** 07/19/2026

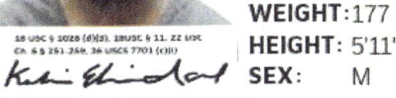

Tribal Travel Id
The Biblical Nation of Israel Registry.World

BACK

American Samoa DRIVER'S LICENSE
Issued by DL services; TRIBAL NATION OF ISRAEL
רישיון נהיגה בינלאומי
אומה שבטית של ישראל-יהודה; IDL מונפקת על ידי שירותי

```
P<XXB980124COJ9FOREIGN<REFUGEE
8307118M3307113XXBAMBASSADOR<9
ISRAEL<JUDAH<<KABIR<ELOHIM<<<<
```
253

Biblical Nation of Israel YHWH

Judahite

Given Name	Surname
Kabir elohim	Israel - Judah

32.242251°N 35.327738°E
Har Kabir, Jerusalem, Kingdom of Judah Southern YHWH

TRIBAL ID

Sex	D.O.B	Nationality
M	07/11/1983	KOJ

Height	Weight	Eye Color	Hair
5'10"	177	Brown	Black

REFUGEE

Date Issued	Date Expires
07/11/2023	07/11/2033

Crown of Judah
EXEMPT

Signature of Holder

OFFICIAL Identification CARD

USC 1101 (14) Self-Governing Dominion
NATIONALITY: 8 USC 1101 (a) (42)
refugee of: The Biblical Nation of Israel

Tribal Identification

The Biblical Nation of Israel Registry.World

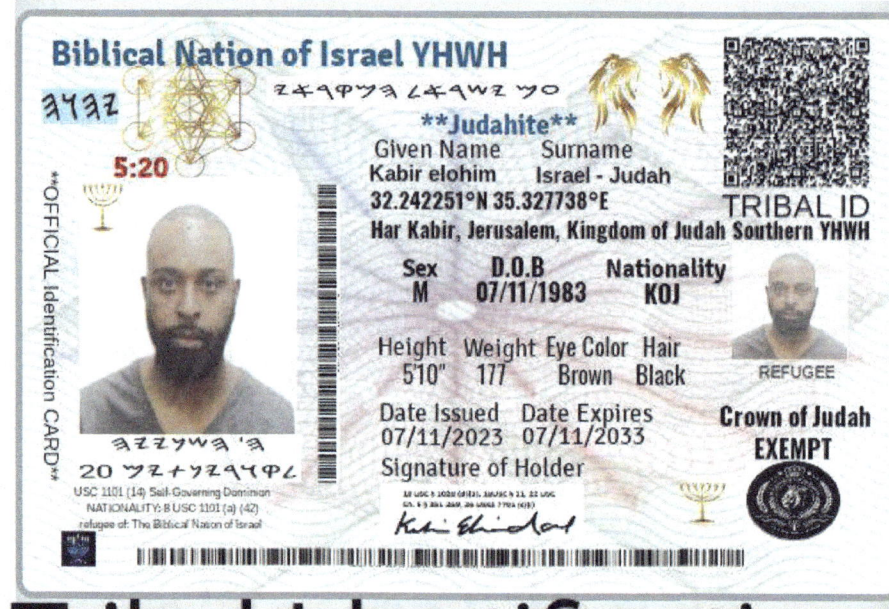

BACK

OFFICIAL INDIGENOUS TRIBAL ID CARD **Tribal MEMBER**
ENHANCED INDIGENOUS IDENTIFICATION

Article 15 affirms that:[3]
Everyone has the right to a nationality.
No one shall be arbitrarily deprived of his nationality nor denied the right to change his nationality.

- ARTICLE 1 (EXODUS 20:3)
- ARTICLE 7 (DEUTERONOMY 6:7)
- ARTICLE 9 (ISAIAH 1:26)
- ARTICLE 11 (LUKE 22:36)
- ARTICLE 12 (MATTHEW 10:32)

OFFICIAL IDENTIFICATION AUTHORIZED BY KINGDOM OF JUDAH.
IF FOUND PLEASE RETURN TO:
THE BIBLICAL NATION OF ISRAEL
P.O. BOX 114
BUCKEYE, ARIZONA (85326)
ALL RIGHTS RESERVED

1951 Refugee Convention
CLASS: FOREIGN

ENDORSEMENTS:
BIBLICAL/ TRIBAL

TheBiblicalNationofIsraelRegistry.World

UNIVERSIAL DECLARATION OF HUMAN RIGHTS

```
P<XXB980124COJ9FOREIGN<REFUGEE
8307118M3307113XXBAMBASSADOR<9
ISRAEL<JUDAH<<KABIR<ELOHIM<<<<
```

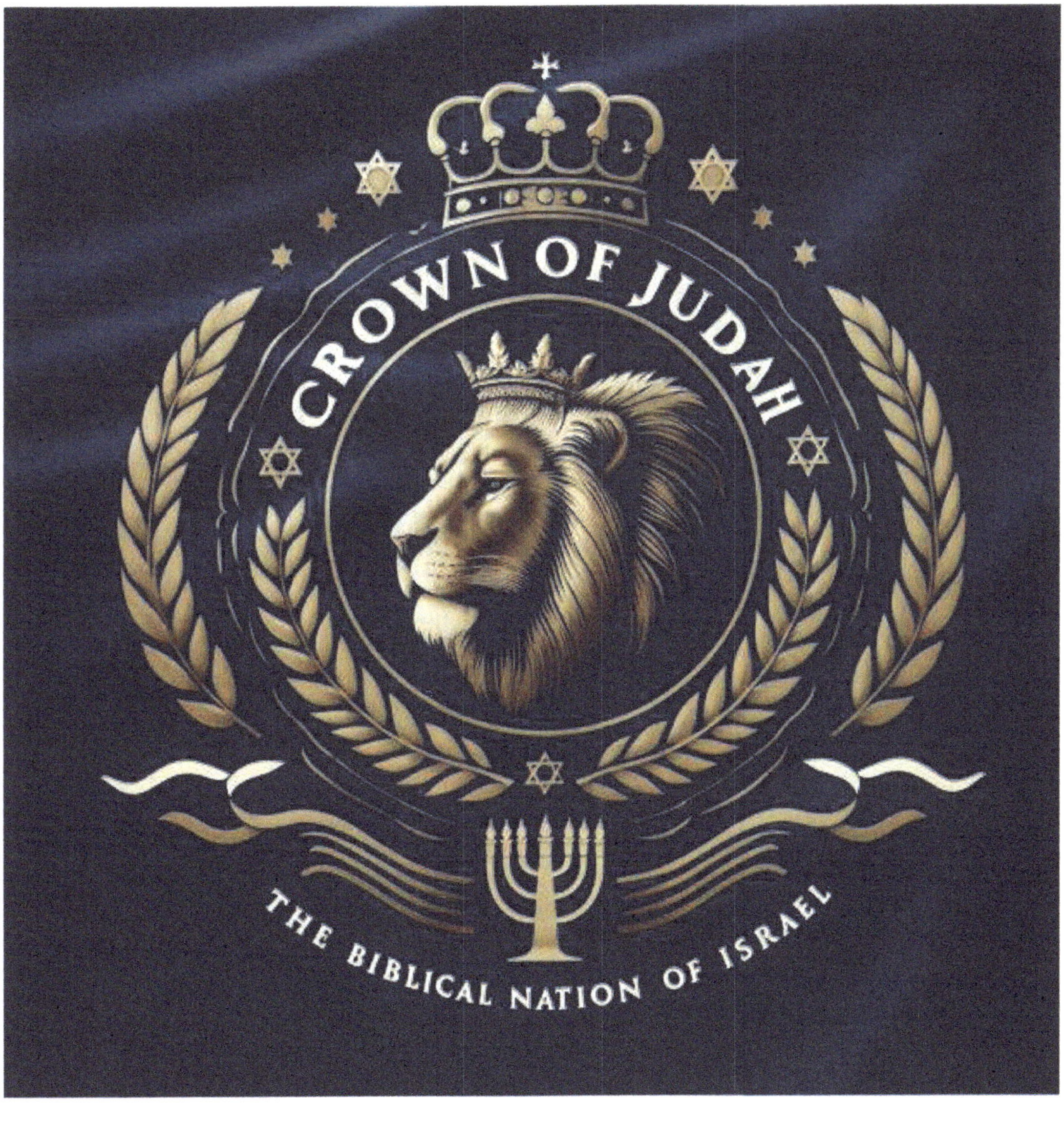
CROWN OF JUDAH
THE BIBLICAL NATION OF ISRAEL

ISBN 979-8-89379-729-9

9 798893 797299

50100

Made in the USA
Las Vegas, NV
28 March 2025